Terence Benedict Snow

Necrology of the English Congregation of the Order of St. Benedict

1600-1833

Terence Benedict Snow

Necrology of the English Congregation of the Order of St. Benedict
1600-1833

ISBN/EAN: 9783744664158

Printed in Europe, USA, Canada, Australia, Japan

Cover: Foto ©Thomas Meinert / pixelio.de

More available books at **www.hansebooks.com**

NECROLOGY

OF THE

ENGLISH CONGREGATION

OF THE

ORDER OF SAINT BENEDICT,

FROM

1600 TO 1883,

BY THE

REV. T. B. SNOW, M.A.,

PRIEST OF THE SAME CONGREGATION,

AND PROCURATOR OF THE PROVINCE OF YORK.

LONDON:

BURNS AND OATES.

—

MDCCCLXXXIII.

Contents.

NECROLOGY

OF THE

ENGLISH CONGREGATION

OF THE

Order of Saint Benedict,

FROM

1600 to 1883.

HE Death Roll of the English Benedictines will enkindle an honourable family pride in the breasts of the English sons of St. Benedict, and will awaken an interest in many who are linked by ties of blood, reverence, and gratitude to the members of the Venerable Order. St. Benedict has never deserted England. From the commencement of its history, throughout its national life, during its catholic ages, in the times of persecution, in the revival of its christian life, the majestic figure of the great Patriarch has hovered over the land. To the old Saxon, he was not the apostle only, but the father, the guide, and the friend: not merely the priest and spiritual father, but the ruler of the church, the mentor of the state, the tiller of the land, the teacher of the children, the mind of the nation, truly a man of light and leading, speaking by the voice of Alcuin and V. Bede, of St. Wilfrid and St. Dunstan, and of all those who made Saxon England the Isle of Saints. When the ruthless Dane ravaged the land he stood before the shrines, and saw the blood of his children stain the sanctuary. In Lanfranc he tempered the stern William, in St. Anselm he curbed the wild will of Rufus, in St. Thomas he stayed the lawless hand of Henry. In Stephen Langton he stood with the barons at Runnymede to wrest from John the liberty of the people, he was foremost in the struggle for the freedom of the serf and the burgher, and when the Red Rose fought with the White he was the mediator, softening the bitterness of strife, soothing the passions of war. Not merely guiding the destinies of the nation, he entered into the social life of the people; his churches arose in the valley and on the hill side, his minsters gathered the people around them, and when in the cathedral cities wondrous temples to the Living God grew out of the soil, he watched his children while they placed stone upon stone, shaped the graceful line, carved the capital and the moulding: when the intellect of the nation was centred in Oxford and Cambridge his spirit and guidance were there: in the city and the village he spoke to the little ones of the burgher and the peasant: he stored up the wisdom of the fathers and the learning of the ancients within the cloistered walls of the homes of his children: he was the scribe and the printer: in the homestead, in the hamlet, in the rising town he was in the midst of the people, lightening their labours and soothing their sorrows: giving food to the poor, shelter to the wanderer, welcome to the traveller: preaching to the people the Word of God, breaking for them the Bread of Life, conveying to them God's pardon, and solacing them on their deathbed. In life and in death, to the sick and the poor, to the wise and the simple, St. Benedict with his paternal mien was ever near.

When Henry VIII. declared war against the Catholic faith in England, the first foe attacked was St. Benedict: the cells, the priories, and the lesser abbeys, those time-honoured homes of generations of black-robed monks were pillaged and seized, their treasures dispersed, and their heirlooms alienated: then followed the onslaught on the greater abbeys, those grand historic monuments that have indelibly emblazoned the name of St. Benedict on England's story: Glastonbury and Westminster, St. Alban's and St. Edmundsbury, Reading and Evesham, and the great temples and cathedrals through whose groined roofs the Benedictine chaunt had re-echoed for centuries, were stripped of their inmates, and the monks sent forth homeless, and outcasts in their own land. Glastonbury, Colchester, and Reading parted not with their sons until the blood of their Abbots had been shed on the block. In Elizabeth's long reign of savage and vindictive persecution, the thousands of Benedictine monks scattered over the land died, one by one, in obscurity, poverty and neglect: no tablet or history records their fate, God alone knows and will one day reveal the years of suffering, the privation and hunger, the desolation and the isolation, the contempt and the affronts, that the homeless children of St. Benedict endured, ere they joined the 'corona fratrum' around their great Patriarch in heaven. Then came the revival. From across the seas, as of old, missionaries landed to commence anew in the seventeenth the old work of conversion of the seventh century, and men's thoughts were taken back to the old Benedictine missionaries who came with their silver cross to Thanet, and spread themselves and the faith over the Saxon land. England was the patrimony of St. Benedict: his name was entwined in the life and activity of the people, every town had its memorials, twelve widowed cathedrals silently mourned for his children ; every page of history, every record and family pedigree, spoke of St. Benedict, and when English Catholic life revived, it could not but influence English hearts, and lead young men of English birth to seek the old familiar habit in a foreign clime, that, returning as children of St. Benedict, they might reclaim their father's inheritance.

Those who have taken part in this revival are recorded in the following pages, which mark the day when the labours of each one ceased, and he commenced above a life of intercession, watching the results of his own work and the progress of his brethren. Three hundred years have passed and still the revival continues, for God's time has not come for the conversion of the English people: one century of persecution and strife, a second of obscurity, a third of development, and still we wait for the grand harvest of souls. Unlike the Benedictine missionaries of old who came few in number and speedily conquered kingdom after kingdom, the missionaries of the second conversion have made but slow and gradual progress. If the progress has been slow, the difficulties have been greater. The first Benedictine missionaries came to a people simple and rude, if barbarous and semi-civilized : the symmetry of the Christian faith was a contrast to their crude religious belief, the beauty of the Christian worship eclipsed their pagan rites, the lustre of the Christian life of love outshone their savage code of morals: the conquest was comparatively easy, it was over the untutored mind, the unoccupied heart: it was the seed falling on the virgin soil. They offered to the wild Saxon not only faith and grace, but temporal benefits: they taught him the arts of civilized life, they cleared his forests, filled up his marshes, tilled his ground, built his houses, instructed him in knowledge, trained his children, so that the Benedictine missionary as before observed, was not merely the Apostle of Saxon England, but the father, the guide and the friend. How altered were the prospects of the second conversion! A people who had known the truth, had through interest and self-indulgence cast off the faith: the veil of heresy had blinded their eyes to the light, the rancour of controversy had steeled their hearts against the truth; with one hand on the spoils of the old church, the other was wielding the sword to chase away the rightful owner; the doctrine of the church was rejected, her rites had no charm, her code of morals was too stringent: all the powers of a strong government were arrayed against the church, her temples were seized, her ministers outlawed, her sacrifice proscribed, her sacraments a crime, her children deprived of civil rights: instead of enriching with temporal benefits her missionaries had nothing to offer but civil death, fine, and imprisonment. With the zeal and self-sacrifice of St. Augustine and St. Paulinus, of St. Aidan and St. Birinus, these second Benedictine missionaries came to a changed and blighted land: the former entered into a land promised to their Patriarch, ripe for the harvest, flowing with milk and honey, the latter entered into the same patrimony devastated and desolated by the hand of the spoiler, who strong in his might had placed barrier and fortification against the entry. They came with a grand tradition, a great name, an illustrious roll of ancestry, and emulating the deeds of their fathers, they faced the tribunal and the dungeon, the fetters and the rack, the halter and the knife of the executioner: in journeys and weariness, in alarms and escapes, in disguise and in hiding places, in hunger and poverty they toiled and struggled to obtain a footing for the faith in the land that their fathers had hallowed. Fifteen won the palm of martyrdom, and the names of Maurus Scot and Alban Roe, of Philip Powel and Ambrose Barlow are as glorious in the heroism of their death as the martyred heroes of the early church. Nine others passed to their crown within the prison walls deprived of the glory of martyrdom, yet suffering more than its pains. Few monks escaped the dungeon or exile in the seventeenth century, and the courage and zeal of these heroic men were tested by their eagerness to return again and again from exile to face toil, prison, and death. Such were the men whose names commence the roll in the following pages: men of indefatigable labour, indomitable energy, invincible courage, and saintly monastic life: of 330 Benedictine priests who died in the seventeenth century, one alone proved unfaithful to his religious vows, and in his old age he repented and returned to obedience. They were alone, separated from their brethren, away from their monasteries, but in their youth they had imbibed the monastic spirit in the cloister, the three great principles of their founder, obedience, 'conversio morum,' and stability had been engraved in their hearts, and they were prepared, like their missionary brethren in the preceding centuries, to practise these monastic virtues in the sight of the world; in spite of danger and persecution, of trial and allurement, to be faithful in their obedience to rule, to be constant in that 'conversio morum' which they had acquired in the cloister, and to be staunch till death in that stability which is the crown of the Benedictine life.

In explanation of the terms that occur in the Necrology the casual reader will need a brief account of the origin and constitution of the present English Benedictine Congregation. After the dissolution of the monasteries by Henry VIII. in 1536 and 1539 the Benedictines were dispersed over the country. The progress of the Reformation during the reign of Edward VI. stopped the supply of catholic priests and the numbers of the clergy both secular and regular gradually diminished. Mary came to the throne nearly twenty years after the dissolution during that interval there had been no professions and death had considerably thinned the ranks of the Benedictine monks: an effort was made to reconstruct the Benedictine Congregation, and a community was gathered together under Abbot Feckenham within the venerable walls of Westminster Abbey. The reign of Mary was too brief to produce any marked progress, and Elizabeth again dispersed the community at Westminster. During her long sway persecution and banishment were added to the loss of the colleges and monasteries for training priests, and the total extinction of the clergy both secular and regular was imminent. A noble effort to establish seminaries abroad was successful, and young men left their native shore to be trained for the arduous work of missionaries, and on their return to take the place of the old clergy: the Jesuits with their characteristic zeal and sacrifice entered strenuously into the work, and took a large share of the toil and suffering. The glory of the old Benedictine name, and and the intimate connection of the order with England inspired many of the heroic band of volunteers with a desire for the Benedictine habit. This spontaneous desire was the more remarkable as there was no Benedictine centre in England, and their missionary fervour could have been satisfied in the seminaries, or in the Jesuit novitiate: it was a sign that St. Benedict had not deserted his patrimony and had obtained these vocations from God. Their attention was directed to Italy and Spain, and the strength of the feeling may be estimated from the fact that no less than fifty-two applied for the Benedictine habit, in the hope that they might be allowed to return to England to resuscitate the Order, and recommence the work of St. Augustine and St. Paulinus. The monasteries in Italy in which these young men made their profession were Monte Cassino, St. Justina at Padua, St. George at Venice, La Cava, St. Paul at Rome, and others: in Spain at St. Emilian, St. Benedict at Valladolid, St. Facundus at Sahagun, St. Martin at Compostella, Montserrat, Najar, Onia, Cella Nouva, St. Sinbert, St. Millan, and others. In 1601 application was made to the Holy See to permit the English, who had been professed in the Cassinese Congregation, to return to their country and undertake the missionary labour, and in 1602 Clement VIII, like St. Gregory the Great, sent these monks with his approval and blessing to work for the conversion of England, and soon after a similiar brief was issued to those in the Spanish Congregation. The missioners entered the proscribed land, and were placed under the jurisdiction of two superiors who acted as the Vicars of the Cassinese and Spanish Generals.

In 1603 at Cisson near Wendlam in Norfolk at the house of Mr. Francis Wodehouse there lived F. Sigebert Buckley, a venerable patriarch of upwards of 85 years of age, who had been professed under Abbot Feckenham at Westminster. He was the last of his race, the sole survivor of the old Benedictines, forty-four years of his long life had been spent within prison walls for refusing the oath of Supremacy: his frame was bent, his step feeble, his eye dimmed, his mind unclouded, and like Simeon of old his days had been prolonged, that he might see the fulfilment of his long hope and prayer for the restoration of the Order in England. In the midst of his solitude and rest, there came to him one day two young and earnest priests, F. Anselm Beech and F. Thomas Preston, who told him that they were Englishmen and Benedictines, and had arrived from Italy with a mission from the Pope to re-establish the Benedictines in England. The meeting was a touching one: on the one hand the speechless delight and gratification of the venerable monk at this answer to his life long prayer, his long deferred hope, his waiting for the dawn of a new day, the opening of a new spring; and on the other the elation and enthusiasm of the young men who at the very threshold of their career, were guided by Providence to the feet of the last survivor of a glorious past. The intercourse was long: the old man's words of welcome and thankfulness mingled with the expressions of attachment and veneration of the young missioners: the records of the past were recalled, the hopes of the future discussed, and they united in the strong determination that, if possible, the old English Congregation and traditions should be perpetuated by the means of the venerable F. Sigebert. The proposal was communicated to the superiors in Italy, and it was arranged that the next postulants should be clothed and professed in England by F. Buckley, that the connection with the old Congregation might be unbroken. Unfortunately at this juncture the fire of bigotry was re-enkindled by the Gunpowder Plot, and one of the victims was F. Sigebert Buckley, who in spite of his great age and infirmity again found himself in the cell of a prison.

The incarceration of the venerable patriarch threatened to overthrow the arrangement, but the importance of the connection and the zeal of the new missioners overcame every obstacle. F. Robert Sadler and F. Edward Maihew, two secular priests who applied to become Benedictines, were clothed with the habit, and passed the year noviceship under the direction of the Italian fathers. On Nov. 21st., 1607, the Feast of the Presentation of Our Lady, they were brought to the Gatehouse prison in London, and conducted to the cell of F. Sigebert Buckley to be professed. It was a strange scene: the dull November light peering through the barred window, shed a dim glimmer on the rough ungarnished walls, the bare table, the rude bench, and the mat that served for the prison bed: the feeble bent figure of the Confessor of the Faith in his 91st. year, with his pale face and glistening eyes that with the excitement had regained their brightness, formed a contrast to the kneeling forms of the two novices in the prime of life with eager faces lit up with religious fervour. He received their vows, with trembling hands he arranged the habits, he gave them the kiss of peace, and then the sight left his eyes and he became stone blind: the last objects that on earth his eyes looked upon were his newly born children of St. Benedict. Never perhaps in the History of the Church is there recorded an act of similar significance, for by that profession were communicated all the rights and privileges of the old Benedictines in England; they were the accumulated rights of a thousand years from St. Augustine in 596, to himself in 1607: the possessions and rights of the Great Abbeys, of the numerous monasteries, of the twelve Cathedral Priories; all the privileges bestowed by Popes and Bishops, the Indulgences conceded by the Holy See, grants and immunities from King and Baron, all that Benedictines could claim for a thousand years were centred in himself as the sole survivor, and communicated to his disciples in that rough cell in the Gatehouse. This act of F. Buckley was formally confirmed by Paul V. in 1612 by the Brief *Cum accepimus.* F. Sigebert was shortly after released from prison, F.F. Anselm Beech, and Robert Preston guided the steps of the blind old patriarch to a safe retreat, ministered to him in his declining years with the affection of children, and, when his days were accomplished comforted his deathbed, and watched him pass away to his reward on Feb. 12th, 1610, at the advanced age of 93.

In the meantime the Anglo - Spanish fathers had
with equal zeal entered into the missionary work: a
number of eager, earnest monks had come from the
Abbeys in Spain, and seeing the difficulties and dangers
of the life, were anxious to obtain more labourers and
to make the work permanent: as the Italians had secured
the connection with the past, they directed their attention
to perpetuation in the future. They saw the necessity
of a centre, a monastery where the monks could be
specially trained for the mission, and to which they
could send young men to whom God had given a
vocation as Benedictine missionaries. F. Augustine
Bradshaw was able in 1605 to commence a monastery
at Douai under the patronage of St. Gregory, and soon
after was instrumental in opening another at Dieulward
in Lorraine dedicated to St. Laurence. In 1611 a third
was commenced at St. Malo in Brittany, under the
special protection of St. Benedict, and in 1615 F.
Francis Walgrave founded the monastery of St. Edmund
at Paris. Thus in a few years there were four monasteries established to supply the demand for missioners,
and there was every prospect of speedy development
when difficulties arose from the nature of the threefold
jurisdiction. The Italian, the Spanish, and the old
English Congregation, each had a superior in England,
and it was felt that it would be difficult to direct the
labours of the Benedictines with success, unless they

amalgamated into one Congregation. Steps were at once taken to procure a union, but the adjustment of the rights and claims of the three Congregations was a matter of tact and delicacy. The negotiations terminated in the appointment by the Holy See of nine Definitors, three chosen from each Congregation, who met under the presidency of Cardinal Bentivoglio the Legate in France, and drew up the Constitutions that were to form the basis of the New English Congregation, which comprised the missionaries then in England and the monks of the newly erected monasteries. Paul V. who throughout the negotiations had taken a deep interest in the construction of the New Congregation, formally ratified the proceedings, and approved of the Constitution and form of government, by the Brief *Ex Incumbenti* in 1619, in which, in order to secure the missionary character of the Congregation, he enacted that, besides the ordinary vows, each monk on profession should take an oath to labour on the mission in England when called upon by his superiors. The first General Chapter under the new Constitution was held 1621. The speedy organisation and rapid development of the New Congregation must be regarded as a signal mark of the blessing of Providence on this second Benedictine Mission to England. In the space of twenty years 52 missionary fathers had come from Italy and Spain, the link with the old Congregation had been secured, four monasteries established, 87 professed in those monasteries and others professed in England, the whole had been welded into one Congregation under one government, and all with the repeated blessing and direct encouragement of the Holy See; and this at a time of persecution and danger, when some were shedding their blood on the scaffold and others were confined in prison, this rapid development of internal organisation will bear comparison with that of the first Benedictine Missionaries. Urban VIII. in 1633 by the Bull *Plantata* crowned the edifice, confirmed all that had been done by his predecessors, endowed the Congregation with privileges, and enacted that it should be the only Congregation in England, commanding all other Benedictines either to join or to return to their monasteries.

Such is a brief outline of the origin of the Congregation, but the terms employed in the Necrology will scarcely be intelligible to the ordinary reader without a sketch of the form of government. A distinctive feature in the structure of the Congregation was the separation of the missioners, and erecting them into corporate bodies distinct from the monasteries. This was a new departure in Benedictine life, but it was adopted by the Definitors in consequence of the missionary character of the English Congregation, as the most efficient means of carrying out its end. To the monastery was consigned the task of instilling the principles of monastic life and of educating and training the missioner, and as soon as he was fit for the Apostolic Ministry, he passed to the care of a superior with a special knowledge and experience of missionary labour, who, living in the midst of the missions, could watch over, guide, control, and teach his subjects. This arrangement, specially sanctioned by the Holy See, avoided the difficulty of obtaining a Superior with capacity and ability sufficient to exact monastic observance and discipline in the monastery, and at the same time to exercise supervision over missionary work, and it moreover secured the advantage of a Superior who, besides having the experience, could give his whole time and undivided attention to the requirements of the mission which was the end of the Institute. The Congregation is composed of distinct corporate bodies, consisting of the two Missionary Provinces of Canterbury and York and the several Monasteries: over each of these is a Superior, a Prelate with regular jurisdiction, in the Provinces called Provincial, in the Monasteries, Prior. Over the whole Congregation, as the Superior of the Superiors, is the President General, who is attached to no Monastery or Province, but holds the highest position of honour and jurisdiction: his interest is that of the whole body as distinct from that of Monastery or Province: he has the power of visitation, the control of the Superiors, he alone can move subjects from monastery to mission, mission to monastery, or from monastery to monastery; his power and jurisdiction are limited only by the Constitutions and Canon Law. In matters of importance he has the assistance of three fathers who are called " Definitors of the Regimen," who are not allowed to hold any office with jurisdiction, in order that their attention may be given to the general interests of the Congregation: they also form a Court of Appeal. Thus the Provinces and Monasteries are presided over by a Superior whose duty it is to attend to the well-being of the separate bodies, while the general interests of the whole are confided to the President General and the Definitors of the Regimen, who are able to adjust any conflict of interest to the advantage of the whole Congregation.

Another distinctive feature adopted by the Definitors was that of temporary superiors instead of superiors for life. All offices, including that of the President General, are held for a term of four years, but at the end of each period of four years the officials are eligible for re-election. A capable superior can thus be continued in office, an unsuccessful one replaced, and moreover greater facility is afforded for employing good administrators in different offices. Every four years the General Chapter assembles and is composed of the Superiors, Definitors, and other officials and dignitaries. It is the supreme legislative authority and ultimate court of appeal:

it controls the elections, examines the accounts of Provinces and Monasteries, receives the report of the visitations, and confirms or rejects the acts of the government during the previous four years.

The Provinces of Canterbury and York each form a corporate body of which the missioners are the community. Each Province has two "Definitors of the Province" to assist and advise the Provincials, a "Procurator" for the transaction of business matters, and holds separate funds and property. The Provincial is a Prelate in the same sense as the Prior in a monastery, and has the same authority and jurisdiction over the missioners as if they were living in the monastery. The Province of York comprises all the missions in the six northern counties together with Derby, Cheshire, Nottingham, Lincoln, and Scotland: the Province of Canterbury includes the rest of England, and Wales.

The Monasteries are distinct from each other, and form separate corporations with superior, council, separate funds and property. Each monk on profession becomes affiliated to the Monastery of profession: when on the mission and removed from the jurisdiction of the Prior, he is not absolutely detached from the Monastery, it is his home to which he returns in infirmity or age, or when not employed on the mission. The principal officials are the Sub-prior, the Novice Master, the Junior Master over the young men after profession, the Cellerarius for matters of business and temporal affairs. The monasteries that have belonged to the Congregation are:—

1.—St. Gregory the Great, founded in 1605 at Douai, by F. Augustine Bradshaw, through the munificence of Abbot Cavarel. At the French Revolution the community was received by Sir E. Smythe at Acton Burnell, Shropshire, in 1793, where it remained till 1814, when it removed to Downside, near Bath.

2.—St. Laurence, founded in 1608 at Dieulward in Lorraine: at the French Revolution, the Community obtained temporary shelter at Acton Burnell, with that of St. Gregory's, in 1794. In 1795 it removed to Birkenhead, in 1796 to Scoles, near Prescot, in 1797 to Vernon Hall, in 1802 to Parbold, and finally towards the end of 1802 to Ampleforth, near York.

3.—St. Benedict, founded in 1611 at St. Malo in Brittany. It was handed over to the Maurist Congregation in 1669.

4.—St. Edmund the King and Martyr, founded in 1615 in Paris. At the Revolution in 1793 the community was imprisoned in the monastery itself for fourteen months. In 1796 the monastery was restored, and in 1804 the monks were again expelled. In 1823 after an interval of twenty years, the community was re-established in the old buildings of St. Gregory's at Douai.

5.—SS. Adrian and Dionysius: an Abbey at Lambspring in Germany, lent to the English Congregation by the Bursfeld Congregation in 1644. In 1803 it was suppressed by the Prussian government, and the monks were allowed to remain till death on a small pension. It was re-established at Broadway, Worcester, in 1834, but relinquished in 1841.

6.—St. Michael and the Angels, founded at Belmont, Hereford, in 1859. A decree of the Holy See ordered a common novitiate, and that at the end of the year of noviceship, the young monks after their simple profession should remain three years in a house of studies before returning to their monastery for solemn profession. This monastery, attached to the Pro-Cathedral of Newport and Menevia, was erected to carry out the designs of the Holy See. The Diocese has a Benedictine Chapter, some of the Canons are resident in the monastery and others are non-resident: the Prior is hence a "Cathedral Prior."

7.—The Abbey of Our Lady of Consolation, which is the only convent of nuns under the jurisdiction of the President General: other convents of English Benedictine nuns are under the jurisdiction of the Bishop of the Diocese and do not belong to the English Congregation. It was founded at Cambray in 1625. At the French Revolution in 1793, the community was imprisoned, and after its release obtained a temporary shelter at Woolton in 1795, whence it removed to Salford, near Evesham in 1807, and finally to Stanbrook, near Worcester, in 1838.

The Cathedral Priors.—Before the Reformation the Benedictines formed the Chapter of twelve of the old Cathedrals. They chaunted the Divine Office and conducted the services of the Cathedral: they had all the privileges of a Chapter of the Diocese and elected the Bishop. The Bishop nominally took the place of the Abbot, and the acting superior of the community was called Cathedral Prior. In recognition of these ancient privileges, Pope Urban VIII. in the Bull *Plantata* in 1633, enacted that these titles should be perpetuated in the new Congregation: the Bull itself nominates the first twelve who were to hold the dignity, and bestows on them the privileges, prerogatives, and immunities of their predecessors before the Reformation. The Bull not only authorizes the Congregation to continue the titles, but commands it never at any time or on any account to abolish or discontinue them, and renders invalid any attempt to do so. The Cathedral Priories perpetuated are those of Canterbury, Winchester, Durham, Ely, Worcester, Norwich, Rochester, Bath, Coventry, Peterboro', Gloucester, and Chester. The offices confer no jurisdiction but are titular merely: they give precedence and a seat in the General Chapter, and are bestowed on those who have been eminent in the Congregation.

The Titular Abbots.—For a similar reason the Holy See has during the present century granted the dignity of Titular Abbot, to perpetuate the great Abbeys that rendered the Benedictine name illustrious before the Reformation. The titles give no jurisdiction, only honour and precedence : at present they are those of Westminster, Glastonbury, St. Albans, St. Edmundsbury, Evesham, and St. Mary's, York.

The Missions have varied in number and character according to times and circumstances. In the days of persecution when liberty and life were at stake, the missionary fathers usually had no settled abode, but passed from place to place to minister to the scattered Catholics, and to elude the attention of spies and informers. With an occasional change of name, as well as concealment of residence, it is difficult to trace the missioner in the seventeenth century : there were no public chapels, mass and other ecclesiastical functions were celebrated in private houses with closed doors and sentinels, means of support for the priest were precarious, he was dependent mostly on the alms of the faithful, and was doubtless often in distress when access to a benefactor was difficult. In every county in England we find records of their labours : London seems to have been the basis of operations, for in the Metropolis there were always Benedictines, and at times regular communities were established at Somerset House and St.

James' Palace under the protection of a Catholic Queen. In the eighteenth century the active persecution diminished, and the Benedictine missions became more fixed: personal liberty was more secure and the missioners could be known and recognized as priests; they were able to erect or hire some room, that bore the name if not the appearance of a Catholic Chapel. The want of funds for support compelled the priests in many cases to remain with a Catholic family of position, and the chapel within, or attached to, the mansion was used by the Catholics of the neighbourhood. Towards the end of the century in the larger towns public chapels were erected usually in retired streets to escape notice. During these two centuries on account of the small number of Catholics, and the meagre means of support, the missions, with the exception of London, were served by one priest only, who lived by himself, receiving regular visits from his superior, and meeting his brethren occasionally at an appointed centre. The Emancipation Act and the immigration from Ireland changed the features of the missionary work. Congregations increased rapidly, funds were more abundant, churches were multiplied, chaplaincies relinquished; in the country the offerings of the people and the endowments of the wealthy, provided both chapel and permanent support; in the towns the labour was too great for one and the means of support sufficient for two or more, so that in many places the number of priests at one mission was gradually increased, thus securing the society of their own brethren, and greater facility for discipline and observance; the rapid means of communication rendered access between the brethren and the superior easy; at the present time the Provincials are within a few hours journey of any of their subjects. Thus commencing in persecution and without home or support, the Benedictine missions have gradually developed into quasi-religious houses with discipline and regular routine.

This preliminary explanation will place the reader in a position to understand the brief references in the Necrology. The names are arranged in three methods, Chronologically, as a Calendar, and Alphabetically. In the Chronological arrangement the names occur as each monk dies, and where the year is uncertain, the name is placed either at the date when he is last known to have been alive, or in the year in which from letters and documents he is supposed to have died. The change from the "Old Style" to the "Gregorian," renders the actual day in some cases uncertain, as it is difficult to ascertain which style the quoted document adopted. The aliases, or names assumed for the purpose of concealment or for other reasons, have been added in order that the individual may be recognized under either name. Besides the mere name and date of death, greater interest has been given by the addition of other dates: the year and place of birth, the year and monastery of profession, the year of ordination, and the year and place of the different missions at which each was stationed. In many the record is imperfect from causes mentioned above, but when complete, sufficient is given to trace any individual from profession till death. Among the many dates that are inserted there are doubtless inaccuracies, but every care and precaution has been taken to secure correctness. F. Allanson's Manuscripts have been freely used, the various necrologies and profession books examined, church registers and memorial tablets referred to, and any source of information consulted that might elucidate a date. The list of the nuns of Our Lady of Consolation has been revised at the Abbey at Stanbrook, and compared with their letters and documents.

The Calendar gives the names in the order of the days of the year. In the necrologies kept in the monasteries, when the actual day of death is unknown, it has been the custom to enter the name on some other day, that of profession, ordination, or birth, in order that the name may not be omitted altogether in the list: and this has given rise to considerable confusion. As all the names are inserted in the chronological arrangement, those with uncertain dates are omitted in the Calendar. Each day in the list records the actual anniversary of the death, and it is hoped that it may secure a special memento in the Holy Sacrifice for those whose names occur on the day.

The Alphabetical arrangement is given to serve for an Index, and accordingly both year and day are inserted to facilitate reference to the Chronological order, and to the Calendar. The second name or alias is repeated, so that an individual may be referred to under either name.

St. Mary's, Liverpool,
    May 20th, 1883.

ABBREVIATIONS AND EXPLANATIONS.

D.—Dom, indicates a priest.   Br.—Brother, one who has not been ordained priest.

The first Christian name is the Baptismal name, the second the name in religion: where one only is given, it may be either.

b.—born; ed.—educated; prof.—professed; ord.—ordained; d.—died.; sec. priest:—secular priest.

St. Greg.:—St. Gregory's Monastery at Douai, Acton Burnell, or Downside.

St. Lau.:—St. Laurence's Monastery at Dieulward, or Ampleforth.

St. Ed.:—St. Edmund's Monastery at Paris, or Douai.

Lambs.:—SS. Adrian and Denis' Abbey at Lambspring.

St. Malo.:—St. Benedict's Monastery at St. Malo.

S. Prov.:—South Province or Province of Canterbury.

N. Prov.:—North Province or Province of York.

Pres. Gen.:—President General.   Pr.:—Prior.   Cath. Pr.—Cathedral Prior.

Prov. of Cant.:—Provincial of Canterbury.   Prov. of York:—Provincial of York.

Def. Reg.:—Definitor of the Regimen.   Def. Prov.:—Definitor of the Province.

Proc. Prov.:—Procurator of the Province.   Gen. Chap.:—General Chapter.

Sec. Gen. Chap.:—Secretary to the General Chapter. Sec. Pres.:—Secretary to the President.

The year of birth or ordination may in some cases be one year wrong: when the authority consulted states the age at death to be e.g. 60, it may mean either 60 last birthday, or in the 60th. year, so that subtracting 60 from the year of death may not in some cases give the actual year of birth.

CHRONOLOGICAL LIST

OF THE

DECEASED MONKS

OF THE

ENGLISH CONGREGATION

OF THE

Order of Saint Benedict.

1601.   Feb. 27th.

MARK BARKWORTH.

b. Lincolnshire; educ. at Rheims and Valladolid where he is supposed to have been professed; came on the English mission and was hanged at Tyburne.

1602.   Oct. 30th.   D. ROBERT GREGORY SAYR.

A protestant; educ. at Cambridge; became a catholic and studied in the Eng. Colleges at Rheims and Rome; ordained sec. priest in Rome; professed at Monte Cassino 1589, and was professor of theology there; removed to St. George's, Venice, to teach theology in 1595, and there died.

1605.   Jan. 20th.   D. AUSTIN DE STO. FACUNDO.
Prof. at the Abbey of S. Facundus at Sahagun, Spain,
and died there.

1608.   April 11th.   D. GEORGE GERVASE.
b. at Boscham, Suffolk, in 1571; taken to the Indies
when young.   On his return went to the Eng. Coll.
at Douai, in 1599.   Ordained sec. priest in 1603.
Laboured on the Eng. mission, 1604-6, banished
1606.   Received the habit at Douai, 1606; returned
to the mission and was hanged at Tyburne.

1608.   ——   D. RAPHAEL.
Educated and was ordained sec. priest at the Eng.
Coll., Rome.   Prof. at St. Paul's, in Rome, about
1594.   Acted as Procurator in Rome for the Eng.
missioners, and d. in Rome.

1609.   April 14th.   D. ANDREW SHERLEY.
Prof. at Najar, in Spain.   Laboured on the Eng.
mission, and d. in Lancashire.

1610.   Feb. 13th.   D. NICHOLAS SADLER.
Suffered martyrdom.

1610.   Feb. 13th.   D. NICHOLAS HUTTON.
Suffered martyrdom.

1610.   Feb. 22nd.   D. ROBERT SIGEBERT BUCKLEY.
b. 1517.   Prof. at Westminster, in Queen Mary's
reign.   Was imprisoned on refusing the Oath of
Supremacy, and remained in prison the whole of
Elizabeth's reign.   Released by James I., but im-
prisoned again after the Gunpowder Plot.   At the
Gate House prison, in London, he received the
Profession of D. Robert Sadler, and D. Edward

Maihew, on Nov. 21st., 1607, and aggregated them to the Abbey of Westminster and the Old Eng. Congregation. He became blind, was soon after released from prison, retired to Wendlam, where he died, and was buried at Pontshall, Surrey.

1610. Dec. 10th. D. JOHN ROBERTS, OR MERVIN.
b. Merionethshire. Educated at the Eng. Coll., Rheims and Valladolid. Prof. at St. Martin's, Compostella, 1595. Ordained, 1600. Came to the mission in England in 1602, and appointed Vicar-General of the Spanish Benedictines in England. Was imprisoned, banished, and returned to the mission four separate times. The fifth time he was taken in his sacred vestments, condemned to death, and hanged at Tyburne.

1611-12. ———— D. MAURUS TAYLOR.
b. Diocese of Ely. Prof. at St. George's, Venice. Was sent on the mission in England and there died.

1612. May 30th. D. WILLIAM MAURUS SCOT.
b. Chigwell, Essex. Educ. at Cambridge. Converted to the Faith and went to the Eng. Coll., Valladolid. Prof. at St. Facundus, at Sahagun. Ordained and sent on the Eng. mission. Was arrested on arrival, remained in prison a year, was banished, and returned. This occurred several times until he was condemned to death and hanged at Tyburne.

———— ———— D. SAMUEL KENNET.
Prof. in the Cassinese Cong., and was on the mission in England in 1611. Date of death uncertain.

1614. Mar. 2nd. D. THOMAS BEDE MERRIMAN.
b. Co. of Durham. Was sent to Eng. Coll., Douai,

1605. Prof. St. Lau., 1610. Went to St. Gregory's to study, was there ordained, and died at Douai, and was buried in the parish church of St. Alban.

1615. Jan. 28th. D. ROBERT EDMUNDS.
b. Kent. Sent to Eng. Coll., Douai, 1602. Ord. sec. priest, and came on the mission in England. Received the habit and was prof. on the mission. Was often in prison and died in the Gate House London.

1615. ———— D. THOMAS DYER.
Stated to have been a Benedictine. Was on the mission, and was executed at Norwich.

1616. Nov. 6th. BR. JOSEPH BROOKS.
Prof. St. Lau., 1615, and d. at Dieulward

1616. ———— D. BARTHOLOMEW.
A secular priest who passed his noviceship, and was prof. on the mission. Date of death uncertain.

1616. ———— D. PLACID.
A secular priest who passed his noviceship, and was prof. on the mission. Date of death uncertain.

1617. July 12th. D. THOMAS MINSHALL.
b. Cheshire. Educ. Eng. Coll., Douai, and ord. sec. priest, 1608. Sent on the Eng. mission, 1609. Received the habit and was prof. on the mission. d. at Harding Castle, Flintshire.

1618. May 4th. D. JOHN AUGUSTINE BRADSHAW, OR WHITE.
b. Worcester, 1576. Educ. Eng. Coll., Valladolid. Prof. St. Martin's, Compostella, 1595, ord. 1600. Sent on the mission 1602. Was Vicar-Gen. of

Span. Bened. in England, 1602-12. Withdrew from mission in 1605, and was instrumental in founding convents at Douai and Dieulward. Resided at Chelles, 1612-15. Appointed superior over the Cluniac monastery at Longueville, in 1615, and died there.

1618. June 14th. D. WM. ANTHONY WINCHCOMB.
b. Henwick, Berks. Educ. Eng. Coll., Douai. Prof. St. Greg., 1614. Ord. and sent to England, and died at Henwick.

1618. Oct. 21st. D. GEORGE BROWN.
b. Essex. Educ. Eng. Coll. Douai. Prof. Abbey St. Sinbert, Spain. Sent to St. Lau., 1609, and the same year went on the Eng. mission. d. at Chelles.

1618. Oct. 30th. D. NICHOLAS BECKET.
Prof. Abbey of Onia, Spain. Sent to St. Lau. and was novice master: appointed to the mission, and d. at Canke, Staffords.

1619. April 18th. D. GREGORY GRANGE.
Prof. St. Martin's, Compostella. Sent to the mission, 1607. Appointed the First Provincial of Canterbury, but did not live to assume office.

16— ——— D. PETER WILCOX.
Prof. in Spain. Was at St. Greg. in 1619. Date of death uncertain.

16— ——— D. JOHN AMBROSE LANGTON.
b. London. Prof. St. Lau., 1615. Date of death uncertain.

16— ——— D. LUKE BENEDICT CAPE.
Prof. at St. Greg., for St. Malo, in 1615. Came on the mission, Date of death uncertain.

1621. June 21st. D. WALTER ROBERT VINCENT SADLER.

b. Collier's Oak, Warwicks. A Convert. Educ. and ord. sec. priest at Rome. Came on the Eng. mission. Was prof. by D. Sigebert Buckley in 1607, and aggregated to the Abbey of Westminster and the Old Eng. Congregation. Was elected one of the nine Definitors to arrange the Constitutions and terms of Union in 1617. Was first Prov. of Canterbury, 1619. d. in London.

16— ——— D. LAMBERT CLIFTON.

Prof. in Spain. Was on the mission in 1619. Date of death uncertain.

1623. Aug. 8th. D. RICHARD AUGUSTINE OWEN.

b. Diocese of St. Asaph, Wales. Educ. Eng. Coll., Douai. Ord. sec. priest, 1599, and the same year was sent on the mission. Received the habit and was prof. on the mission for St. Greg., 1616. d. in Yorkshire.

1623. Sep. 13th. D. JOHN COLUMBAN MALONE.

b. Lancashire. Educ. Eng. Coll., Douai. Prof. St. Greg., 1609. Was Professor of Philosophy, and Sub-prior. Elected Prior of St. Lau., 1621, and d. at Dieulward.

1624. June 24th. D. JOSEPH HAWORTH.

b. Lancashire. Educ. Eng. Coll., Douai. Prof. St. Lau., 1609. Was for a time a Conventual at St. Greg., and then at St. Malo. Elected Definitor in 1621. d. at St. Malo, and was buried at Claremont.

1624. July 25th. Br. Ralph Epiph. Stapylton.
b. Carleton, Yorks. Prof. St. Greg., 1620. Ord. Subdeacon, and d. on his way to Paris, at Roy, Pierrone, Picardy.

1624. Aug. 8th. D. Thomas Green or Houghton.
Prof. at Valladolid, and sent on the Eng. mission. Was in prison in Newgate, and banished in 1606. In exile he taught Theology at St. Greg. and St. Malo. He returned to the mission, was again in prison, and in ·1622 was released on account of infirmity.

1624. Dec. 19th. D. Thos. Torquatus Latham.
b. Rainfaith, Lancashire. Educ. Eng. Coll., Douai. Prof. St. Martin's, Compostella. Went to St. Greg., 1608. Professor of Philosophy at Marchienne Coll., Douai. Elected one of the nine Definitors to arrange the terms of the Union, in 1617. Chosen Definitor 1621. d. at Douai.

1625. Sep. 14th. D. Edward Maihew.
b. Dinton, Salisbury, 1570. Educ. Eng. Coll., Rheims and Rome. Sent on the Eng. mission, and was prof. by D. Sigebert Buckley, and aggregated to the Abbey of Westminster and the Old Eng. Congregation. Prior of St. Lau., 1614-20. One of the nine Definitors in 1617. Vicar of Nuns at Cambray, in 1625, where he died and was buried in the parish church of St. Vedast.

162- —— D. Anthony Athanasius Martin.
Educ. Eng. Coll., Rome. Ord. sec. priest. Prof. at La Cava, 1594. He died some time before 1626.

1626.　Jan. 8th.　Br. Oliver John Toudelle.

b. Lancashire.　Prof. St. Lau., 1625, and d. at Dieulward.

1626.　Feb. 20th.　D. Thomas Placid Hilton,
or Musgrave.

b. Carlisle.　Educ. Eng. Coll., Douai.　Ord. sec. priest
at Rheims, 1609.　Prof. St. Lau., 1610.　Went to
St. Malo and acted as superior in 1612.　Sent on
the mission, 1619.　d. in Middlesex.

1626.　Feb. 29th.*　D. Richard Hodgson.

b. Groumond, Yorks.　Educ. Eng. Coll., Douai.　Prof.
St. Greg., 1614.　Sent to St. Martin's, Compostella,
and there died.

1626.　Mar. 4th.　D. John Austin. Richardson.

b. Somerset.　Was a sec. priest on the mission.　Received the habit on the mission, was banished and
prof. St. Greg., 1618.　Returned to the mission and
d. in London.

1626.　June 10th.　D. Ralph Francis Atrobas.

b. Chester.　Was a Calvanist minister.　Converted
and went to the Eng. Coll., Douai.　Prof. at Onia,
Spain.　Prior of St. Greg., 1620-1.　Sent on the
mission 1621.　Was some time in prison.　d. in
Staffords.

16—　———　D. Arthur Michael Godfrey.

b. Suffolk.　Educ. Eng. Coll., Douai.　Prof. in Italy,
passed to the mission.　Date of death uncertain.

---

* As 1626 was not leap year Feb. 29th must be wrong.　It may
be either Feb. 28th or Mar. 1st, or by error in change of style either
Feb. 19th or Mar. 10th.　In the uncertainty the date given by the
authorities is retained.

1628. Nov. 20th. D. ROBERT AMANDUS VERNER, OR FERMOR.

b. Devon. Educ. Eng. Coll., Douai. Ord. 1609, and passed to the mission. Banished and prof. St. Lau., 1614. Returned to the mission, suffered long imprisonment, and d. in London.

1629. Jan. 24th. D. THOMAS BEDE HELME.

b. Kendal, Westmoreland. Educ. Eng. Coll., Douai. Prof. at Montserrat and passed to the mission. Was First Provincial of York, 1620-5. d. in Durham.

1629. April 10th, D. WILLIAM GABRIEL GIFFORD.

b. Hants, 1554. Educ. Lincoln Coll., Oxford, Louvaine, Rheims, and Rome. Professor of Theology at Rheims, 1582. D.D., 1584. Was Chaplain to Card. Allen, in Rome, 1595. Dean of Lisle, Flanders, 1597-1607. Chancellor of the Archdiocese of Rheims, 1607. Received the Benedictine habit at Rheims, 1608, and prof. St. Lau., 1609. Prior of St. Lau., 1609-10. Prior of St. Malo's, 1611-18. One of the nine Definitors to arrange the Union in 1617. Consecrated Bp. of Archidale and Coadj. to Rheims in 1618, Succeeded to the Archbishopric, 1622. d. at Rheims.

1629. June 6th. D. BEDE BANESTER, OR GAILE.

b. Yorkshire. Prof. St. Greg., 1620. Passed to the mission in the N. Prov., and d. in Northumberland.

1629. Oct. 25th. D. JOHN CELESTINE TREMBIE.

b. 1591. Prof. at St. Greg. for St. Malo, 1614. Went to St. Malo, and there died.

1629. Oct. 28. D. RUPERT GUILLET.

b. Wales, 1595. Prof. St. Malo, 1618, and there died.

163— ——— D. Edward Ashe, or Fesand.

b. London. Educ. Eng. Coll., Valladolid. Prof. in Spain. Passed to the mission, and d. at Midhurst, shortly after 1629.

1630. Mar. 15th. D. Maurus Hanson.

Prof. in Spain. Sent on the mission in the N. Prov. d. in Lancashire.

1630. Oct. 10th. D. Thomas Emerson.

Prof. at Sahagun, Spain. Took Degree of D.D. Passed to the mission, was several times in prison and banished. d. on the mission.

1631. Feb. 5th, D. John Norton.

b. Sussex. Prof. St. Greg., 1624, and d. at Douai.

1631. May 25th. D. Joseph Prater.

Prof. at St. Martin's, Compostella. Sent on the mission. Was Prov. of Canterbury, 1621-5.

1631. June 4th. D. Francis Foster.

b. Shrops. Educ. Eng. Coll., Rome, and Douai. Ord. 1598. Sent on the mission, 1599. Imprisoned in Newgate. Banished, 1606, but returned. Was professed on the mission, frequently in prison, and died at Stafford Castle.

1631. Oct. 24th. D. Augustine Heath.

b. Winchester. Was a secular priest. Prof. St. Lau., 1612. Sent to Chelles. d. at Dieulward.

16— ——— D. Augustine Smith.

b. Lancs. Educ. Eng. Coll., Rome. Ord. sec. priest. Prof. Monte Cassino, 1592. Made Vicar of the Abbey. Passed to the mission 1605, and acted as Superior of the Italian Benedictines in England. Date of death uncertain.

16— ———— D. DAVID CODNER.
Prof. in Italy. Sent on the mission, 1626. Date of death uncertain.

1632. May 8th. D. PLACID FRERE.
b. Essex. Prof. St. Greg., 1624. Ord. 1631. d. at Rintelin, Westphalia.

1632. June 27th. D. GREGORY HAYWARD.
b. Oxfords, 1602. Prof. at Paris for St. Greg., 1621. Ord., 1628. d. at Douai.

1632 July 6th. D. JOHN PLACID MUTTLEBERRY.
b. Wells, Somerset. Educ. Eng. Coll., Douai. Ord., 1601 and passed to the mission. Banished in 1606. Prof. St. Lau., 1610 or 1611, and died at Dieulward.

1632. Nov. 9th. D. MICHAEL BLAKESTONE.
b. Co. of Durham. Prof. St. Greg., 1625, and died at Douai.

1632. Nov. 17th. D. JEROME PORTER, OR NELSON.
Prof. at Paris for St. Greg., 1622, and d. at Douai.

163- ———— BR. HENRY FRANCIS WHITENHALL.
b. Kent. Prof. St. Ed., 1629. He was sent to St. Greg., and St. Lau., and then in 1632 on account of his health to England, where he died soon after.

1633. Jan. 14th BR. CELESTINE DE LANDRES.
b. Lorraine. Prof. St. Lau., 1630. Sent to St. Greg. for his studies, and d. at Douai.

1633. Jan. 21st. D. MAURUS SMITH.
b. London. Prof. St. Greg., 1625, and d. at Douai.

16— ———— D. GEORGE HATHERSAL.
Prof. St. Greg., 1615. Date of death uncertain.

1633. Aug. 19th. D. Sigebert Bagshaw.
  b. Derbyshire. Was a secular priest. Prof. on the mission and stated to have been aggregated to the Abbey of Westminster. He was Procurator in Rome for the old Eng. Cong. Was one of the nine Definitors to arrange the Union in 1617. Pr. of St. Ed., 1621-9. Pres. Gen. 1630 till death at Douai.

1633. Oct. 13th. D. Laurence Lowick.
  b. Osmotherly, Yorks. Prof. St. Lau., 1620. Sent on the mission in the S. Prov., and d. at Stoke, Gloucester.

1633. Oct. 23rd. D. Walter William Kemble.
  b. Herefords. Prof. St. Greg., 1620, and passed to the mission in the S. Prov., and d. at Faunethorpe, Herefords.

16— ——— D. Amatus Legatt.
  b. Shaftesbury. Joined the Cluny Cong., then prof. St. Greg., 1626, and passed to the mission. Date of death uncertain.

16— ——— Br. Robert Theodore Barlow.
  b. Manchester. Prof. St. Greg., 1630. Sent to England, and died there.

1634. March 22nd. D. Boniface Blandy.
  Prof. at St. Facundus, Sahagun, Spain. Acted as Proc. for the Eng. Cong. in Spain. d. at Madrid.

1634. April 2nd. D. Felix Thompson, or Pratt.
  b. Northampton. A sec. priest. Imprisoned and banished. Prof. St. Malo, 1614. Was Novice Master of St. Malo, Chelles, and Paris. Returned to the mission, and d. in Staffords.

1634. Aug. 15th. D. WM. ROMUALD DANVERS.

b. Suffolk. Was a Minister of the Established Church. Deprived of his living, imprisoned and banished. Went to Eng. Coll., Douai. Ord. 1619. Prof. St. Greg., 1620. d. at St. Malo, and buried at Claremont.

1634. Nov. 21st. D. GREGORY GEORGE GAIRE.

Prof. St. Lau., 1611. Went to St. Ed., 1615. Passed to the mission, suffered imprisonment and exile, and d. in London.

1634-5. Dec. 28th. D. ANSELM BEECH.

b. Manchester. Educ. Eng. Coll., Rome. Ord. sec. priest. Prof. St. Justina, Padua, 1591. Sent on the mission, 1603. Went to Rome as Procurator in 1607. Returned to England and appointed Superior of the Italian Benedictines in 1613. Retired in his old age to Padua, and there died.

1635. March 10th. D. WILLIAM MAURUS ATKINS.

b. Oatwell, Norfolk. Prof. St. Greg., 1614. Was Cellerarius. Passed to the mission, and died in England.

1635. March 31st. D. GABRIEL LATHAM.

b. Lancashire. Prof. St. Ed., 1622. Ord. 1627. d. at La Celle.

1635. April 23rd. D. JUSTUS EDNER, OR RIGG.

Prof. Valladolid. Passed to the mission in the S. Prov., and d. in Oxfordshire.

1635. June 20th. D. JOHN MAURUS CURRE.

b. Sandonfee, Berks. Prof. St. Greg., 1614. Sent on the mission, was imprisoned, banished, and returned. d. in Yorkshire.

1635.   June 30th.   D. JOHN ALLEN.
b. Middlesex.   Educ. Eng. Coll., Douai.   Prof. St. Greg., 1624.   d. at Douai.

1635.   Dec. 27th.   D. JOHN LEANDER JONES.
b. London, 1575.   Educ. St. John's Coll., Oxford.   Became a Catholic.   Prof. St. Martin's, Compostella, 1600.   Ord. and took D.D. at Salamanca.   Was Novice Master at St. Greg., 1607.   Appointed Vic. Gen. of Spanish Benedictines, 1612.   One of the nine Definitors to arrange the terms of Union in 1617.   Was the First Pres. Gen., 1619-21.   Pr. of St. Greg., 1621-5.   First Definitor, 1625-9.   Pr. of St. Greg., 1629-33.   Cath. Pr. of Canterbury, 1633, and Abbot of Cismar, 1629.   Pres. Gen., 1633, till his death in London.   He was buried at Somerset House.

1636.   Jan. 8th.   D. ANSELM WILLIAMS.
Prof. St. Lau., 1622   Hanged from a tree in Lorraine by the heretical army of Saxon Weimar.

1636.   Jan. 8th.   BR. LEANDER NEVILLE.
Prof. St. Lau., 1628   Hanged in Lorraine with D. Ans. Williams.

1636.   April 1st.   D. BERNARD EDMUNDS.
b. Kent.   Prof. St. Lau., 1610 or 1611.   Sent away to avoid the pestilence, but d. at Pont-a-Mousson.

1636.   May 11th.   D. BENEDICT D'ORGAINE.
b. Dieulward.   Prof. St. Lau., 1612.   Sent to St. Malo and there ord.   Went to Cluny and there died.

1636.   July 4th.   BR. BONIFACE MARTIN.
b. London.   Prof. St. Lau., 1622.   Ord. Deacon.

Accompanied D. Benedict D'Orgaine to Cluny, and d. at the monastery of "La Charité."

1636. Aug. 3rd. D. ALEXIUS BENNET.

A Protestant soldier converted by D. Rob. Sadler. Prof. St. Lau., 1615. d. of pestilence at Dieulward.

1636. Aug. 7th. D. JOSEPH FOSTER.

b. Yorks. Prof. St. Lau., 1630. d. of pestilence at Dieulward.

1636. Aug. 15th. D. ALDHELM PHILLIPS.

b. Herefords. Prof. St. Lau., 1620. d. of pestilence at Dieulward.

1636. Aug. 31st. BR. ANTHONY BENEDICT JERNINGHAM.

b. Norfolk. Prof St. Lau., 1625. d. of pestilence at Dieulward.

1636. Sep. 6th. D. ROBERT INGLEBY.

b. Lawkland, Yorks. Prof. St. Lau., 1626. d. of pestilence at Dieulward.

16— ——— D. DUNSTAN GIBSON.

b. Yorks. Prof. St. Ed., 1629. Ord. 1634. Date of death uncertain.

1637. July 21st. D. EDWARD BENEDICT SMITH.

b. Whalley, Lancs. Prof. at Chelles, 1617. Sent on mission, 1618. Appointed Vicar of Nuns at Cambray, 1625. Definitor, 1629. Cath. Pr. of Chester, 1633. Sent as Procurator to Madrid and died there.

—— March. 27th, D. Dunstan Grove, or Craffe.

Prof. at Chelles. Went to St. Ed. Was stationed with the Benedictine Nuns at Jouar, and died there, the year being uncertain.

1638. Feb. 2nd. D. John Cuthbert Fursden.

b. Thorverton, Devon. Prof. St. Greg., 1620. Sent to the mission in the S. Province and d. in London.

1638. Aug. 19th. D. Richard Wolstan Ingham, or Walmsley.

Prof. St. Ed., 1630. Ord. 1634. Master of Novices, 1636. d. at Paris.

1638. Sep. 14th. D. William Gordon.

A Scotch Benedictine aggregated to the Eng. Cong., and d. at Paris.

1639. Oct. 19th. D. William Benedict Jones, or Price.

b. London. A convert. Educ. Eng. Coll., Douai. Prof. at St. Facundus, Sahagun, Spain. Was Procurator in Rome for the Span. Benedictines. One of the nine Definitors to draw up the terms of the Union in 1617. Instrumental in establishing the nuns at Cambray. Was many years on the mission. Cath. Pr. of Winchester, 1633. d. in London.

1639. Nov. 2nd. D. Bernard Berington.

Prof. at Onia, Spain. Pr. of St. Ed., 1616-8. Cath. Pr. of Worcester, 1633. d. at Paris.

1639. Nov. 28th. D. JOHN HARPER.

Prof. at Emilian's in Spain. Was Novice Master at St. Malo in 1612. Sent on the mission. Suffered imprisonment and banishment, but returned and d. in London.

1639. Dec. 24th. D. JOHN STANISLAUS TANKE.

b. Wales. Prof. St. Greg., 1625, and passed to the mission and d. in England.

1640. Jan. 13th. D. HENRY STILES.

Prof. in Italy. d. at St. Gislin.

1640. Mar. 3rd. D. VINCENT LATHAM.

b. Lancashire. Prof. St. Greg., 1622. Sent on the mission in the N. Prov. d. in Yorkshire.

1640. March. 31st. D. AUGUSTINE LEE, OR JOHNSON.

b. Mortlake, Surrey. A secular priest. Prof. on the mission for St. Greg. in 1624. d. in Sussex.

1640. April 3rd. D. THOMAS PRESTON.

b. Shropshire. Educ. Eng. Coll., Rome. Ordained sec. priest. Prof. at Monte Cassino, 1590, was sent on the mission in 1602. Suffered long imprisonment, and d. in the Clink, London.

1640. Nov. 13th. BR. BENEDICT PRESTON.

b. Lancashire. Prof. St. Greg., 1639, and d. at Douai.

1640. Dec. 9th. BR. JEROME HESKETH.

b. Lancashire. Prof. St. Greg., 1639, and d. at Douai.

1640. Dec. 15th. D. WM. SWITHBERT LATHAM.

b. Rainfaith, Lancs. Educ. Eng. Coll., Douai. Prof. St. Lau., 1614. Sent on the mission in the N. Prov., and d. at Mosborrow, Lancs.

1641. Feb. 22nd. D. JOHN LONE.
b. Kent. Prof. St. Greg., 1620. d. at Douai.

1641. April 6th. D. GERVASE GRAY.
Prof. in Italy. Passed to the mission, and d. at Westby, Lancs.

1641. July 20th. D. LAURENCE MABBS.
b. Leicestershire. Prof. St. Greg., 1620. Sent on the mission. Suffered imprisonment, and d. in Newgate.

1641. Aug. 9th. D. DAVID AUGUSTINE BAKER.
b. Abergavenny, 1575. Educ. at Oxford. Studied for the Law. Was Recorder of Abergavenny. Became a Catholic. Received the habit at St. Justina, Padua, in 1605. Prof. in England. Ordained. Served on the mission. Went to St. Greg., 1624, and then to the nuns at Cambray. Was Definitor in Chapter, 1633, but resigned. Sent to the mission, 1638. d. of the plague in London, and was buried at St. Andrews, Holborn.

1641. Sep. 20th. D. EDWARD AMBROSE BARLOW.
b. Manchester, 1586. Educ. Eng. Coll., Douai, and Valladolid. Prof. St. Greg., 1616. Ord. 1617. Sent on the mission in the N. Prov., and laboured in Lancashire. Was hanged at Lancaster.

1642. Jan. 31st. D. BARTHOLOMEW ALBAN ROE.
b. Suffolk, 1583. Educ. at Cambridge. Became a Catholic. Went to the Eng. Coll., Douai. Prof. St. Lau., 1612. Sent to St. Ed., and then to the mission. Was imprisoned and banished, but returned to be again imprisoned. Was hanged at Tyburne.

1642. June 12th. D. Thomas Monington.

b. All Hallows, Herefords. Prof. St. Greg., 1610. Was Novice Master at St. Greg. Pr. of St. Ed., 1620-1. Definitor, 1621-5. Passed to the mission in the S. Prov. was at Whitefield, Gloucestersh. in 1625, where he d. and was buried at Dirhurst.

1643. Aug. 19th. D. Thomas John Hutton.

Prof. St. Martin's, Compostella. Passed to the mission. Prov. of York, 1629-33. Cath. Pr. of Ely, 1633. d. in Yorkshire.

16— —— D. Christian Goaverdt.

b. Bruges. Prof. St. Greg., 1624. Sec. of Pres., 1633. Date of death uncertain.

1644. May 5th. D. Matthew Sandeford.

b. Shropshire. Educ. Eng. Coll., Douai. Prof. St. Malo, 1613. Pr. of St. Ed., 1618-9. Joined Archbp. Gifford at Rheims, 1619. Took degree of D.D. Appointed Prior of St, Nivards. Was at St. Ed., 1629-32, and then returned to St. Nivards, where he died.

1644. July 26th. D. Wm. Alphonsus Hanson, or Hesketh.

b. Barrowford, Lancs. Educ. Seminary, Seville. Ord. sec. priest. Prof. St. Greg., 1615. Sent on the mission. Returned to teach Philosophy at St. Greg. and St. Ed. Again on the mission in Yorkshire. Worried to death by the Parliamentary troops in Yorkshire.

1644. July 26th. D. Francis Boniface Kemp, or Kipton.

Prof. at Montserrat. Was Sub-prior at St. Malo's in 1612. Sent to the mission. Imprisoned in Newgate and banished, but returned. Worried to death by Parliamentary troops in Yorkshire.

1644. July 26th. D. William Middleton, or Hethcote

Prof. on the mission. Worried to death by the Parliamentary troops in Yorkshire.

1644. Aug. 7th. D. Edmund Thomas Hill.

b. 1560 Ord. secular priest, 1591, and D.D. Received the habit in prison and professed on his release, 1613. Laboured many years on the mission. Cath Pr. of Gloucester, 1633. In old age retired to St. Greg., and d. at Douai.

1644. Nov. 27th. Br. William Sheldon.

b. Warwickshire. Prof. St. Ed., 1640. Ord. deacon. d. at Douai.

1645. April 15th. D. Anselm Turberville.

Prof. at Montserrat. Sent on the mission, and d. in Glamorganshire.

1645. Nov. 27th. D. Paulinus Greenwood.

b. Brentwood, Essex. Prof. St. Greg., 1612. Was Sub-prior and Professor of Philosophy. Sent on the mission and suffered long imprisonment, and on release, returned to St. Greg. Prior of St. Malo, 1620-5. Definitor and Procurator in Rome, 1655. Cath. Pr. of Norwich, 1633. Sent again on the mission, and was Prov. of Canterbury, 1641, till his death at Oxford.

1645. Dec. 31st.   D. Francis Hull.

b. Devonshire. Prof. St, Lau., 1615. Appointed Vicar of Nuns at Cambray, 1629. Definitor, 1633. Vicar in France, 1639-45. Resided at St. Ed., and then at St. Malo, where he died.

1645. ———   D. Paulinus Appleby.

Prof. Onia, Spain. Pr. of St. Lau., 1610-4. Sent on the mission in the N. Prov., 1614, and d. in Yorkshire.

1645. ———   D. Paulinus Hird, or Laton.

b. Yorkshire. Prof. St. Greg., 1631. Passed to the mission and d. in the N. Prov.

———   ———   D. Renatus Deodatus Langevin.

b. St. Malo. Prof. at St. Greg. for St. Malo, 1614. Pr. of St. Malo, 1629-40. Afterwards resided at St. Ed.

1646. Mar. 12th.   D. Peter Boniface Wilford.

b. London, 1556. A sec. priest. Prof. St. Greg., 1609. Was at Chelles in 1612, and at St. Greg., 1616, and passed to the mission. Suffered imprisonment and d. in Newgate, upwards of 90 years of age.

1646. May 22nd.   D. John Moundeford, or Mumford.

b. Wenhamrow, Norfolk. Educ. Eng. Coll., Douai. Prof. St. Greg., 1614. Sent to Compostella, St. Ed., and St. Greg., and then passed to the mission in the S. Prov. d. at Worcester.

1646. June 11th.   D. George Joseph Latham.

b. Rainfaith, Lancs. Educ. Eng. Coll., Douai. Prof. St. Greg., 1617. Was Cellerarius, and sent to St. Ed., and passed to the mission in the S. Prov. in 1625. d. at Hereford.

1646. June 30th. D. ROGER PHILIP POWEL, OR MORGAN OR PROSSER.

b. Tralon, Brecknock, 1594. Studied Law in the Temple. Prof. St. Greg., 1620. Passed to the mission in the S. Prov. in 1622, and stationed in Devon and Somerset. Hanged at Tyburne and buried in Moorfields.

1646. Aug. 27th. D. JAMES ANDERTON.

b. Lostock, Lancs. Prof. St. Greg., 1623. Sent on the mission in the S. Prov., and d. at Harding Castle, Flints.

1646. Dec. 13th. D. PLACID LOADER, OR IRELAND.

b. London. Prof. St. Greg., 1620. Ord., 1624. Sent on the mission.

1646. ——— D. MARTIN CUTHBERT HARTBURN.

b. Stillington, Durham. Prof. St. Greg., 1614. Passed to the mission.

——— ——— D. MICHAEL MIDDLETON.

A conventual at St. Greg. in 1646, but there is no record of his Profession, or death.

1648. Jan. 24th. D. FRANCIS GICOU.

b. Brittany, 1585. A sub-deacon. Prof. at St. Ed. for St. Malo, 1617. Superior of St. Malo, 1640-3 and died there.

1648. May 23rd. D. ROBERT BENEDICT COX.

Prof. St. Lau., 1612. Sent on the mission. Imprisoned and d. in the Clink under sentence of death.

1649. ———— D. Edward Constantius Nathal, or Matthews.

Educ. Eng. Coll., Douai. Prof. in Spain. Was at St. Ed. in 1619. Passed to the mission and suffered imprisonment. d. in Norfolk.

1649. Aug. 5th. D. Nicholas Curre.

Prof. St. Lau., 1610 or 1611. Was Sub-prior of St. Greg., 1624. Definitor, 1625. Vice-prior of St. Ed., 1631. Passed to the mission in the S. Prov., 1632. d. at Weston, Warwicks.

——— ——— D. William Romanus Grossier.

b. Paris. Prof. St. Ed. for St. Malo, 1620. Was Cellerarius at St. Ed., 1625. Went to St. Malo. Date of death uncertain.

——— ——— D. Humphrey Placid Peto, or Budd.

Prof. St. Facundus, Sahagun, Spain. Passed to the mission, was in prison and escaped, 1615. Laboured many years on the mission, was again in prison, and d. in Newgate under sentence of death.

——— ——— Br. Peter Gifford.

b. Whiston, Staffords. Prof. St. Ed. 1640. d. in England, the date uncertain.

1650. Feb. 8th. D. Rob. Haddock, or Benson.

Prof. St. Martin's, Compostella. Passed to the mission, 1607. Appointed Superior of Span. Benedictines in England. One of the nine Definitors to arrange the terms of the Union, 1617. Prov. of York, 1625 - 9. Cath. Pr. of Durham, 1633. d. in Staffordshire.

1650. Feb. 10th. D. DUNSTAN EVERARD.
b. Suffolk. Prof. at St. Greg. for St. Malo, 1616. Sent on the mission. Suffered imprisonment and banishment. Was at St. Ed. in 1641. d. in Jersey and buried at St. Malo.

1650. March 6th. D. FRANCIS BLAKESTON.
b. in the Co. of Durham. Prof. St. Greg., 1626. Laboured many years on the mission. In the Civil war was Chaplain in the Royal army.

1650. Oct. 21st. D. BERNARD WARREN.
b. Cheshire. Prof. at. La Celle, 1648. Ord. 1649. d. in Paris.

1650. Nov. 22nd. D. JOHN GARTER.
b. Northamptons. Prof. St. Ed., 1639. Was cellerarius, 1642. Ord., 1643. Sent to La Celle, 1644. Returned to St. Ed. to be Cellerarius again. Appointed Superior of La Celle, 1648, and there died.

1651. Jan. 12th. D. WILLIAM ANTHONY BATT.
b. Wiltshire. Educ. Eng. Coll., Douai. Ord. 1604. Prof. St. Lau., 1615. Sent on the mission and returned to St. Ed. Cath Pr. of Peterboro', 1633. Superior and Novice Master at La Celle, 1641. Returned to St. Ed., 1642. d. in Paris.

1651. Mar. 17th. D. CLEMENT REYNER.
b. Yorks, 1589. Prof. St. Lau., 1610. Sent to St. Greg. for studies. Took the degree of D.D. Was Sec. to Pres., 1621-9. Was sent to Germany to negotiate the transfer of monasteries from the Bursfield Cong. Definitor, 1633. Pres.-Gen., 1635-41. Obtained the Abbey of Lambspring, 1643. Confirmed Abbot, 1645. d. at Hildesheim and buried at Lambspring.

1651. July 1st. D. Felix Jocelin Elmer.
b. Worcestershire. Prof. St. Lau., 1610 or 1611. Pr. of St. Lau., 1620-1. Pr. of St. Malo, 1625-9. Pr. of St. Lau., 1629-41. Pres.-Gen., 1641-5. Definitor, 1645. Pr. of St. Malo, 1649, till death there.

1652. May 16th. D. Nicholas Fitzjames.
b. Redlynch, Somerset, 1560. Educ. Eng. Coll., Douai. Ord. 1601. Passed to the mission, 1601. Prof. St. Greg., 1608. Went to St. Lau. and was Novice Master, also Prior for a short time in 1610. Sent again on the mission and d. at Stourton, Wilts.

1652. July 9th. D. Thomas Cuthbert Risden.
Prof. St. Ed., 1640, and d. at Paris.

1652. Nov. 13th. D. Andrew Simpson.
Prof. St. Ed., 1641, and d. in Normandy.

1652. ——— D. Edw. Gloster, or Glasscock.
b. Essex. Prof. at St. Greg. for St Ed., 1640. Was Novice Master at La Celle, 1642. Cellerarius at St. Ed., 1645. d. at La Celle.

1653. Jan. 27th. D. Thos. Woodhope, or White.
b. Worcestershire. Prof. St. Greg., 1622. Passed to mission in S. Prov., and was stationed at Beoley, Worcesters. Was vice-prior of St. Greg. in 1649, and d. at Douai.

1653. Feb. 17th. D. Henry Placid Cary.
Prof. St. Ed., 1641. Sec. to Pres., 1649.

1653. June 8th. D. Robert Amandus Southcot.
b. Devon. Prof. St. Greg., 1624. Sent on the mission in the S. Prov., and d. at Bidwell, Exeter.

1653. July 1st. Br. John Barter.

Took the habit at St. Greg. on the same day as his father, in 1653, and d. of the plague at Douai.

1653. July 11th. D. Christopher Anderton.

b. Lostock, Lancs., 1607. Educ. Eng. Coll., Douai. Prof. St. Greg., 1624. Elected Definitor, 1641-5. Sec. to Pres., 1645-9, and went to Rome with him. Definitor again, 1649, residing at St. Greg., where he died of the plague.

1654. Jan. 6th. D. John Owen.

b. St. Asaphs, Wales. Educ. Eng. Coll., Valladolid. Prof. in Spain. Passed to the mission and d. Drury Lane, London.

1654. May 28th. D. Francis Constable.

Prof. St. Lau., 1615. Sent on the mission and d. Drury Lane, London.

1654. May 29th. D. Rob. Mellitus Bapthorpe.

Educ. Eng. Coll., Valladolid. Prof. at Rheims for St. Lau., 1609. Went to St. Malo. Passed to the mission, 1619, to the N. Prov. and d. in the N. of England.

—— ——— Br. Laurence Errington.

Prof. St. Greg., 1654. Date of death uncertain.

1655. Jan. 8th. D. George de Sto. Ildephonso.

b. Sculthorpe, Norfolk. A secular priest prof. on the mission for St. Greg., 1622. d. on the mission.

1655. Feb. 12th. D. Gregory Moore.

b. Carlisle. A sec. priest prof. on the mission for St. Greg., 1622. d. on the mission.

1655. May 30th. D. John Placid Hartburn,
or Commings, or Foorde.

b. Stillington, Durham. Educ. Eng. Coll., Douai.
Ord., 1609. Passed to the mission, 1610. Prof.
St. Greg., 1617. Went to St. Ed., 1629, and thence
to the mission again, 1639, in the N. Prov. Proc.
of the Province in 1633. d. on the mission.

1655. May 31st. D. William Palmer.

b. 1575. Prof. in Italy, passed to the mission in
the S. Prov. and d. at Longwood, Hants.

1655. Oct. 14th. D. William Claude White,
or Bennet.

b. Bangor, 1583. Educ. Eng. Coll., Douai. Ord.,
1605. Place of prof. is doubtful, but he was
aggregated to St. Lau., 1610 or 1611. Was a
conventual at St. Ed., 1620, and thence on the
mission for the second time. Was Prov. of Canterbury, 1629-33. Pres.-Gen. for a short time in
1633. Definitor, 1633. Prov. of Canterbury, 1645-
53. Pres.-Gen., 1653, till death at St. Ed. He
was buried at St. Germains. During the 36 years
of missionary life he was for some time chaplain
to Lord Windsor, and for four years at Weston,
Warwicks, 1649-53.

1655. Nov. 26th. D. Richard Huddlestone.

b. Farrington Hall, Lancs, 1583. Educ. Eng. Coll.,
Rheims, Douai and Rome. Ord., 1607. Passed to
the mission. Returned to Italy and was prof.
Monte Cassino. Again sent on the mission in
1619, and d. at Stockeld, Yorks.

1656. July 22nd. D. FERDINAND EMILIAN THROCKMORTON.
b. Antwerp. Prof. St. Ed., 1623. Ord., 1627. d. in Paris.

1656. Sep. 19th. D. WM. RUDESIND BARLOW.
b. Manchester, 1585. Educ. Eng. Coll., Douai. Prof. at Cella Nuova, Gallicia, 1605. Ord., 1608. Took the degree of D.D. at Salamanca. Sent to St. Greg., 1611. Was Pr. of St. Greg., 1614-21. One of the nine Definitors for the Union, 1617. Pres.-Gen., 1621-29. Definitor, 1629. Prof. of Theology for 40 years at the Coll. of St. Vedast, Douai. Cath. Pr. of Canterbury, 1633. d. at Douai.

1657. Feb. 18th. D. RICHARD WILFRID READE, OR SELBY.
b. Northumberland. Prof. St. Greg., 1620. Was Procurator in Rome, 1629-45. Cath Pr. of Chester, 1642. Pres.-Gen., 1645-9. d. in Rome.

1657. Feb. 20th. D. JOHN HILARION WAKE, OR MERRIMAN.
b. Carryhouse, Durham. Prof. St. Greg., 1639. Sent to Lambspring, 1645. Returned to Douai. Was sec. to chapter, 1649. Sec. to Pres., 1653. Procurator in Rome, 1654. d. in Rome.

1657. April 22nd. D. MAURUS HAMES.
Prof. St. Malo, 1630, and died there.

1657. April 25th. D. THOMAS JAMES SHERBURNE.
b. Whalley, Lancs. Educ. Eng. Coll., Douai. Prof. St. Greg., 1614. Sent to Chelles, and St. Malo, and returned to St. Greg., whence he passed to the mission, suffered imprisonment, and d. on the mission.

1657. July 31st. D. NICH. MAURUS PRITCHARD.
  b. Monmouths. Prof. St. Greg., 1620. Passed to the
  mission, 1633, in the S. Prov. Proc. of Province,
  1649. Cath. Pr. of Durham, 1650. Definitor of
  Prov., 1653. d. at Rouen.

1657. ——— D. ILDEPH. CLIFFE, OR COWPER.
  A sec. priest. Banished. Prof. St. Greg., 1615. Sent
  to St. Malo, returned to Douai, and passed to the
  mission. Was Sec. to Chapter, 1629. Date of death
  uncertain.

165- ——— D. ROBERT GREGORY HUNGATE.
  b. Saxton Hall, Lancs. Educ. Eng. Coll., Douai. Prof.
  St. Greg., 1610, and passed to the mission in the
  N. Prov. Prov. of York, 1653, and d. before the
  expiration of his term of office.

1657. Aug. 20th. D. JAMES MAURUS ROE.
  b. Suffolk. A convert. Educ. Eng. Coll. Douai. Prof.
  St. Lau., 1626. d. at St. Malo.

1657. Aug. 21st. D. PET. WARNFORD, OR WEST.
  b. Winchester. A secular priest who took the habit
  on the mission in 1619. The date of profession
  doubtful.

1657. ——— D. THOMAS HUNGATE.
  b. Saxton Hall, Yorks. Educ. Eng. Coll., Douai. Prof.
  in Spain and passed to the mission.

1657. Oct. 17th. D. MICHAEL GASCOIGNE.
  b. Barnbow, Yorks. Prof. St. Ed. for St. Greg., 1622.
  Passed to the mission in the N. Prov. Was Sec.
  to Chapter, 1641. Proc. of Province, for many
  years. Was stationed at Welton, Northumberland,
  where he died.

1657. Dec. 12th. D. MICHAEL WITHAM.
b. Clyff, Yorks. Prof. St. Greg., 1636, and was sent on the mission in the N. Prov. and there died.

1658. Mar. 9th. D. GEORGE BERNARD SALKELD.
b. Cumberland. Prof. St. Greg., 1650, and passed to the mission in the N. Prov. where he died.

1658. Mar. 14th. D. JOHN MARK CROWTHER, OR BROUGHTON.
b. Shropshire. Prof. St. Greg., 1609. Sent to St. Lau. and thence to the mission in the S. Prov. Suffered imprisonment in London and on release laboured in Gloucestershire. Was Prov. of Canterbury, 1625-9. In old age retired to Lambspring, and d. there.

16— ——— D. LAURENCE NEVILLE.
Prof. St. Lau., 1630. Sent on the mission in the S. Prov. Date of death uncertain.

1660. Jan. 16th. D. BONIFACE CHANDLER.
Prof. St. Lau., 1615. Assisted D. Clement Reyner in Germany, and on the acquisition of Lambspring was cellerarius. d. at Lambspring.

1662. Feb. 2nd. D. MAURUS ROBINSON.
b. Yorks. Prof. St. Ed., 1653. Sent on the mission in the N. Prov. and d. there.

1662. May 11th. D. BASIL CHERITON.
b. Oxfords. Prof. St. Ed., 1651, and d. in Paris

1662. Nov. 18th. BR. DUNSTAN DUCK.
Prof. St. Lau., 1655, and d. at Dieulward.

1663. April 4th. D. GEORGE BACON.
b. 1597. A secular priest prof. on the mission. d. at Little Stoke, Gloucesters.

1663. June 9th. D. WILLIAM MAURUS DAVIS,
OR BENNET.
b. Flintshire. Prof. St. Ed., 1642. Sent on the mission
in the N. Prov. Proc. of Province, 1653. d. on the
mission.

1663. Oct. 22nd. BR. BEDE SHERBURNE. ·
b. Lancashire. Prof. St. Ed., 1660, and died in Paris.

1663. Oct. 28th. D. WM. JOHNSON, OR CHAMBERS.
b. Carlisle, 1583. Educ. Eng. Coll., Douai. Prof. St.
Martin's, Compostella. Passed to the mission and
d. in London.

1663. Nov. 10th. D. WM. ELPHEGE SHERWOOD.
b. Bath, Somerset. Prof. St. Lau., 1626. Sent on the
mission, returned to St. Lau.. and d. at Dieulward.

1663. Dec. 25th. D. GEORGE BERNARD PALMES.
b. Naborne Castle, Yorks. Prof. St. Greg., 1643. Sent
to Lambspring, 1645. Was confessor to the nuns at
Brussels, 1646-9. Professor at St. Greg., 1649. Pr.
of St. Greg., 1653-7. Procurator in Rome, 1657. d.
at Gratz, Styria, on his way to Rome.

1664 ——— D. LAURENCE APPLETON,
b. Essex. Prof. St. Greg., 1635. Sent to Lambspring,
1645, and made Prior. Passed to the mission in the
S. Prov. Date of death uncertain.

1664. April 8th. D. CLEMENT LAURENCE REYNER.
b. Yorkshire, 1582. Educ. Eng. Coll., Douai. Prof. St.
Lau., 1609. Sent on the mission. Was Pr. of St. Lau.,
1623-8. Went to Cambray then again on the mission.
Prov. of York, 1649-53. Again Pr. of St. Lau., 1653-5.
Pres. Gen., 1655-7, after which he returned to the
mission. Was Cath. Pr. of Worcester, 1641.

1664. May 19. D. George Berington.
b. 1576. Prof. at St. Emilian's, Spain. Passed to the mission and d. at Hereford.

1664. June 16th. D. Bernard Ribertierre.
b. St. Malo. Prof. St. Greg. for St. Malo., 1621. Was Sec. to Pres., 1641. Pr. of St. Malo, 1651-3. d. at St. Malo.

1664. July 2nd. D. Richard King, or Scott.
b. Bedfordshire. Prof. St. Ed., 1639. Ord., 1639. Cellerarius, 1641. Sent on the mission in the S. Prov. 1643. Was at Leighland, Somerset, 1641, till death.

1664. Dec. 11th. D. Robert Benedict Meryng.
b. Tardebig, Worcestersh. Accompanied Sir Walter Raleigh in his voyages. Prof. Lams., 1658, when upwards of 60 years of age, and there died.

1664. ———— D. Mansuetus Powel.
b. in Ireland. Prof. St. Malo, 1621, and there died.

1665. Jan. 3rd. D. William Bede Witham.
b. Coken Castle, Durham. Prof. St. Greg., 1649. Sent on the mission in the N. Prov. Stationed at Cliffe, Yorks. Was Proc. of the Prov., 1661, also Definitor Prov., 1661. d. on the mission.

1665. Jan. 17th. D Robert Sherwood.
b. Bath, Somerset, 1588. Prof. St. Greg., 1613. Was Sub-prior. Professor of philosophy. Sent to Chelles and St. Malo. Procurator in Rome, 1621-4. Passed to the mission in 1624 in the S. Prov. Cath. Pr. of Bath, 1629. Prov. of Canterbury, 1633-41. d. at Kiddington, Oxfords.

1665.   Jan. 18th.   D. Robert Corham.
b. Antwerp.   Prof. St. Greg., 1643, and d. at Douai.

1665.   Jan. 21st. D. Wm. Walgrave, or Pleiall.
b. Barneston, Essex, 1588.   A secular priest.   Prof. St. Greg., 1650.   Was vicar of nuns at Cambray, 1653-7. Passed again to the mission in the S. Prov. and was at Flixton, Suffolk, 1657, where he died.

1665.   Aug. 12th.   D. Robert Gabriel Brett.
b. White Stanton, Somerset, 1599.   Prof. St. Malo, 1615.   Ord., 1627.   Was Pr. of St. Ed., 1633-40. Passed to the mission, 1640.   Cath. Pr. of Winchester, 1641.   Pr. of St. Malo, 1645-9.   Definitor 1649. Pr. of St. Malo, 1657-61.   Went again on the mission and d. of the plague in London.

1665.   Aug. 15th.   D. Dunstan Pettinger.
b. 1586.   Prof. St. Lau., 1615.   Sent to St. Ed., 1615, and there ord.   Passed to the mission in the S. Prov., 1619.   Was in London, 1626.   Sent into the N. Prov.   Was proc. of the N. Prov., 1653.   In the same year he was made Definitor, and Cath. Pr. of Worcester, and vicar of nuns at Paris.   He went on the mission again in 1656 to the S. Prov., and d. of plague at Drury Lane, London.

1665.   Sep. 8th.   D. Leander Normington.
Educ. Cambridge.   A convert.   Prof. St. Greg., 1649. Was vicar of nuns at Cambray, 1657-61.   Procurator in Rome, 1661.   d. in Rome.

1666.   May 5th.   D. Arthur Anselm Crowther,
or Broughton.
b. Montgomeryshire, 1588.   Prof. St. Greg., 1611.   Was Sub-prior and professor of philosophy.   Definitor,

1621. Passed to the mission in the S. Prov. Cath. Pr. of Rochester, 1633, then Canterbury, 1657. Prov. Canterbury, 1653-66. d. at the Old Bailey, London.

1666. May 5th. D. JOHN MEUTISSE, OR NORTHAL. b. Shropshire. Prof. St. Greg.,1626. Went to St. Ed. Was vicar of nuns at Cambray, 1633-41. Sec. to Chapter, 1639. Pr. of St. Greg., 1641-53. Cath. Pr. of Norwich, 1645. Pr. of St. Malo, 1653-7. Passed to the mission. Retired in old age to Douai and there died.

1667. April 9th. D. GEO. BERNARD MILLINGTON. b. 1627. Prof. St. Lau., 1651. Was Sec. to Pres., 1659. Sec. to Chapter, 1661. Sent on the mission in the S. Prov. to Leighland in 1664, and there died.

1667. April 19th. D. FRANCIS CRATHORNE. b. Ness Hall, Yorks, 1598. Prof. St. Greg., 1621. Sent on the mission in the S. Prov. Was proc. of the Prov., 1657. Cath. Pr. of Rochester, 1657. Definitor of the Prov., 1661. d. at Three Sister Comerford House, Warwickshire.

1667. June 23rd. D. THOMAS SWINBURNE. b. Northumberland, 1607. Prof. St. Greg., 1625. Was Sub-prior of St. Ed. Returned to St. Greg., 1643-53. Confessor to nuns at Paris, 1653-5. Returned to St. Greg., 1655, and d. at Douai.

1667. Aug. 6th. D. ROBERT PAUL ROBINSON. b. 1601. A Protestant barrister. Became a Catholic. Prof. St. Lau., 1625. Sent to St. Ed. for studies. Was Cath. Pr. of Ely, 1643. Pr. of St. Malo, 1643-5. D.D. of Sorbonne. Pres.-Gen., 1657-9. Def. Reg., 1661. Came on the mission and d. at Longwood, Hants.

1667. Aug. 11th. D. JOHN BARTER.
b. 1599. A soldier and married. On the death of his wife took the habit with his son at St. Greg., 1653. Prof., 1654. Sent on the mission in the S. Prov. and d. at Sutton Hall, Surrey.

1667. Sep. 12th. D. RICHARD GODERIC BLOUNT.
b. Fawley. Berks, 1617. Prof. St. Greg., 1649. Pr. of St. Greg., 1666, till death at Douai.

1668. Jan. 29th. D. MICHAEL CAPE.
b. Sussex, 1609. Prof. St. Lau., 1628. Sent to St. Ed. for studies and ord., 1638. Sent to St. Malo and returned to St. Greg., 1644. Passed to the mission in the N. Prov., 1652. Was Definitor of the Prov., 1661. Went to St. Malo, 1662. Pr. of St. Ed., 1666, till death at Paris.

1668. Jan. 30th. D. FRANCIS CAPE.
b. Sussex, 1608. Prof. St. Greg., 1620. Was Novice Master at St. Ed., 1628. Sent on the mission, 1629. Pr. of St. Ed., 1641-53. Definitor, 1653-7. Again Pr. of St. Ed., 1657-66. d. in Paris.

1668. April 18th. D. AUGUSTINE STOKER.
b. Brabant, 1598. Prof. St. Greg., 1621. Sent on the mission in the S. Prov. Was Def. Reg. in 1666 and d. in London.

1668. Nov. 3rd. D. PLACID JOHNSON.
b. Yorkshire. Prof. St. Lau., 1652. Was Cellerarius and d. at Dieulward.

1668. Nov. 6th. D. ANTH. FRANCIS WALGRAVE.
b. Northamptonshire. Was a secular priest. Passed his novitiate at Rheims. Prof. St. Lau., 1609. Was

chaplain to nuns at Chelles, 1611. Was at Marmontier, 1627, Paris, 1632. Took D.D. at Rheims, 1637. Was at La Celle, 1641. Retired in old age to St. Ed., and d. in Paris.

1668. ———— D. THOMAS TANKE.
b. Wales. Prof. St. Greg., 1623. Sent on the mission. Date of death uncertain.

1669. Feb. 7th. D. DAVID GUILLIAM.
b. Monmouthshire. Prof. St. Ed., 1652. d. at La Celle.

1669. Mar. 21st. D. PETER HUNT.
Prof. St. Lau., 1615, and d. at Dieulward.

1669. Mar. 25th. BR. BENEDICT SPARREY.
Prof. St. Lau., 1668. and d. at Dieulward.

1669. May 11th. D. EDWARD WOLSELEY.
b. Staffordshire. Prof. St. Greg., 1632. Sent on the mission in the S. Prov. and d. in Oxfordshire.

1669. June 5th. D. BERNARD SANDERSON.
b. Paris. Prof. Lams., 1663, and d. at Herbipolis, Germany.

1669. Sep. 8th. D. FRANCIS MORGAN.
b. Weston, Warwickshire, 1600. Prof. St. Greg., 1623. Sent to the mission in the S. Prov. Was Cath. Pr. of Winchester, 1666. Def. Prov., 1669, and d. at Stoke Charity, Hants.

1669. Sep. 30th. D. RICHARD LEANDER THOMPSON, OR JACKSON.
b. Co. of Durham. Prof. St. Greg., 1635. Passed to the mission.

1669. Oct. 2nd. D. Maurus Flutot.
b. Dieulward, 1610. Prof. St. Lau., 1630, and d. at Dieulward.

16— ——— D. Ambrose Bride.
Prof. St. Greg., 1657. Was sent to St. Malo, and La Celle, and returned to St. Greg. Date of death uncertain.

1670. Jan. 30th. D. Matthew Cheriton.
b. Oxfordshire. Prof. St. Lau., 1656. Sent to the mission in the N. Prov. and d. on the mission.

1670. Aug. 6th. D. Denis Sanderson.
b. Northumberland. Prof. Lams., 1664, and there died.

1671. Oct. 9th. D. Thomas Anderton.
b Euxton, Lancs., 1611. Prof. St. Ed., 1630. Ord., 1636. Was Novice Master, Sub-prior, Pr. of St. Ed., 1640-1. Definitor, 1641. Sec. to Chapter, 1657. Retired for a time to a hermitage. Pr. of St. Malo, 1661-6. Again Pr. of St. Ed., 1668-9. d. on the mission at Saxton Hall, Yorks.

1671. Oct. 28th. D. Anselm Cassey.
b. Herefordshire, 1610. Prof. St. Greg., 1626. Sent on the mission in the S. Prov. d. in Herefordshire.

1671. Nov. 3rd. D. Gregory Scroggs.
b. Chichester, 1615. Prof. St. Greg., 1634. Sent on the mission in the S. Prov. Was Proc. of the Prov., 1669. d. in London.

1672. Jan. 2nd. D. Roger Augustine Hungate.
b. Saxton Hall, Yorks., 1584. Educ. Eng. Coll., Douai. Prof. at Montserrat and passed to the mission in the N. Prov. Was Prov. of York, 1633-49, and again 1657-61. Pres.-Gen., 1661-9. d. on the mission.

1672. April 30th. D. JOHN MARTIN.

b. Balsbury, Somerset. Prof. St. Greg., 1661. Sent
on the mission in the S. Prov. and d. at Wells,
Somerset.

1672. July 9th. D. JOHN MAURUS SCROGGS.

b. Chichester, 1617. Prof. St. Greg., 1634. Sent on
the mission in the S. Prov. and d. at Bidwell, Essex.

1672. Nov. 30th. D. BENEDICT WINCHCOMB.

b. Henwick, Berks, 1643. Prof. St. Lau., 1660. Sent
on the mission in the S. Prov. and stationed in
London, where he died.

1673. Mar. 24th. D. BASIL ROAN.

Prof. St. Greg., 1654. Sent on the mission in the
N. Prov. where he died.

1673. Mar. 29th. D. GEORGE GREGORY GRAINGE,
OR CARNABY.

b. Yorks. Prof. St. Greg., 1624. Sent on the mission
in the N. Prov. and stationed at Kilvington, Yorks,
where he died.

1674. Jan. 12th. D. MELLITUS HESKETH.

b. Lancashire, 1644. Prof. St. Lau., 1664. Sent on
the mission in the N. Prov. and d. in Lancashire.

1674. Aug. 10th. D. HUGH SERENUS CRESSY.

b. Thorp Solvin, Yorks, 1605. Educ. Merton Coll.,
Oxford. Was M.A. and fellow. Ord. in the established Ch. Was chaplain to Lord Wentworth, and
in 1638 chaplain to Lord Falkland in Ireland.
Canon of Windsor, 1642. Converted in Rome, 1646.
Prof. St. Greg., 1649. Ordained and went to the
nuns at Paris, 1651-2. Returned to St. Greg., 1653-
60. Sent on the mission in the S. Prov. and

stationed at Somerset House as chaplain to Queen Henrietta. Was Def. Prov., 1666. Cath. Pr. of Rochester, 1669, d. at East Grinstead, Sussex.

1674. —————— D. WM. CHAS. PHILIP, OR PUGH.

b. St. Asaph, Flintshire. Prof. St. Ed., 1660. Sent on the mission in the S. Prov. and stationed at Rotherwas, Hereford, where he died.

1675. Jan. 22nd. D. PETER SALVIN.

b. Thornton, Durham, 1605. Prof. St. Greg., 1632. Sent on the mission in the S. Prov. Proc. Prov., 1653. Confessor to nuns at Paris, 1657-65. Again sent on the mission in the W. of England, in old age retired to St. Lau. and d. at Dieulward.

1675. Aug. 20th. D. ROLAND DUNN.

A Scotch monk of Wurzburg, Germany, who was aggregated and d. on the mission in Northumberland.

—————— —————— D ANDREW RYCAUT.

b. London. Prof. St. Ed., 1664, and d. in Paris, the date uncertain.

1676. Jan 25th D ELEYSON BENEDICT BRYCHAN, OR THOMAS.

b. Brecknockshire, 1610. Prof. St. Greg., 1625. Sent on the mission in the S. Prov. d. at Fawley, Berks.

1676. Feb 21st D AUGUSTINE KINDER.

b. Nottinghamshire, 1596. Prof. St. Greg., 1621. Was Sub-prior of St. Ed., 1625. Vicar of nuns at Cambray, 1641-5. Sent on the mission in the S. Prov. and stationed at Orleton Park, Herefords, where he died.

1676. Sep. 26th. Br. EDWARD CUTHBERT BRENT.
Prof. at St. Greg. for St. Lau. about 1674, and d. at
Douai.

1677. Feb. 16th. D. AMATUS ILDEPHONSUS
WILLOUGHBY, OR RIDER.
Prof. St. Greg., 1668. Sent on the mission and there
died.

1677. May 17th. D. EDMUND WOLSTAN SHUTTLE-
WORTH, OR DALTON.
b. Bedford, Lancs. Prof. St. Ed., 1640. Sent on the
mission in the N. Prov. and there died.

1677. Nov, 13th. D. HENRY AUGUSTINE LATHAM.
b. Mosborrow, Lancs.. 1619. Prof. St. Ed., 1640. Ord.,
1642. Cellerarius and Sub-prior, 1646. Sent on
the mission in the S. Prov. Was Pr. of St. Ed.,
1653-4. Again on the mission in S. Prov., 1654.
Proc. of Prov., 1661. Def. Prov., 1661. Stationed
at Somerset House, 1666-75. Def. Reg., 1666.
Procurator in Rome, 1675-7. Pr. of St. Ed., 1677,
and d. in Paris.

1677. Dec. 21st. D. THOMAS CUTHBERT HORSLEY.
b. 1597. Prof. St. Lau., 1626. Was Pr. of St. Lau.,
1641-53. Definitor, 1653. Again Pr. of St. Lau.,
1655-9. Pres.-Gen., 1659-61. A third time Pr. of
St. Lau., 1661-77, and d. at Dieulward.

1677. Dec. 23rd. D. THOMAS FURSDEN.
b. Thovorton, Devon, 1585. Prof. St. Lau., 1620, and
d. at Dieulward.

——— ——— D. ALEXIUS CARYL.
Prof. St. Greg., 1654. Was confessor to nuns at

Brussels, 1661-9. Vicar of nuns at Cambray, 1673-5. Sent on the mission in the S. Prov. Date of death uncertain.

1678. Sep. 15th. D. THOS. CUTHBERT MIDDLETON.
b. Stockeld, Yorks. Prof. St. Greg., 1643.

1678. Oct. 13th. D. LIONEL SHELDON.
b. Beoley, Worcesters., 1633. Prof. St. Greg., 1653. Ord., 1657. Sent on the mission in S. Prov. and stationed at Somerset House for 15 years. Def. Reg., 1673. Banished, 1675. Retired to Douai and Brussels, where he died.

1679. April 13th. D. ROGER ANS. COLLINGWOOD.
b. Eslington, Northumberland. Prof. Lams., 1663. Sent to the mission in the N. Prov. Cast into prison where he died.

1679. Aug. 25th. D. ROBERT AMBROSE BOOTH.
Prof. St. Lau., 1673, and d. at Dieulward.

1680. Aug. 4th. D. GREG. BENEDICT STAPYLTON.
b. Carlton Hall, Yorks, 1623. Prof. St. Greg., 1643. Ord., 1647. Was Professor of theology and philosophy for 16 years. D.D. Definitor, 1655. Pr. of St. Greg., 1657-61. Passed to the mission and was superior at Somerset House, 1661. Cath. Pr. of Canterbury, 1666. Pres.-Gen., 1669-80, and d. at Dieulward.

1681. Jan. 19th. D. THOMAS VINCENT FAUSTUS SADLER.
b. Warwickshire, 1604. A convert. Prof. St. Lau., 1622. Sent on the mission in S. Prov. Was Cath. Pr. of Chester and Def. Prov., 1661. d. at Dieulward.

1681. ———— D. Philip Constable.
Prof. St. Greg., 1660. Sent on the mission in the
N. Prov. Date of death uncertain.

——— ——— D. John Placid Adelham.
b. Wiltshire. Was a Protestant minister and became
a Catholic. Prof. St. Ed., 1652. Was Pr. of St.
Lau., 1659-61. Sent on the mission in the S. Prov.
and stationed at Somerset House, 1661-1675. Banished, 1675. In prison in 1679, and d. in Newgate.

——— ——— D. Rob. Anderton, or Ashton.
b. Lancs. Prof. St. Ed., 1636. Ord., 1639. Sent on
the mission in the S. Prov., 1641. Proc. of the
Prov., 1666. Def. Reg., 1666-73. Cath. Pr. of Ely,
1669. Was accused at Oates' Plot and retired to
the continent. Date of death uncertain.

1681. July 24th. D. John Placid Gascoigne.
b. Barnbow, Yorks, 1599. Prof. St. Lau., 1615. Sent
to St. Ed. for studies. Ord., 1623. Was Pr. of
St. Ed., 1629-33. Sec. to Chapter, 1633. Definitor,
1633. Sent on the mission in N. Prov. in 1633,
and was in Yorks. for 16 years. Pres.-Gen., 1649-53.
Abbot of Lambspring, 1651-81, and d. at Lambspring.

1681. Sep. 6th. D. John Gregory Mallet, or
Jackson.
b. 1604. Prof. St. Lau., 1625. Ord., 1627. Sent to
St. Ed. and to St. Greg., 1628. Passed to the
mission in the S. Prov. Was Definitor, 1645.
Vicar of nuns at Cambray, 1645-50. Cath. Pr. of
Peterboro', 1653. Prov. of Canterbury, 1666-81.
Was stationed at Weston, Warwicks., till death at
Long Compton, Warwicks.

1681. Nov. 24th. D. Placid Shaftoe.

b. in Co. of Durham, 1634. Prof. Lams., 1655. Ord., 1659. Was on the mission in the N. Prov., 1663-73. Vicar of nuns at Cambray, 1673-81. d. at Lambspring.

16— ——— D. Augustine Conyers.

b. Yorks. Prof. St. Greg., 1638. Was Sec. to Chapter, 1645. Procurator in Rome 1645-53. Sent on the mission in the S. Prov., 1653. Sec. to Chapter, 1669. Accused at Oates' Plot and retired to the continent. Date of death uncertain.

1682. April 12th. D. Bede Taylard, or Taylor.

b. 1593. Prof. St. Lau., 1622. Sent to St. Ed. for studies. Ord., 1630. Sent on the mission in the N. Prov., 1630, and spent his life in the county of Durham. Was Prov. of York, 1661-77.

1683. Nov. 19th. D. Edward Johnson.

b. Yorkshire. Prof. St. Lau., 1663, and d. at Dieulward.

1683. Dec. 11th. D. David Benedict Constable.

b. Yorkshire. Prof. Lams., 1669. Sent on the mission in the N. Prov. and on arrival was cast into prison in Durham and there died.

1684. Jan. 5th. D. Thomas Stourton.

b. Stourton, Wilts. Prof. St. Greg., 1645. Sent on the mission in the S. Prov. and d. at Paris.

168— ——— D. Anthony Basil Skinner.

b. Yorkshire. Prof. St. Greg., 1657. Sent on the mission in the N. Prov. Was stationed at Walton, Yorks. 1672. d. before chapter, 1685.

168– ———— Br. Augustine Cornwallis.

b. Norwich. Prof. St. Ed., 1654, and d. in Paris before chapter, 1685.

1685. April 16th. D. Edward Sheldon.

b. Weston, Warwicks. Prof. St. Greg., 1644. Was Definitor, 1657. Sent on the mission but returned to Douai, 1682, and there died.

1685. Dec. 17th. Br. Adrian Kirke.

b. Northamptonshire. Prof. Lams., 1653, and there died.

168–. ———— D. Leander Pritchard.

b. Monmouthshire. Prof. St. Greg., 1623. Was Definitor, 1649. Cath. Pr. of Gloucester, 1653. Definitor, 1657. Vicar of nuns at Cambray, 1661-9. Passed to the mission in the S. Prov., 1669, and d. after chapter, 1685.

1686. ———— D. Richard Clement Meutisse, or Northall.

b. Yorkshire. Prof. Lams., 1645. Was at St. Lau., 1648, returned to Lambspring and was cellerarius. Sent to Bened. Monasteries at Munster and Salzburg in Germany, where he took the degree of D.D. Sent on the mission in the S. Prov. and stationed in London. d. at Dieulward.

1687. June 4th. D. Augustine Mather.

b. Fishwick Hall, Lancs. Prof. St. Lau., 1666. Sent on the mission in the N. Prov. and stationed at Leigh, Lancs., where he died.

1687. ———— D. RICHARD BEDE HOUGHTON, OR FARNABY.

b. Lancs. Prof. St. Ed., 1642. Ord., 1644. Sent on the mission in the N. Prov. Was Def. Reg., 1669. d. on the mission.

1688. Feb. 4th. D. EDMUND HAWET.

b. Ormskirk, Lancs. Prof. St. Ed., 1683. Sent on the mission in 1688, and went to Ireland as chaplain to Col. Parker's regiment and d. in Dublin.

1688. Feb. 12th. D. HENRY HUGH STARKEY.

b. Darley, Cheshire, 1618. Prof. Lams., 1649. Was confessor to nuns at Paris, 1660. Sent on the mission in the S. Prov., 1661, into Lincolnshire. Was Def. Prov., 1673-81. Condemned at Oates' Plot, but reprieved and released. Retired to the continent and was confessor to nuns at Paris till death. Was Def. Reg., 1681-5. Cath. Pr. of Peterboro', 1685. d. in Paris.

1688. May 10th. D. NICHOLAS HESKETH.

b. Lancs. Prof. St. Lau., 1668. Sent on the mission in the N. Prov. where he died.

1688. Oct. 8th. D. ANDREW WHITFIELD.

b. Hexham. Prof. St. Greg., 1638. Sent on the mission in the N. Prov. Was Cath. Pr. of Bath, 1666. Def. Reg., 1669. Retired to Douai, 1682, and there died.

16— ———— D. BEDE TATHAM.

b. Yorkshire. Prof. St. Greg., 1657. Was Sub-prior, 1676. Sent on the mission in the S. Prov. Date of death uncertain.

1689.   Mar. 10th.   Br. Maurus Fermor.
Prof. St. Lau., 1686, and d. at Dieulward.

1689.   March 15th.   D. Francis Porter.
b. Co. of Durham.   Prof. Lams., 1658.   Sent on the mission in the N. Prov.   Stationed at Beaufront, Northumberland, where he died.

1689.   ———   D. Edw. Placid Betenson.
b. Essex.   Prof. St. Greg., 1649.   Was Cellerarius, Sub-prior, Novice Master.   Sent on the mission in the S. Prov., 1666.   Was Sec. to Pres., 1668.   Def. Reg., 1673.   Banished and retired to Douai.   Returned to the mission in the N. Prov., where he died.

1689.   July 2nd.   D. Mellitus Walmesley.
b. Lancs.   Prof. at St. Ed. for St. Lau., 1679.   Pr. of St. Lau., 1687, and d. at Dieulward.

168—   ———   D. George Anselm Touchet.
b. Stalbridge, Dorset.   Prof. St. Greg., 1643.   Sent on the mission in the S. Prov. and stationed at Somerset House.   Banished in 1675.

1689.   Sept. 14th.   Br. Chas. Jerome Bruning.
b. Hambledon Park, Hants.   Prof. St. Ed., 1688, and d. in Paris.

16—   ———   D. Fran. Ildephonsus Radcliffe.
b. Northumberland.   Prof. Lams., 1669.   Sent on the mission in the N. Prov.   Date of death uncertain.

1690.   May 3rd.   D. Maurus Nelson.
b. Fairhurst, Lancs.   Prof. St. Ed., 1681.   Was Sub-prior, Cellerarius, and Novice Master.   d. in Paris.

1690. June 26th. D. Joseph Sherwood.
b. Flanders. Prof. Lams., 1653. Was Cellerarius,
Prior, Coadjutor to the Abbot, 1673, and Abbot,
1681. d. at Lambspring.

1691. Feb. 22nd. D. Zachary Alban Fuller.
b. Norfolk. Prof. St. Lau., 1674. Was Sub-prior. d.
at Dieulward.

1692. Jan. 15th. D. Wm. Willibrord Wilson.
b. Co. of Durham. Prof. Lambs., 1684, and there died.

1692. April 5th. D. Placid Scroggs, or
Windsor.
b. Berks. Prof. St. Greg., 1634. Sent on the mission
in the S. Prov., retired in old age to Douai, and
there died.

1692. Oct. 13th. Br. William Sheldon.
Prof. St. Greg., 1690, and d. at Douai.

1693. Oct. 31st. Br. Richard Wilfird Reeve.
b. Gloucester, 1642. Educ. Cambridge. Became a
Catholic, 1667. Prof. St. Greg., 1676. Not ordained
on account of lameness. Was professor at St. Greg.
till 1685. At La Celle, 1685-7. Taught at Magdalen Coll., Oxford, and the Bluecoat School, Gloucester, 1687. Took charge of a school at Burton-on-
the-Water. At the Revolution, 1688, was eight
months in prison. On release went to Kiddington,
Oxfords, and thence to Westminster, where he died
and was buried in St. Martin's in the Fields.

1693. ——— D. George Alban Porter.
b. Cumberland. Prof. Lambs, 1664. Sent on the
mission in the N. Prov. and there died.

1693. ——— D. Anselm Williams.
A monk of Cluny. Prof. St. Malo, 1657. Sent on
the mission in the S. Prov. Founded the mission
at Bath and there died.

1693. ——— D. Roger Jerome Hesketh.
b. Lancs. Prof. St. Greg., 1639. Sent on the mission
in the N. Prov. Was Proc. of Prov., 1657. Confessor to nuns in Paris, 1675-8 Went again on
the mission in the S. Prov., 1678. Was 15 months
in prison in Newgate. Pr. of. St. Greg., 1681-5.
d. after chapter, 1693.

1694. Jan. 10th. D. Joseph Frere.
b. Essex, 1598. Prof. St. Greg., 1620. Pr. of St.
Greg., 1633-41. Definitor, 1645-54. Cath. Pr. of
Coventry, 1641. Pr. of St. Greg., 1662-6. Definitor,
1681. d. at Douai.

**1694. April 10th. D. William Bede Thornton,
or Foster.**
b. Galley Hill, Northumberland. Prof. at St. Greg.
for St. Malo, 1634. Was Sub-prior, 1657. Sent
on the mission in the N. Prov. Retired in old
age to St. Ed. and St. Lau., and d. in Paris.

1694. Aug. 22nd. Br. Fran. Bern. Hornyold.
b. Worcestershire, 1658. Prof. St. Ed., 1688. Ord.
deacon and d. in Paris.

1694. Sept. 30th. D. Martin Stone.
b. Euxton, Lancs., 1655. Prof. St. Ed., 1685, and d.
in Paris.

1694. Oct. 22nd. D. Thomas Hesketh.
b. Mawdesley, Lancs., 1655. Prof. St. Ed., 1673. Was
D.D., Sorbonne. d. in Paris.

1694.   Oct. 30th.   D. FRANCIS FENWICK.
  b. London, 1645. Prof. St. Ed., 1664. Was Sec. to
   Pres., 1673. D.D., Sorbonne, 1675. Sent on the
   mission in the S. Prov. and stationed in London.
   Def. Reg., 1685. Pr. of St. Ed., 1689-93. Sent to
   Rome in 1693, and there d. and was buried at the
   Eng. Coll.

1694.   Nov. 29th.   BR. RICHARD YOWARD.
  b. London, 1645. Prof. St. Ed., 1663. d. at La Celle.

1694.   Nov. 29th.   BR. JOHN SMITH.
  b. Wootton, Warwicks., 1632. Prof. St. Ed., 1677. d.
   at La Celle.

1695.   ———   BR. GEORGE CANNING.
  b. Foxcote, Warwicks. Prof. St. Greg., 1688, and d.
   at Douai.

1695.   Jan. 25th.   D. BARTHOLOMEW GREGORY
                                  HESKETH.
  b. Lancs. Prof. St. Lau., 1653. Sent on the mission
   in the N. Prov. Was Def. of Prov., 1685-93. d.
   at Fishwick, Lancs.

1695.   Nov. 13th.   D. GEORGE BEARE.
  Prof. St. Greg., 1660. Sent on the mission in the S.
   Prov. and d. on the mission.

1695.   ———   D. FRANCIS AUGUSTINE ACTON.
  b. London. Prof. St. Greg., 1681. Was sent on the
   mission in the N. Prov., 1685, and d. on the mission.

1696.   Aug. 11th.   D. GREGORY HELME.
  b. Lancs. Prof. St. Lau., 1686. Sent on the mission
   in the N. Prov. and d. there.

1697. April 9th. D. JOSEPH SHERBURNE.
b. Lancs., 1628. Prof. St. Ed., 1652. Was Pr. of St. Ed., 1669-77. Cath. Pr. of Rochester, 1677. Pres.-Gen., 1681, till death at Paris.

1697. June 11th. D. LAURENCE WOOLFE.
b. Shropshire, 1632. Prof. St. Ed., 1656. d. at La Celle.

1697. July 20th. D. JAMES PLACID SKINNER.
d. Yorks. Prof. St. Greg., 1662. Was Cellerarius. Sec. to Chapter, 1673. Sent to the mission in the S. Prov. d. at Douai.

1697. ——— D. THURSTON CELEST. ANDERTON.
b. Lancs. Ord. sec. priest, 1646. Uncertain where professed. Was on the mission in the N. Prov. and d. at Sefton, Lancs.

1697. ——— D. ROGER SERENUS ROTTON.
b. Harbourne, Staffordshire. Prof. St. Greg., 1679. Sent on the mission in the S. Prov. and there died.

1697. ——— D. FRANCIS MUTTLEBERRY.
b. Somersets. Prof. St. Ed., 1658. Sent to the mission in the S. Prov. and there died.

1697. Oct. 30th. D. BENEDICT SIES.
b. Antwerp. Prof. Lambs., 1689, and there died.

1698. Sept. 22nd. D. JOHN HUDDLESTONE.
b. Cumberland, 1609. Was a volunteer in the army of Charles I. Ord. sec. priest. Prof. on the mission. At the Restoration went to Somerset House where he died. Was Sec. Chapter, 1666, and then made Cath. Pr. of Worcester.

1699.   Jan. 3rd.   D. MARTIN ADRIAN BARNARD.
b. Lancashire.   Prof. Lambs., 1690, and d. there.

1699.   Jan. 6th.   D. AMBROSE LINDLEY.
b. Yorkshire.   Prof. Lambs., 1670.   Sent on the mission
in the S. Prov., returned to Lambs. and d. there.

1699.   April 9th.   D. CHAS. DOMINIC GREEN.
b. Windsor, 1665.   Was a convert.   Prof. St. Ed., 1688,
and d. at La Celle.

1699.   June 1st.   D. JOHN COLUMBAN PHILLIPS.
b. Pembrokeshire, 1613.   Prof. at St. Lau. for St. Ed.,
1632.   Ord. 1639.   Sent on the mission, returned to
St. Ed. and d. in Paris.

1699.   July 25th.   BR. THOS. AUGUSTINE LUMLEY.
b. Yorkshire.   Prof. St. Ed., 1699, and was drowned
at La Celle.

1699.   Sept. 3rd.   D. WM. BENEDICT NELSON.
b. Mawdesley, Lancs, 1618.   Prof. St. Ed., 1640.   Pr.
of St. Ed., 1654-7.   Pr. of St. Malo, 1666.   Def.
Reg., 1673-7.   Pr. of St. Ed., 1677-85.   Def. Reg.,
1685.   Cath. Pr. of Durham, 1685.   d. at Paris.

1699.   Sept. 26th.   BR. EDMUND JOHN GREEN.
Prof. St. Lau., 1693.   Ord. deacon and d. at Dieulward.

1699.   Dec. 7th.   D. MAURUS POSS, OR NICHOLS.
Prof. St. Greg., 1650.   Sent on the mission in the S.
Prov.   Was Proc. of Prov., 1685.   Returned to St.
Greg. in 1693 and d. at Douai.

1699.   ———   D. ALEX. MACARIUS BROWN.
A Scotch Benedictine who was incorporated, and was
on the mission in the N. Prov.

1700. —————— D. JOHN JEROME WILSON.
b. Yorkshire. Prof. St. Greg., 1685. Was Sub-prior, 1689. Sent on the mission in the S. Prov. and d. on the mission.

1700. Aug. 28th. D. RICHARD JOSEPH ASHTON.
b. Lancashire. Prof. St. Greg., 1688, and d. at Douai.

1701. Jan. 11th. D. JOHN BRUNO JENNINGS.
b. Middlesex. Prof. St. Greg., 1668. Sent on the mission in the S. Prov., retired in ill health to St. Greg. and d. at Douai.

1701. Aug. 29th. D. JN. BYFLEET, OR WORSLEY.
b. Devon. Prof. St. Greg., 1624. Was Sec. to Pres., 1638-41. Sent to the mission in the S. Prov. Was at Stourton, Wilts, 1652, and d. there. Was Def. Reg., 1677.

1702. Jan. 29th. D. CHARLES SUMPNER.
b. Hellingly Castle, Sussex, 1645. Educ. at Oxford. Became a Catholic. Prof. St. Greg., 1672. Sent on the mission in the S. Prov. Returned to Douai, 1683, and was Pref. of studies, Vicar of nuns at Cambray, 1701, and d. there.

1702. May 6th. D. WILLIAM CUTHBERT HUTTON, OR SALVIN.
b. Co. of Durham. Prof. St. Greg., 1685. Sent on the mission in the N. Prov. and d. at Plompton, Yorks.

1702. June 5th. D. GEO. BENEDICT HEMSWORTH.
Prof. St. Greg., 1657. Sent on the mission in the N. Prov. and stationed at Whenby, Yorks. Returned to Douai, 1673. He was sent again on the mission, and retired to Douai, and there died.

1702. Oct. 20th. D. Nicholas Colston.

b. Quarry Hill, Durham. Prof. Lambs., 1673. Sent on the mission in the N. Prov. returned to Lambspring and d. there.

1703. ———— D. Roger Joseph Hesketh.

b. Lancas. Prof. St. Greg., 1681. Sent on the mission in the S. Prov. and d. on the mission.

1703. July 25th. D. Joseph Aprice.

b. Northamptonshire, 1650. Prof. St. Lau., 1666. Sent on the mission in the S. Prov. Was at Somerset House, 1683. Accompanied James II. to St. Germains, 1688. Cath. Pr. of Rochester, 1697. d. at Paris.

1703. Oct. 25th. D. John Lumley.

b. Yorkshire. Prof. St. Lau., 1656. Sent on the mission in the S. Prov. Was Def. Prov., 1681-93. d. on the mission.

1703. Dec. 4th. D. Charles Barker.

b. Sussex. Prof. St. Lau., 1688. Sent on the mission in the S. Prov. and d. at Tixall, Staffords.

1704. Jan. 2nd. D. John Placid Scudamore.

b. Middlesex. Prof. Lambs., 1695. Sent on the mission, 1699, to the S. Prov. and d. at Hawkwell Place, Kent.

1704. Oct. 4th. D. William Cuthbert Wall, or Marsh.

b. Alburgh, Norfolk. Educ. St. Omer's and Eng. Coll., Douai. Ord. sec. priest and sent on the mission in 1652. Prof. on the mission for Lambs., 1668. Tried at the Old Bailey, for Oates' plot, in 1679, and acquitted. Tried again for priesthood and sentenced to death, but reprieved and kept in prison till 1685. At the Revolution he retired to St. Greg., 1688, and to Lambspring in 1691 and d. there.

1704. Nov. 8th. D. FRANCIS LEANDER GREEN.
b. Monmouthshire. Prof. Lambs., 1660. Sent to the mission in the N. Prov. and stationed at Brindle, Lancs., where he died.

1704. Dec. 9th. D. VINCENT CRAVEN.
b. Lancs. Prof. St. Lau., 1686, and d. at Dieulward.

1705. March 20th. D. JOHN ELPHEGE SKELTON.
b. Cumberland. Prof. Lambs., 1688. Sent on the mission in the N. Prov. and stationed at Swinburne Castle, Northumberland, and d. there.

1705. April 9th. D. JOHN BASIL SMEATON.
b. Cumberland. Prof. Lambs., 1664. Sent on the mission in the N. Prov. and stationed in the County of Durham. Was Proc. of Prov., 1689. Was some time at Gateshead. Returned to Lambspring in 1697, and d. there.

1705. Aug. 16th. D. BARTHOLOMEW BEDE ADDY.
b. Co. of Durham. Prof. Lambs., 1665. Sent to Rome to assist the Procurator. Passed to the mission in the N. Prov., 1681, and was placed at Beaufront. He then went into the S. Prov. and d. in London.

1705. Oct. 30th. D. CUTHBERT PARKER.
b. Marscough, Lancs. Prof. St. Ed., 1673. Was Sec. to Pres., 1681-9. Sent on the mission in the S. Prov. and stationed at St. James', and passed to the N. Prov. He returned to St. Ed. in ill health. Was Cellerarius. Def. Reg., 1705, and d. in Paris.

1706. Feb. 14th. D. Anselm Brown.
Prof. St. Lau., 1688, and d. at Dieulward.

1706. June 21st. Br. Richard Lanning.
b. Dorset. Prof. St. Greg., 1698. and d. at Douai.

1706. Oct. 2nd. Br. Joseph Dunstan Porter.
b. Cumberland. Prof. St. Greg., 1676. d. at Douai.

1707. Jan. 19th. D. Ralph James Nelson.
b. Mawdesley, Lancs., 1638. Prof. St. Ed., 1660. Was
Pr. of St. Ed., 1685-9. Def. Reg., 1689-97. Cath.
Pr. of Worcester, 1700. d. in Paris.

1707. Mar. 11th. D. Patrick Curwen.
Prof. St. Lau., 1668. Sent on the mission in the S.
Prov. and d. on the mission.

1707. Aug. 22nd. D. Philip Blakey.
b. Northumberland. Prof. Lambs., 1690, and d. there.

1708. April 28th. D. John Maurus Knightly.
b. Warwicksh. Prof. Lambs., 1670. Sent on the
mission in the S. Prov. and stationed at St. James'
in 1685. Was Sec. to Chapter, 1685. At Revolution
returned to Lambspring, 1688. Was Prior. Procurator in Rome, 1692. Was at St. Greg., 1693.
Returned to Lambspring, 1695. Abbot of Lambspring, 1697, and d. there.

1708. Oct. 7th. D. Placid Bagnal.
Prof. St. Lau., 1693, and d. at Dieulward.

1709. Feb. 7th. D. George Whall.
b. Norfolk. Prof. St. Lau., 1666. Went to St. Ed.
1687. Returned to St. Lau. and d. at Dieulward.

1709. July 27th. Br. Joseph Roskow.

b. Runshaw, Lancas. Prof. St. Ed., 1708, and d. at Paris.

1709. Aug. 20th. Br. Bernard Bradley.

Prof. St. Lau., 1707, and d. at Dieulward.

1709. Dec. 12th. D. Henry Gregory Timperly.

b. Hintlesham, Suffolk, 1631. Prof. St. Ed., 1677. Sent on the mission in the S. Prov. and stationed at St. James', 1685. Passed into Suffolk in 1688. Retired in old age to St. Ed. and d. in Paris.

1709. Dec. 29th. D. Francis Joseph Kennet.

Prof. St. Lau., 1685. Sent on the mission in the N. Prov. and stationed in Lancashire where he died.

1710. Feb. 28th. D. John Dakins.

b. Leicesters, 1668. Prof. St. Ed. 1688. Sent to St. Greg. and ord. 1695. Sent on the mission in the S. Prov. and stationed at Bath. Returned to St. Ed. and d. at La Celle.

1710. July 30th. D. Robert Killingbeck.

b. Yorks. Prof. Lambs., 1653. Sent on the mission in the N. Prov. Prov. of York, 1685-93. Cath. Pr. of Peterboro,' 1689. Def. Prov., 1693-1701. In old age retired to Lambspring and d. there.

1710. Aug. 1st. D. Gregory Dalyson.

b. Lincolns. Prof. Lambs., 1670. Sent on the mission in S. Prov. Was stationed in London and there died.

1711. Jan. 27th. D. Wm. Bernard Gregson.

b. Lancas, 1650. Prof. St. Lau., 1668. Was Pr. of St. Lau., 1681-5. Sent on the mission in the S.

Prov. and stationed at St. James'. Cath. Pr. of Gloucester, 1688. Def. Prov., 1693-7. Pres. Gen., 1697-1701. Prov. of Canterbury, 1701-5. Pres. Gen., 1705-10. Prov. of Canterbury, 1710, till death in London.

1711. Feb. 9th. D. JOHN JEROME FARNWORTH.
b. Runshaw, Lancas. Prof. St. Ed., 1696. Sent on the mission in the N. Prov. and stationed in Lancashire where he died.

1711. Aug. 10th. D. WILLIAM HITCHCOCK, OR NEDAM.
b. 1617. Educ. St. Omer's and ord. sec. priest. Prof. St. Greg., 1649. Was Sec. to Pres., 1663. Pr. of St. Greg., 1668-74. Cath. Pr. of Norwich, 1670, then Winchester, 1674. Again Pr. of St. Greg., 1675-7. Def. Reg., 1678-85. Again Pr. of St. Greg., 1685-93. Def. Reg., 1693-7. Pr. of St. Ed., 1697-1701. Def. Reg., 1701. d. at Douai.

1711. Oct. 14th. D. EDWARD AUGUSTINE LLEWELLYN.
b. Yorks. Was a convert. Prof. St. Ed., 1658. Sent to St. Malo, then to La Celle, and then to the mission in the S. Prov. Prov. of Canterbury, 1681-93. Cath. Pr. of Bath, 1689. Def. Reg., 1697-1710. Was on the mission at Bath, 1693, till death there.

1711. Dec. 8th. D. JOHN TEMPEST.
b. Yorks. Prof. Lambs., 1661. Sent on the mission in the N. Prov. Was Def. Prov., 1685. Sec. to Chapter, 1689. Retired in old age to Lambspring and d. there.

1712. Jan. 26th. D. JAMES FERREYRA.

A Portuguese. Prof. St. Lau., 1676. Sent on the mission to the S. Prov., and stationed at Somerset House, and d. in London.

1712. March 18th. D. THOMAS ILDEPHONSUS APRICE.

b. Northamptons. Prof. St. Lau., 1668. Sent on the mission in the S. Prov. Was Proc. Prov., 1681. Placed at St. James', 1685. Went to St. Greg., at Revolution, 1688. Returned to the mission in 1692 into the S. Prov. Def. Prov., 1697. Cath. Pr. of Gloucester, 1697. Was in London, 1705. Prov. of Canterbury, 1711, till death in London.

1712. April 12th. D. RICHARD PAUL CHANDLER.

b. Maryland, America. Prof. St. Greg., 1705. Ord., 1710. d. at Douai.

1712. Nov. 12th. D. THOMAS AUGUSTINE CONSTABLE.

b. Eagle Castle, Lincolns. Prof. St. Greg., 1649. Was Sec. to Pres., 1657-9. Sent on the mission in the N. Prov. Was Proc. Prov. and Def. Prof., 1666. Cath. Pr. of Norwich, 1673. Passed to the S. Prov., 1677. Was at St. James', 1685. Def. Prov., 1689. Prov. of Canterbury, 1693-7. Def. Reg., 1697. Cath. Pr. of Durham, 1701. d. on the mission.

1712. Nov. 15th. D. FRANCIS LAWSON.

b. Yorks. Prof. St. Greg., 1650. Sent on the mission in the N. Prov. Returned to St. Greg. and was Sub-prior, 1672. Again on the mission in the N. Prov. Was Prov. of York, 1677-05. Cath. Pr. of Chester, 1681. Def. Prov., 1701. Was stationed for some time at Middleton Lodge, Yorks, where he died.

1712. Dec. 7th. D. James Winton.
  b. Middlesex, 1672. Prof. Lambs., 1690. Sent on the
  mission in the N. Prov., 1704. d. at Lambspring.

1713. April 18th. D. Wolstan Crosby.
  Prof. St. Greg., 1660. Sent on the mission in the N.
  Prov. Returned to St. Greg., 1701, and d. at Douai.

1712-3. ——— D. Thomas Wilson.
  b. Yorks. Prof. St. Greg., 1667. Sent on the mission
  in the N. Prov. and d. there.

1713 Nov. 23rd. Br. Ralph Benedict Welden.
  b. London, 1674. Became a Catholic, 1687. Prof. St.
  Ed., 1692. Went to La Trappe, 1694. Returned to
  St. Ed., 1695. Was at La Celle, St. Greg., and other
  monasteries and d. in Paris.

1714. July 9th. D. Edmund Taylor.
  b. London. Prof. St. Greg., 1680. Sent on the mission,
  1688. Returned to St. Greg., 1692. Was Sub-prior,
  1693-8, and also 1701-14. Def. Reg., 1710. d. at
  Douai.

1715. Jan. 18th. D. Alban Berriman.
  b. Somerset. Prof. St. Ed., 1661. Sent on the mission
  to the S. Prov. and d. in London.

1715. ——— D. Joseph Berriman.
  b. Somerset. Prof. St. Greg., 1654. Was Sub-prior,
  1678. Sent on the mission in the S. Prov. Was
  at Leighland, Somerset, 1689-97. Def. Prov., 1701.
  Cath. Pr. of Peterboro', 1710. d. on the mission.

1715. July 27th. D. Alban Placid Francis.
  b. Middlesex. Prof. Lambs., 1670. Sent on the
  mission to the S. Prov. in Cambridgesh. At Revolution withdrew to Lambspring, 1688, then to St.

Greg., 1699, and again on the mission in the S. Prov. and d. there.

1715. Sep. 9th. D. PHILIP SYLVESTER METHAM. b. Yorksh. Prof. St. Greg., 1683. Sent on the mission in the N. Prov. Proc. Prov., 1701. Prov. of York, 1705-10. Def. Prov., 1710-3. Pr. of St. Greg., 1713, till death at Douai.

1715. Dec. 22nd. D. JAMES MAURUS CORKER. b. Yorks, 1636. Was a convert. Prof. Lambs., 1656. Sent on the mission in the S. Prov., 1665. Tried and acquitted at Oates' plot, 1679. Condemned for priesthood and was in Newgate till 1685. Pres. Gen., 1680-1, and installed in Newgate. Cath. Pr. of Canterbury, 1681. On release laboured in London. Abbot of Lambspring, 1690. Resigned, 1695. Again the mission in the S. Prov., and d. at Paddington, and was buried at St. Pancras.

1716. Sep. 6th. D. RICHARD GEORGE BRENT. b. Worcestersh. Prof. Lambs., 1696, and d. there.

1716. Nov. 19th. D. FRS. PLACID HAGGERSTONE. b. Northumberland. Prof. St. Greg., 1701. Ord., 1708. d. at Douai.

1717. ———— D. RICHARD MAURUS HARRISON. b. Stokesley, Yorks. Prof. St. Greg., 1701. Ord., 1707. Sent on the mission in the N. Prov. and stationed at Stay House, Yorks, 1710, and d. there.

1717. ———— D. ANSELM NELSON. b. Fairhurst, Lancas. Prof. St. Ed., 1683. Sent on the mission in the N. Prov. and stationed in Yorkshire. Drowned at Dover.

1717.   Aug. 24th.   D. JOS. WILFRID HUTCHINSON.
b. Northumberland.   Prof. of Lambs., 1679.   Sent on
the mission in the N. Prov., 1697, and stationed in
Lancashire.   Was at Brindle in 1704 and d. there.

1717.   Dec. 18th.   D. RICHARD HOLMES.
b. Lancas.   Prof. St. Greg., 1676.   Sent on the mission
in the N. Prov. in Lancashire.   Was at Sefton in
in 1697 and d. there.

1718.   Feb. 10th.   D. FRANCIS JAMES POYNTZ.
b. Northamptons.   Was a convert.   Prof. St. Ed., 1688.
Sent on the mission in the S. Prov.   Was at Fawley,
Berks, 1703, and d. there.

1718.   April 4th.   D. WM. PLACID ANDERTON.
b. Euxton, Lancas.   Prof. St. Ed., 1696.   Sent on the
mission in the N. Prov.   Was Pr. of St. Ed., 1713-7.
Again on the mission in the S. Prov. and there died.

1718.   April 13th.   D. JAMES CUTHBERT TATHAM.
b. Barton, Yorks.   Prof. St. Greg., 1678.   Was Sub-prior.
Vicar of nuns at Cambray, 1685-1701.   Sent on the
mission in the S. Prov., 1701.   Pr. of St. Greg., 1705-
10.   Again on the mission in the S. Prov., 1701, and
d. there.

1718.   July 4th.   D. JOHN JOHNSON.
b. Lancas.   Prof. Lambs 1674.   Took D.D. in Paris.
Sent on the mission in N. Prov.   Went to St. Greg.
1693, and to Lambspring 1695.   Retired to Hildesheim in 1705 and d. there.

1718.   July 14th.   D. EDWARD CHORLEY.
b. Lancas.   Prof. St. Greg., 1698.   Ord., 1704.   Was
Cellerarius, 1706.   Sec. to Chapters, 1710 and 1713.

Sec. to Pres. 1710. Pr. of St. Greg., 1715-7. Def. Reg., 1717.

1718. July 15th. Br. Bede Knight.
b. Somerset. Prof. St. Greg., 1714, and d. at Douai.

1718. Aug. 17th. D. Laurence Swale.
b. Yorks. Prof. Lambs., 1670. Sent on the mission in N. Prov. and d. there.

1718. Aug. 26th. D. Thos. Augustine Howard.
b. Cumberland, 1644. Prof. St. Greg. 1662. Ord., 1668. Prof. of St. Greg., 1677-81. Cath. Prov. of Ely, 1681. Sent on the mission in S. Prov. and stat. at St. James'. Def. Prov. 1693-7. Pres. Gen. 1697-8. Prov. of Canterbury 1698-1701. Pres. Gen. 1701-5. Prov. of Cant., 1705-10, also 1713-7. Was for many years on the mission in London and d. there.

1719. Aug. 6th. D. Thomas Bruning.
b. Hambledon Park, Hants. Prof. St. Ed., 1696. Sent on the mission in the S. Prov. Was stat. at Bonham, Wilts., 1714, and d. there.

1719. Sept. 8th. D. Ralph Jerome Wilson.
b. Yorks., 1652. Prof. St. Greg. 1668. Ord. 1677. Sent on the mission in the N. Prov. to Lancashire. Def. Prov. 1701-10. Was stat. at Broughton, Yorks., 1703, then at Woolstan, Lancs., where he died.

1720. March 7th. D. John Rous.
b. Lancas. Prof. St. Lau., 1711. and d. at Dieulward.

1720. June 15th. D. William Philipson.
b. Streitly, Berks. Prof. St. Ed., 1684. Sent on the mission in the N. Prov., 1697. Was Def. Reg., 1717. d. on the mission.

1720. June 23rd. D. HENRY BERNARD LOWICK. b. Stoxley, Yorks. Prof. St. Ed., 1673. Sent on the mission in the S. Prov. and stationed at St. James', 1685. At Revolution retired to St. Ed., 1681. Was Sub-prior. Pr. of St. Lau., 1713-7. d. at La Celle.

1720. Dec, 6th. D. FRANCIS MILDMAY. b. Amersden, Oxfords. Prof. Lambs., 1674. Sent on the mission in the S. Prov. Was at Leighland, Somerset, 1697 - 1701. Returned to Lambspring, 1701, and d. there.

1720. Dec. 16th. D. JOSEPH BERNARD GREAVES. b. Northumberland. Prof. St. Greg., 1676. Sent on the mission in the N. Prov., 1685. Was stationed in Newcastle on Tyne. Def. Prov., 1693-1701. Proc. Prov., 1693-1701. Passed to the S. Prov., 1701-8. Again on the mission in the N. Prov., 1708, and stationed at Bedal, Yorks, Def. Reg., 1713-7. Prov. of York, 1717, till death at Bedal.

1720. ——— D. RICHARD PLACID BRUNING. b. Hambledon Park, Hants. Prof. St. Ed., 1663. Sent on the mission in the S. Prov. Was Sec. to Chapter, 1681. Vicar of nuns at Cambray, 1681-5, then to the S. Prov. till death. Cath. Pr. of Canterbury, 1717.

1721. Feb. 10th. D. ANTHONY TURBERVILLE. b. Glamorgans. Prof. St. Ed., 1664. Sent on the mission in the S. Prov. Pr. of St. Ed., 1701-5. Again to the S. Prov. Pr. of St. Ed., 1710-3. Cath. Pr. of Durham, 1713. d. at Paris.

1721. —————— D. Celestine Shaftoe.
b. Co. of Durham. Prof. Lambs., 1672. Was confessor to nuns at Paris, 1690-8. Sent on the mission in the S. Prov. and d. at Marville.

1721. Oct. 22nd. D. John Gregory Skelton.
b. Cumberland. Prof. St. Greg., 1681. Ord., 1686. Sent on the mission in the N. Prov., 1686. Stationed at Beaufront, Northumberland. Was Prov. of York, 1721, till death at Beaufront.

1722. Mar. 8th. D. Thos. Augustine Townson.
b. Lancas. Prof. Lambs., 1688. Sent on the mission in the N. Prov. and d. there.

1723. Jan. 1st. D. Benedict Gibbon.
b. Westcliffe, Kent. Prof. Lambs., 1673. Was Prior, 1681. Sent on the mission in the S. Prov., 1684. Stationed at St. James'. Was Proc. Prov., 1689. In 1693 returned to Lambs. for two years. Again on on the mission, 1695. Confessor to nuns at Paris, 1698, till nearly the end of his life. Def. Reg., 1710. Cath. Pr. of Bath, 1713. d. at Douai.

1723. Jan. 22nd. Br. John Osland.
b. Sutton, Shrops. Prof. Lambs., 1702, and d. there.

1733. Feb. 3rd. D. Michael Pullien.
b. Hampswith, Yorks. Prof. St. Greg., 1672. Sent on the mission in the N. Prov. Was Prov. of York, 1693-7. Cath. Pr. of Coventry, 1697. Pr. of St. Greg., 1701-5. Cellerarius, 1708. Pr. of St. Greg., 1710-3. Cellerarius again. Def. Reg., 1721. d. at Douai.

1723.   Mar. 7th.   D. RALPH MAURUS WILSON.
b. Co. of Durham.   Prof. Lambs., 1688.   Sent on the
mission to the S. Prov., 1704.   Stationed at Barmingham, Norfolk, till 1711.   Returned to Lambspring
and was Cellerarius there till death.

1723.   May 2nd.   D. WILLIAM ANSELM BLAKEY.
b. Northumberland.   Prof. Lambs., 1682.   Sent on the
mission to the S. Prov.   Retired in old age to Lambs.,
1721 and d. there.

1723.   July 9th.   D. HENRY JOSEPH JOHNSTON.
b. Methley, Yorks.   Prof. at St. Lau. for St. Ed., 1675.
Sent on the mission in the S. Prov., and stationed at
St. James', 1685.   Pr. of St. Ed., 1697, but resigned.
Retired to St. Farons at Meaux.   In 1700 was at
St. Greg., and in 1701, at St. Ed. and Sub-prior.   Pr.
of St. Ed., 1705-10.   Def. Reg. 1710.   Cath. Pr. of
Durham, 1717.   d. at Paris.

1724.   Jan. 16th.   D. JAMES MATHER.
b. Fishwick, Lancas.   Prof. St. Lau., 1668.   Pr. of St.
Lau., 1685-7, also 1689-93.   Sent on the mission in
the S. Prov. and was stationed in London for 30 years.
Def. Prov. 1701.   Cath. Pr. of Chester, 1713.   d. in
London.

1724.   Jan. 26th.   D. RICHARD PLACID NELSON.
b. Fairhurst, Lancas.   Prof. St. Ed., 1679.   Sent on the
mission in the S. Prov., 1689.   Pr. of St. Ed., 1693-7.
Then was on the mission in the N. Prov., 1697.
Passed to the S. Prov. 1706, and was at Stourton,
Wilts., till 1711; then went to Burton on the Water,
Gloucestershire; then to the N. Prov., to Cuerdon,
Lancas., where he died,

1724. June. 2nd. D. CLEMENT PASTON
b. Barmingham, Norfolk. Prof. St. Ed., 1683. Sent on the mission to the S. Prov. and retired to St. Ed., 1697, and d. in Paris.

1725. Jan. 26th. D. RALPH ANTHONY ORD.
b. Northumberland. Prof. St. Greg., 1685. Sent on the mission to the N. Prov. 1690. Was at Gilling Castle 1708-22. Pr. of St. Greg., 1722-5, and d. at Douai.

1725. July 4th. D. AMBROSE EASTGATE.
Prof. St. Lau., 1715, and d. at Dieulward.

1725. July 8th. D. JOHN BENEDICT WILSON.
b. Softly, Durham. Prof. St. Greg., 1678. Was Sub-prior, 1686. Sent on the mission in the N. Prov., 1688, and stationed at Blaydon, Durham, and d. there.

1725. Aug. 15th. D. GEORGE FITZWILLIAMS.
b. Lancas. Prof. St. Greg., 1695. Sent on the mission in the N. Prov., 1710. Stationed at Bedal, Yorks., 1720, and d. on his way to Douai.

1725. Oct. 10th. D. EDWARD SALISBURY.
b. Devon, 1685. Prof. Lambs., 1703. Sent on the mission to the S. Prov., 1711. Stationed at Bonham and then at Farmcote and there d.

1725. Oct. 16th. D. BART. DENIS BISHOP.
b. Oxfordsh. Prof. Lambs., 1682. Sent on the mission to the S. Prov., 1699. Vicar of nuns at Cambray, 1702-5. Again on the mission in London, 1705, till death there. Was Def. Prov., 1717.

1725.   Dec. 26th.   D. OSWALD SMITHERS.
b. Middlesex.   Prof. Lambs., 1694.   Sent on the mission in the S. Prov.   Stationed at Hawkwell Place, Kent, and then at Kiddington, 1701, and d. there.   Was Proc. Prov., 1717.

1726.   May. 16th.   D. WILLIAM BANESTER.
b. Lancas.   Prof. St. Greg., 1688.   Sent on the mission in the S. Prov.   Was Proc. Prov., 1701-13.   Stationed at Bath, 1714, till death there.   Was Prov. of Canterbury, 1721-5.   Cath. Pr. of Bath, 1725.

1726.   June 22nd.   BR. JOHN MAURUS DALE.
b. Yorksh., 1708.   Prof. St. Ed., 1725, and d. in Paris.

1726.   July 4th.   D. WILLIAM AUSTIN. FENWICK.
b. Northumberland.   Prof. St. Greg., 1693.   Ord., 1694, Sent on the mission in the N. Prov., 1700, and d. there.   Was Proc. Prov., 1710-7.

1726.   Sep. 21st.   D. JOHN BAPTIST SAVORY.
b. Oxford.   Prof. St. Greg., 1697.   Sent on the mission in the S. Prov.   Was stationed at Colkerk, Norfolk, in 1711, and probably died there.

1726.   Nov. 16th.   D. MICHAEL PHILIP ELLIS.
b. Waddesden, Bucks, 1653.   A convert.   Prof. St. Greg., 1675.   Sent on the mission in the S. Prov. and stationed at St. James', 1685.   In 1688 consecrated Bp. of Aureliopolis and Vic. Ap. of Western District.   Left England at the Revolution and was in Rome, 1693.   Translated to the See of Segni in the Campagna, 1708, and d. there.

1727. Feb. 6th. D. JOSEPH WYCHE.
  b. Middlesex, 1672. Prof. Lambs., 1620. Was Prior, 1715. Vicar of nuns at Cambray, 1717, till death there. Was Def. Reg., 1725.

1727. Nov. 25th. D. JOHN PLACID ACTON.
  b. London. Prof. St. Greg., 1685. Sent on the mission in the N. Prov., 1699. Was stationed at Low, Lancas.

1727. ———— D. GEORGE ANSELM CARTER.
  b. Worcestersh. Prof. St. Greg., 1670. Was Sub-prior and Cellerarius. Sent on the mission in the N. Prov., 1685, into Yorkshire. Was Def. Prov., 1710-3. Proc. Prov., 1717-20. Prov. of York, 1720-1. Def. Prov., 1721. d. at Hazlewood.

1628. Feb. 13th. D. CHRIS. MAURUS BARBER.
  b. London. Prof. St. Greg., 1683. Was Sub-prior, 1691. Sent on the mission in the N. Prov., 1693, and stationed at Pomfret, Yorks, and then at York, where he died.

1729. Mar. 14th. BR. WILLIAM THOMAS SHORT.
  b. London, 1670. Prof. St. Ed., 1689. Ord. deacon. d. at La Celle.

1729. ———— D. AUGUSTINE STELLING.
  b. Co. of Durham. Prof. at St. Lau, for St. Ed., 1676. Sent on the mission in the S. Prov. and d. there.

1729. ———— D. JOHN MAURUS BUCKLEY.
  b. Yorks. Prof. St. Greg., 1714. Sent on the mission in the N. Prov., stationed at Plompton, Yorks., 1725; Whitehaven, 1726; Corby Castle, 1727; Lotherton, Yorks, 1729, and d. there.

1729. Aug. 15th. D. JOHN GIRLINGTON.
b. Thurstland, Lancas. Prof. St. Ed., 1653. Pr. of St. Lau., 1677-81. Sent on the mission in the N. Prov. and d. at Sunderland.

1729. Nov. 17th. D. FRANCIS AUSTIN TEMPEST.
b. Yorks. Prof. Lambs., 1664. Was at St. Lau., 1671-3. Sent on the mission in the N. Prov., 1673, and stationed at Gilling Castle, Yorks. Was Proc. Prov. 1685. Prov. of York, 1701-5. Def. Prov. 1705-8. Abbot of Lambspring, 1708, till death there.

1729. Nov. 23rd. D. THOMAS WITHAM.
b. Cliffe, Yorks. Prof. St. Greg., 1685. Sent on the mission in the N. Prov, 1693. Was at Blaydon, Durham, 1725, and d. there.

1730. Jan. 6th. D. JOHN BENEDICT CUMBERLEGE.
b. Newcastle-under-Lyne. Prof. Lambs., 1703. Sent on the mission in the S. Prov. Was some time at Fonthill. d. on the mission.

1730. Mar. 1st. D. GEORGE GREGORY RIDDELL.
b. Northumberland. Prof. Lambs., 1688. Was at St. Greg., 1695, and took degree of D.D. Was Sub-prior 1698-1701. Sec. to Chapter, 1701. Returned to Lambs., 1705. Pres. Gen. 1710-3. Cath. Pr. of Winchester, 1713. Def. Reg. 1718. Abbot of Cismar, 1729. Was in the mission in London from 1713 until his death there.

1730. May 24th. D. JOHN AUGUSTINE SOUTHCOT.
b. Witham Place, Essex. Prof. St. Ed., 1689. Sent on the mission in the S. Prov. Was Def. Prov., 1717. Cath. Pr. of Chester, 1725. Retired to St. Ed., and d. in Paris.

1730. Sep. 11th. D. JOHN ALEXIUS WALL.
b. Ludshott, Hants. Prof. Lambs. 1715, and d. there.

1730. Dec. 2nd. D. MATT. DUNSTAN HUTCHINSON.
b. Northumberland. Prof. Lambs., 1685. Was novice
master. Pr. 1720 and d. there.

1731. Jan. 14th. D. RICHARD FELIX TASBURGH.
b. Flaxton Hall, Suffolk. Prof. St. Ed., 1682. Sent
to St. Greg., and there ord. Sent on the mission in
S. Prov. Stationed in London, and d. there.

1731. June 24th. D. ANTONY CHAS. DELATRE.
b. London. Prof. Lambs. 1711. Ord. 1715. Sent on
the mission in the S. Prov. 1726, and there died.

1731. Sep. 1st. D. BERNARD QUYNEO.
Prof. St. Lau., 1693. Sent on the mission in the S.
Prof. 1702. Was stationed at Kiddington, Oxfords.
1703, at Bath, 1711. Was Proc. Prov. 1713. Con-
fessor to Nuns at Lisbon, 1714. Sec. to Pres. 1725-7.
Vicar of nuns at Cambray, 1727, till death there.
Was Def. Reg., 1729.

1732. April 21st. D. WM. LAURENCE CHAMPNEY.
b. London, 1667. Prof. St. Lau., 1684. Pr. of St.
Lau., 1693-1701. Sent on the mission in the N.
Prov, 1701. Again Pr. of St. Lau., 1717-21. Again
in the N. Prov. and stationed at Bedal 1721-31, then
at Woolton, Lancas., where he died.

1732. April 29th. D. THOMAS BASIL WARWICK.
b. Warwick Hall, Cumberland. Prof. St. Greg., 1698.
Sent on the mission in the N. Prov., and stationed at
Warwick Hall. Pr. of St. Greg., 1729 till death at
Douai.

1732. Sep. 5th. D. LAURENCE CASSE.

b. Knaresboro'. Prof. St. Ed., 1689. Spent some time in Maurist Monasteries. Sent on the mission in the N. Prov. Stationed at Parlington, Yorks, where he died. Was Proc. Prov. 1710-3. Def. Prov. 1713-21. Cath. Prof. Gloucester, 1713. Prov. of York, 1721-5. Def. Prov. 1725-9. Def. Reg. 1729.

1732. Sep. 23rd. D. JOHN AUGUSTINE HUDSON.

b. Lancas. Prof. St. Lau., 1686. Sent on the mission in the S. Prov. and stationed at Flixton, 1704, till death there. Was Proc. Prov., 1721. Def. Prov., 1729.

1733. Feb. 17th. D. OBED ALBAN DAWNEY.

b. Lancas. Prof. Lambs., 1683. Sent on the mission in the S. Prov. Def. Prov., 1721. Procurator in Rome, 1725, till death there. Was Abbot of Rintelin, 1733.

1733. May 1st. D. EDW. AUGUSTINE DELATTRE.

b. London. Educ. Eng. Coll., Rome. Ord. sec. priest. Prof. St. Ed., 1706. Was Sub-prior in 1715. d. at La Celle.

1733. Aug. 15th. D. ARTHUR FRANCIS WATMOUGH.

b. Lancas, 1665. Prof. St. Lau., 1684. Was Cellerarius. Sent on the mission in the N. Prov. and stationed in Lancashire. Was Procurator in Rome, 1698-1701. Pr. of St. Lau., 1701-10. Cath. Pr. of Worcester, 1710. Pres. Gen., 1713-7. Prov. of Canterbury, 1717-21. Stationed at Fonthill. Pr. of St. Lau., 1721-33. d. at Douai.

1733. Sep. 16th. D. WILLIAM JOSEPH HOWARD.
b. Corby Castle, Cumberland. Prof. St. Greg., 1712.
Sent on the mission in N. Prov. Was Proc. Prov.,
1721. Sec. to Pres., 1729. Def. Prov., 1732. d.
at Wootton, Warwicks.

1734. Sep. 1st. D. JOHN LEANDER DAVIS.
b. Middlesex, 1670. Prof. Lambs., 1689. Sent on
the mission in the S. Prov., 1708. Stationed at
Brise Norton, 1712, afterwards in London, where
he died.

1734. Sep. 8th. D. GILBERT KNOWLES.
b. Hants, 1667. Prof. St. Greg., 1692. Ord., 1700.
Sent on the mission in the N. Prov., 1705. Stationed
at Newboro', Yorks, 1710, and then at Whenby.
Returned to St. Greg. and d. at Douai.

1735. Jan. 4th. D. VINCENT PALIN.
Prof. St. Lau., 1717. Sent on the mission to the
N. Prov., stationed at Wetherby, Yorks. Passed
to the S. Prov. to Witham Place, Essex, and d. there.

1735. Jan. 18th. D. JOHN BARTHOL. HAVERS.
b. Kelveton, Norfolk. Prof. St. Greg., 1729, and d. at
Douai.

1735. Feb. 12th. D. RICHARD BERN. BARTLETT.
b. Worcesters. Prof. St. Greg., 1692. Sent on the
mission to the N. Prov. and stationed in Yorks.
and Lancas. Retired to St. Greg. and d. at Douai.

1735. April 23rd. D. BENJAMIN BEDE MOORE.
b. London. Prof. St. Ed., 1681. Sec. to Pres. and
Chapter, 1689 and 1693. Sent on the mission in
the S. Prov. Returned to St. Ed., 1701, was Cellerarius, 1705-6. At St. Greg., 1707., St. Lau., 1712,

then came to England. Was Def. Reg., 1717-21.
d. in England.

1735. May 12th. D. RICHARD ANS. WALMESLEY.
b. Lancas. Prof. St. Lau., 1710. Sent on the mission
in the N. Prov. and stationed at Woolstan, Lancas,
1719-35. d. at Ormskirk.

1736. Feb. 22nd.· D. EDWARD JOSEPH RIDDELL.
b. Northumberland. Prof. Lambs., 1719. Was Prior,
1735. d. at Hildesheim.

1736. April 14th. D. WM. PESTEL, OR PHILIPS.
b. Winchester. Prof. St. Greg., 1682. Was Cellerarius,
1693. Sent on the mission to the S. Prov., 1694.
Stationed at London. Was Proc. Prov. and Def.
Prov. 1705. Pr. of St. Greg., 1721-3. Def. Reg.,
1725, till death in London.

1736. April 24th. D. WM. BENEDICT WINTER.
b. Huntingdons. Prof. St. Greg., 1692. Ord., 1707.
Went to Lambs., 1715. Returned to St. Greg., 1724,
and d. at Douai.

1736. Dec. 6th. D. SIMON AUSTIN DUNSCOMBE.
b. Devon, 1702. Prof. Lambs., 1722, and d. there.

1737. Feb. 11th. D. ARTHUR BEDE HALSALL.
b. Northumberland. Prof. St. Greg., 1687. Was
Cellerarius. Sent on the mission in the N. Prov.,
1693. Was in Yorkshire, 1703. Prov. of York,
1713-7, at Newboro', 1713, Stockeld, 1715, Beaufront,
1721, and d. there. Was Def. Prov., 1729.

1737. Mar. 10th. D. WM. EDMUND BATCHELOR.
b. Yorksh., 1709. · Prof. St. Ed., 1726. Sent on the
mission to the S. Prov., 1735. d. at Bromley, Kent.

1737. July 1st. D. WILLIAM BENEDICT LAWSON.
b. Brough Hall, Yorksh. Prof. Lambs., 1685. Sent
on the mission in the N. Prov. d. at Marseilles.

1737. Sep. 3rd. D. WILLIAM AMBROSE GAWEN.
b. Middlesex. Prof. Lambs., 1690. Was Sub-prior,
1729. Prior, 1730. Sent on the mission in the
N. Prov., 1731, and stationed at Bedal, Yorks., and
d. there.

1738. Jan. 8th. D. WILLIAM JOSEPH KENNEDY.
b. 1661. Was a convert. Prof. St. Ed., 1692. Went
to Cambray and then to St. Greg. Ord., 1694.
Returned to St. Ed., 1705, and was Cellerarius.
Sent on the mission in the S. Prov., 1705. Was at
St. Greg., 1716, St. Ed. 1718. Again in the S. Prov.
Retired to St. Ed., 1633, and d. in Paris.

1738. Feb. 5th. D. HENRY AUSTIN BRIGHAM.
b. Wyton Hall, Yorks. Prof. St. Greg., 1731, and d.
at Douai.

1738. Feb. 8th. D. THOMAS NELSON.
b. Lancas. Prof. St. Greg., 1703. Ord., 1707. Was
Sub-prior, 1713. Sec. to Chapter, 1721. Pr. of St.
Greg., 1733-7. d. in England.

1738. Feb. 12th. D. WILLIAM ODO DUDDELL.
b. Middlesex, 1670. Prof. Lambs., 1689. Sent on
the mission in the S. Prov. and d. there.

1738. July 17th. D. WILLIAM METCALFE.
b. Yorks. Prof. St. Greg., 1690. Ord., 1698. Sent
on the mission in the N. Prov. into Yorks. Retired
in old age to St. Greg. and d. at Douai.

1739. Feb. 10th. D. Placid Robinson, or Fairfax.
b. Yorkshire. Prof. Lambs., 1701. Sent on the mission to the S. Prov. and d. in London.

1739. Sep. 18th. D. John Philipson.
b. Streitly, Berks. Prof. St. Greg., 1676. Was Cellerarius, 1685. Sub-prior, 1688. Pr. of St. Greg., 1693-1701. Cath. Pr. of Norwich, 1701. Sent on the mission in the S. Prov. Was Def. Prov., 1710. Def. Reg., 1732. d. upwards of 80.

1740. Jan. 11th. D. William Champney.
b. Lancas. Prof. St. Lau., 1711. Sent on the mission in the N. Prov. and stationed at Little Mosna, Walton-le-Dale, 1724, till death there.

1740. Feb. 7th. D. John Joseph D'Ognate.
b. Bruges. Prof. St. Ed., 1700. Sent on the mission to the N. Prov., 1718. Retired to La Celle and d. there.

1740. April 5th. D. Francis Rich.
b. Kent. Prof. St. Greg., 1692. Ord., 1698. Sent on the mission in the N. Prov., 1706. Stationed in Cumberland and then in Yorks. Was at Plompton, in 1726, and d. there.

1740. July 7th. D. Robert Thomas Riddell.
b. Swinburne, Northumb., 1698. Prof. Lambs., 1715. Was at St. Greg., 1726. Returned to Lambspring, 1738, and d. there.

1741. Mar. 13th. D. John Francis Moore.
b. Fawley, Berks. Prof. St. Ed., 1698. Sent to England, 1701. Returned to St. Ed., 1710. Ord.,

1711. Procurator in Rome, 1713-7. Pr. of St. Ed., 1717-21. Cath. Pr. of Canterbury, 1721. Sent on the mission in the S. Prov. and stationed in London. Was Def. Reg., 1723. d. at Coventry.

1741. July 17th. D. JOHN DENIS BULMER.
b. Middlesex. Prof. Lambs., 1732. Ord., 1736, and d. there.

1741. Dec. 27th. D. ROBERT HARDCASTLE.
Prof. St. Lau., 1690. Was Sec. to Pres., 1705. Sub-prior. Pr. of St. Lau., 1710-3. Sent on the mission to the S. Prov., 1717, and stationed in London. Cath. Pr. of Peterboro', 1717. Def. Prov., 1721. Prov. of Canterbury, 1737-41. d. in London.

1742. Jan. 2nd. D. THOMAS WILFRID. HELME.
b. Goosnargh, Lancas. Prof. St. Ed., 1699. Was sent on the mission in the S. Prov. for 3 or 4 years, and then passed to the N. Prov. and stationed at Kilvington, Yorks. Was Proc. Prov., 1725. Prov. of York, 1725-9. Pr. of St. Ed., 1729-33. Cath. Pr. of Chester, 1733. Retired to St. Lau., 1737, and d. at Dieulward.

1742. Nov. 19th. D. WM. BENEDICT SHAFTOE.
b. Northumberland. Prof. St. Ed., 1715. Was confessor to nuns at Lisbon and d. there.

1743. Feb. 15th. D. FRAN. BENEDICT KNIGHT.
b. Reasby, Lincolns, 1716. Prof. Lambs., 1732, and d. there.

1743. Feb. 15th. D. JOHN BERNARD WYTHIE.
b. Cambridgesh. Prof. St. Greg., 1708. Ord., 1716. Was Sec. to Chapter, 1725. Was sent on the mission

in the S. Prov., 1726, and stationed at Weston, Bucks.
In London, 1730. Was Proc. Prov., 1733. Def.
Prov. 1737. Procurator in Rome, 1737, till death
there. Cath. Pr. of Gloucester, 1741.

1743. June 21st. D. JOHN BEDE POTTS.
b. Northumberland, 1674. Prof. Lambs., 1691. Was
Cellerarius. Sent on the mission to the N. Prov.,
1701, and stationed at York, and removed to Everingham, 1730, till death there. Was Def. Prov.,
1721. Cath. Pr. of Durham, 1733.

1743. July 18th. D. LAURENCE KIRBY.
b. Lancas. Prof. St. Lau., 1710. Sent on the mission
in the N. Prov. and stationed at Childwall, Lancas.,
where he died.

1744. Aug. 3rd. D. GREGORY GREENWOOD.
b. Brise Norton, Oxfords. Prof. St. Greg., 1688. Was
Cellerarius, 1698. Sent on the mission in the S.
Prov., 1702, and stationed at Brise Norton. Was
Def. Prov., 1721. Cath. Pr. of Coventry. 1725.
Prov. of Canterbury, 1725-37. Def. Reg., 1737, till
death. Was at Coughton, Warwick., 1726, and died
there.

**1745. Jan. 3rd. D. JOHN RICHARD ISHERWOOD,
OR SHERBURNE.**
b. Lancashire. Prof. Lambs., 1685. Sent on the
mission in the S. Prov., 1699. Was stationed at
Leighland, Somerset, 1701-27. Fawley, Berks., 1727,
till death there. Was Def. Reg., 1729-41.

1745. Mar. 13th. D. EDWARD SHERBURNE.
b. Parringdon, Essex, Prof. St. Ed., 1699. Sent on

the mission to the N. Prov., 1713. Stationed at
Swinburne. d. at Beaufront.

1745. Mar. 16th. D. BERTRAM EDWARD BULMER.
b. Yorks. Prof. Lambs., 1685. Sent on the mission
to the N. Prov., 1693, in Yorks. Was at Stockeld,
1701-15; Chester-le-Street, 1727, till death there.
Was Def. Prov., 1717. Def. Reg., 1721. Cath. Pr.
of Durham, 1725. Def. Prov., 1725. Def. Reg.,
1731. Cath. Pr. of Canterbury, 1733.

1745· Mar. 19th. D. DAVID EDMUND COX.
b. London, 1662. Prof. St. Ed., 1698. Sent on the
mission to the N. Prov., 1721. Passed to the S.
Prov., 1730, retired to St. Ed. and d. at Paris.

1746. Mar. 4th. D. THOS. ANSELM CRATHORNE.
b. Ness Hall, Yorks. Prof. Lambs., 1703. Went to
St. Ed., 1708. Took degree of D.D. at Sorbonne.
Returned to Lambs, 1716. Was Prior. Sent on
the mission to the S. Prov., 1718. Returned to
Lambs., 1730. Abbot of Cismar, 1733. Def. Reg.,
1736. d. at Lambspring.

1746. May 27th. D. EDWARD DUNSTAN ROGERS.
b. Co. of Denbigh. Prof. St. Ed., 1714. Sent on the
mission to the N. Prov., 1727. Stationed at Hazlewood, till 1731, and then at Parlington till death.
Proc. Prov., 1733-46. Def. Prov., 1745. Cath. Pr.
of Norwich, 1745.

1746. June 4th. D. LEWIS LAURENCE FENWICK.
b. Northumberland. Prof. St. Greg., 1685. Sent on
the mission to the N. Prov. and stationed at Bedal.
Passed to the S. Prov., 1697. Again to the N. Prov.,

1707, to Whenby and then Bedal.   Def. Reg., 1713-7.
Pres. Gen., 1717-21.   d. at Chelsea, London.

1746.   Oct 25th.   Br. WALTER MAURUS BLOUNT.
b. Maple Durham, Berks., 1727.   Prof. St. Greg., 1745,
and d. at Douai.

1747.   Jan 27th.   D. WILLIAM HEWLETT.
b. Winchester.   Prof. St. Ed., 1699.   Was Cellerarius,
1706-14.   Sent on the mission to the N. Prov., 1714,
to Lancashire.   Went into Yorkshire in 1725, and
then to Whitehaven.   Returned to St. Ed., 1726,
and d. in Paris.

1747.   April 29th.   D. THOMAS EAVES.
b. Lancas., 1659.   Prof. St. Lau., 1684, and d. at
Dieulward.

1747.   May 26th.   D. FRANCIS BRUNING.
b. Berks., 1675.   Prof. Lambs., 1699.   Sent on the
mission to the S. Prov., 1704.   Def. Prov., 1725.
Was at Bath, 1726-30; Salford, Warwicks., 1730:
Spetchley, 1741, till death there.   Was Cath. Pr.
of Ely, 1737.   Def. Reg., 1745.

1747.   June 29th.   D. FRANCIS WALMESLEY.
b. Lancas., 1717.   Prof. St. Lau., 1735.   Was Sub-prior.
d. at Dieulward.

1748.   Feb. 20th.   D. ROBERT PAUL GILMORE.
b. Ramsbury, Wilts.   Prof. Lambs., 1685.   Went to
St. Ed. and then was sent on the mission to the
N. Prov. and stationed at Parlington where he died.

1748.   April 8th.   D. ARTHUR ALBAN ASHTON.
b. Warrington, 1680.   Prof. St. Ed., 1699, and d. in
Paris.

1748.   April 8th.   D. JOHN STOURTON.
b. Stourton, Wilts.   Prof. St. Greg., 1693.   Ord., 1699.
Was Cellerarius, 1704.   Vicar of nuns at Cambray,
1705-17.   Pr. of St. Greg., 1717-21.   Pr. of St. Ed.,
1725-9.   Cath. Pr. of Bath, 1729.   Sent on the
mission in the N. Prov.   Was at Whenby, 1730-3,
then Gilling Castle.   Def. Reg., 1741.   Confessor to
nuns at Antwerp, 1741, till death there.   Was Cath.
Pr. of Winchester, 1745.

1748.   Oct. 24th.   D. THOMAS SOUTHCOT.
b. Surrey, 1670.   Prof. St. Greg., 1688.   Was Cellerarius, 1694-8.   Took degree of D.D. at Douai.   Sent
on the mission in the S. Prov. and stationed in
London, 1700; Standon, Herefords., 1705.   Was Sec.
to Chapter, 1705.   Def. Reg., 1713.   Abbot of Cismar,
1717.   Pres. Gen., 1721-41.   Vicar of nuns at
Cambray till death.

1749.   April 17th.   D. JAMES BUCKLEY.
b. London.   Prof. St, Ed., 1708.   Sent on the mission
in the S. Prov. and d. there.   Was Def. Prov., 1745.

1749.   Aug. 20th.   D. EDWARD GREGORY PIGOTT.
b. Oxfords.   Prof. St. Greg., 1711.   Sent on the mission
to the S. Prov., 1721.   Was at Spetchley, 1747, and
d. there.

1749.   Oct. 25th.   D. GREGORY ROBINSON.
b. 1710.   Prof. St. Lau., 1730.   Sent on the mission to
to the N. Prov., 1738.   Returned to St. Lau. in ill
health, 1740, and d. at Dieulward.

1749.   Nov.   18th.   D.   SIMEON   BENEDICT
RIGMAIDEN.
b. Lancas.   Prof. St. Lau., 1707.   Sent on the mission

to the S. Prov. Stationed at Burton on the Water, Gloucester. Was Sec. to Pres., 1717-25. Retired to St. Lau., 1744, and d. at Dieulward.

1750. Mar. 19th. D. FRANCIS ROOKWOOD.
b. Coldham Hall, Suffolk. Prof. St. Greg., 1680. Sent on the mission to the S. Prov. Was Proc. Prov., 1693. Def. Prov., 1697-1701. Sec. to Chapter, 1697. Sec. to Pres., 1701. Def. Prov., 1705-12. Cath. Pr. of Rochester, 1705. Prov. of Canterbury, 1712-3. Def. Prov., 1713. Was stationed at Witham Place, Essex. At Acton Burnell, 1724-37, and afterwards in Worcestershire where he died.

1750. Sep. 3rd. D. ROBERT ELPHEGE DOBSON.
b. Tunbridge, Kent. Prof. Lambs., 1709. Sent on the mission to the N. Prov., 1726, but returned the same year. Was Novice Master, 1731. d. at Lambspring.

1751. Mar. 16th. D. FRANCIS DUNSTAN PIGOTT.
b. London. Prof. St. Greg., 1727. Sent to Lambspring. Returned to St. Greg., 1739. Was Cellerarius, 1749. d. at Douai.

1751. Aug. 26th. D. EDWARD HOUGHTON.
b. Parkhall, Lancas. Prof. St. Lau., 1710. Sent to Lambspring, 1717. Ord., 1720. Sent on the mission to the N. Prov. and stationed at Parkhall, Low, and Hindley and d. there. Was Def. Prov., 1745.

1752. April 24th. D. JOHN GREGORY METCALFE.
b. Lancas., 1724. Prof. Lambs., 1740, and d. there.

1752. July 15th. D. JAMES HAWKINS.
b. Gloucesters. Prof. Lambs., 1705. Sent on the mission in the S. Prov., 1718. Retired to Lambspring, 1719. Was Prior, 1752, and d. there.

1753. Mar. 14th. D. ABRAHAM MAURUS COUPE.
b. Owlerton, Lancas. Prof. St. Ed., 1731. Was Sec.
to Pres., 1741. Pr. of St. Ed., 1745-9. Cath. Pr.
of Ely, 1749, d. in Paris.

1753. Oct. 12th. D. WM. ILDEPHONSUS BYERLY.
b. Leicestersh. Prof. St. Greg., 1708. Ord., 1711.
Sent on the mission to the S. Prov., 1721. Stationed
at Brise Norton, Oxfords., and d. there.

1754. Jan. 1st. D. RALPH CUTHBERT FARNWORTH.
b. Runshaw, Lancas., 1680. Prof. St. Lau., 1701. Went
to St. Greg., and returned to St. Lau. Sent on the
mission to the N. Prov. Was at Wetherby, Yorks.,
1726, at Capheaton, 1727. Prov. of York, 1729-41.
Cath. Pr. of Winchester, 1733, then Canterbury, 1745.
Pres. Gen., 1741-53. Def. Reg., 1754. d. in Paris.

1754. Mar. 14th. D. JOSEPH STARKEY, OR HANMER.
b. London. Prof. St. Greg., 1703. Sent on the mission
to the S. Prov., 1709. Was at Witham Place, Essex,
1750, and d. there.

1754. Aug. 1st. D. WILLIAM AMBROSE DAVIS.
b. London. Prof. St. Ed,, 1688. Was at St. Lau., 1694,
La Celle, 1695. Ord., 1697. Sent on the mission to
the N. Prov. Was at Kilvington, Yorks., 1728. Bedal,
1731-2. d. near York.

1755. Feb. 2nd. D. WM. AMBROSE BROWN.
b. Westmoreland. Prof. St. Greg., 1700. Ord., 1706.
Was Cellerarius, 1713-7. Sent on the mission to the
S. Prov., 1717, and was at Winchester till 1741, at
Bath, 1741-5. Was Proc. Prov., 1729. Cath. Pr. of
Worcester, 1737. Def. Prov., 1741. Def. Reg., 1744.
d. on the mission.

1755. May 16th. D. HUGH FRANKLAND.

b. York. Prof. St. Greg., 1700. Ord., 1705. Was at St. Ed., 1707, and Sub-prior, 1708. Returned to St. Greg., 1709. Was Cellerarius, 1710-3. Sent on the mission in the N. Prov., 1713, to Yorks. Was at Middleton Lodge, 1719-45. Capheaton, 1745. Huddleston Hall, 1748, and d. there. Was Def. Prov., 1745.

1755. May 17th. D. THOMAS PLACID HUTTON.

b. Eldon, Durham. Prof. Lambs., 1714. Ord., 1720. Novice Master, 1722. Sent on the mission to the N. Prov., 1729. Was at Woolton, 1732, till death there. Was Def. Prov., 1752.

1755. Aug. 3rd. D. THOMAS ALEXIUS SHEPHERD.

b. Warwicksh. Prof. St. Greg., 1721. Sent on the mission to the S. Prov. Was at Winchester, 1741. Pr. of St. Greg., 1745, till death at Douai. Cath. Pr. of Bath, 1749.

1755. Aug. 10th. D. JOHN ALEXIUS JONES.

b. Middlesex, 1681. Prof. St. Greg., 1699. Ord., 1705. Sent on the mission to the S. Prov., 1708. Passed to the N. Prov. and again to the S. Prov. to Bury, Suffolk, and then to Hongrave, where he died.

1755. Dec. 12th. D. FRANCIS HOWARD.

Prof. St. Lau., 1708. Was Cellerarius. Sent on the mission to the S. Prov. Was at Coldham Hall, Suffolk, 1717-37, Hongrave, and Bury, 1737, till death there. Was Def. Prov., 1749. Cath. Pr. of Norwich, 1749.

1756. May 29th. D. WILLIAM BEDE HUTTON.

b. Eldon, Durham. Prof. Lambs., 1713. Ord., 1720.

Sent on the mission to the N. Prov., 1731. Was at Blaydon, Durham. Kendal, 1735. Hesleyside, 1747, and d. there.

1757. July 30th. D. ROBERT AUSTIN TURNER.
b. Lancas., 1721. Prof. Lambs., 1740. Was at St. Greg., 1750. Sent on the mission to the N. Prov., 1752. Was at Hesleyside, 1756, and d. there.

1758. Dec. 29th. D. ANTHONY LEANDER RAFFA.
b. London. Prof. St. Greg., 1733. Sent on the mission to the N. Prov. Was at Swinburne, 1743-6. Chester-le-Street, 1746, and d. at Birtley.

1759. Jan. 8th. D. JOHN MAURUS RIGMAIDEN, OR SMITH.
b. Lancas., 1672. Prof. St. Lau., 1693. Sent on the mission to the S. Prov. Was at Barmingham, Norfolk, 1701-5. Stourton, Wilts, 1712-5. Colley Wood, 1715, then Oxburgh Hall, where he died. Was Def. Prov. many years.

1759. Feb. 6th. D. EDWARD GREGORY SELBY.
b. Yardhill, Northumberland. Prof. Lambs., 1726. Sent on the mission to the N. Prov. and was at Beaufront, 1737, till death at Hesleyside.

1760. April 13th. BR. ROLAND ANSELM MACDONALD.
b. Lochabers, Scotland, 1738. Prof. St. Greg., 1757. Ord. Sub-deacon. d. at Douai.

1760. July 2nd. D. ANTH. CUTHBERT HUTCHINSON.
b. Yorksh. Prof. St. Greg., 1723. Sent on the mission to the S. Prov. Had charge of a school at Redmarley, Gloucesters., 1733. Passed to the N. Prov. and was

at Plompton, Yorks., 1740-5.   Middleton Lodge,
1745-59, and d. at Aberford.

1760.   Aug. 15th.   D. JORDAN MAURUS LANGDALE.
b. Holme Hall, 1734.   Prof. St. Greg., 1751.   d. at Douai.

1760.   Sep. 5th.   BR. BENEDICT HARSNIP.
b. Ormskirk, 1737.   Prof. St. Ed., 1753.   Ord. deacon
and d. at Paris.

1761.   Feb. 1st.   D. FREDERICK ALEXIUS LATHAM.
b. Hamburg.   Prof. Lambs., 1743, and d. there.

1761.   April 26th.   D. RICHARD PLACID ASHTON.
b. Warrington, 1707.   Prof. St. Ed., 1725.   Sent on
the mission to the S. Prov.   Was at Flixton, Suffolk,
1737.   Returned to St. Ed., 1741, and d. at Paris.

1761.   Sep. 14th.   D. THOMAS ADRIAN HARDISTY.
b. Yorksh., 1686.   Prof. Lambs., 1703.   Was Cellerarius.
Cath. Pr. of Coventry, 1745.   d. at Lambspring.

1761.   Nov. 6th.   D. GEORGE JOSEPH ROKEBY.
b. Middlesex, 1688.   Prof. Lambs., 1703.   Sent to St.
Greg., 1717.   Took degree of D.D.   Sent on the
mission to the N. Prov. and stationed at Everingham,
Yorks.   Was Sec. to Chapter, 1729.   Abbot of
Lambspring, 1730, and d. there.

1762.   Mar. 12th.   D. GEORGE ROBERT ROBINSON.
b. Middlesex.   Prof. Lambs., 1722.   Sent on the mission
to the N. Prov., 1729.   Vicar of nuns at Paris, 1735,
till death there.   Was Sec. to Chapter, 1749.

1762.   May 15th. D. JOHN NICHOLAS RICHARDSON.
b. Lancas.   Prof. St. Lau., 1737.   Sent on the mission
to the S. Prov., 1747.   Returned to St. Lau. and d.
at Dieulward.

1762. Aug. 1st. D. JOHN ASPINWALL.
b. Yorksh. Prof. St. Ed., 1714. Sent on the mission
to the N. Prov., 1726. Was at Stockeld, 1729.
Passed to the S. Prov. and stationed at Witham
Place, Essex, 1735. Returned to St. Ed. Passed
to Lambspring, 1755, and d. there.

1763. Nov. 22nd. D. JOHN DENIS WAREHAM, OR
WENHAM.
b. Middlesex. Prof. Lambs., 1744, and d. there.

1764. July 5th. D. THOMAS SIMPSON.
b. Lancas. Prof. St. Lau., 1737. Sent on the mission
to the N. Prov. Stationed at Cuerdon, Lancas. d.
at Ormskirk.

1764. Sep. 9th. D. JAMES WILFRID WITHAM.
b. Cliff, Yorks. Prof. Lambs., 1715. Sent on the
mission to the N. Prov. Was at Whenby, 1721-30.
Whitehaven and Kendal. Returned to Lambs, 1731.
Again to the N. Prov. and was at Whenby, 1733-7.
Bedal, 1736-43. Returned to Lambspring. Was
Prior and d. there.

1764. Sep. 24th. D. JOHN PLACID RIGBY.
b. Lancas. Prof. St. Lau., 1725. Was Sub-prior. Sent
on the mission to the S. Prov. and was at Hanley,
Worcestersh., 1736, Passed to the N. Prov., 1746.
Again to the S. Prov. and was at Bidwell, Exeter,
1755, and at Welshpool. Returned to St. Lau. and
d. at Dieulward.

1764. Nov. 30th. D. JOHN ANSELM MANNOCK.
b. Gifford's Hall, Suffolk, 1681. Prof. St. Greg., 1700.
Sent on the mission to the S. Prov. Was at Foxcote,

1709-59. Kelvedon Hall, Essex, 1759, till death
there. Was Proc. Prov., 1729. Def. Prov., 1755.
Cath. Pr. of Worcester, 1757. Def. Reg., 1757.

1764. Dec. 27th. D. PHILIP WILFRID CONSTABLE.
b. Everingham Hall, Yorks., 1706. Prof. St. Ed., 1725.
Sent on the mission to the S. Prov. Was at Weston,
Bucks., 1733-47. Spetchley, 1749, till death there.

1766. July 5th. D. JOHN PLACID HOWARD.
b. Corby Castle, Cumberland, 1698. Prof. St. Greg.,
1719. Was Cellerarius. Sent on the mission to
the N. Prov. Was at Corby, 1728. Passed to the
S. Prov. and stationed in London. Was Def. Prov.,
1737. Proc. Prov., 1741. Prov. of Canterbury,
1745-53. Cath. Pr. of Bath, 1745, then Winchester,
1749, then Canterbury, 1757. Pres. Gen., 1653,
till death at Douai.

1766. July 13th. D. ROBERT AMBROSE BOUCHER.
b. Middlesex, 1726. Prof. Lambs., 1744, and d. there.

1767. Jan. 4th. D. JAMES BERNARD PRICE.
b. Standish. Prof. St. Lau., 1737. Sent on the mission
to the N. Prov., 1744. Was at Standish, 1744. Pr. of
St. Ed., 1757-65. Again on the mission in the S. Prov.
and stationed at Ugbrooke, 1765, where he died and
was buried at Chudleigh.

1768. Jan. 4th. D. AUGUSTINE SULYARD.
b. Haughley Hall, Norfolk. Prof. St. Lau., 1708. Was
confessor to nuns at Lisbon. 1725, till death there.

1768. Nov. 30th. D. MATTHEW PAUL ALLANSON.
b. Woodal, Yorksh. Prof. Lambs., 1713. Sent on
the mission to the N. Prov., 1731. Was at Whitehaven, 1731-5. Passed to the S. Prov. and was

at Leighland, Somerset, 1736-46. Woolter's Hill, Worcester, 1746-68. Retired in old age to Lambspring, 1768, and d. there.

1769. Feb. 20th. D. AUGUSTUS LAURENCE TURCK. A German. Prof. Lambs., 1751. Was Cellerarius, 1764, and d. there.

1769. Aug. 30th. D. HENRY WYBURNE. b. Hawkwell Place, Kent. Prof. St. Ed., 1723. Sent on the mission to the S. Prov. Was at Weston, Bucks., 1730. Pr. of St. Ed., 1737-45. Cath. Pr. of Chester, 1745, then Winchester, 1757. Def. Reg., 1745-53. Prov. of Canterbury, 1750, till death in London.

1770. Mar. 18th. D. DUNSTAN WORSWICK. b. Brindle, Lancas. Prof. St. Lau., 1758. Sent to Lambspring and d. at Hildesheim.

1770. April 12th. D. FRANCIS BASIL BRADSHAW. b. Esk, Durham. Prof. Lambs., 1762, and d. there.

1770. April 20th. D. WILLIAM LAURENCE YORK. b. London, 1687. Prof. St. Greg., 1705. Ord., 1711. Was Cellerarius, 1719. Sent on the mission to the N. Prov., 1720. Pr. of St. Ed., 1721-5. Pr. of St. Greg., 1725-9. Sec. to Pres., 1729. Again on the mission in the S. Prov. 1729. Was at Bath, 1730. Def. Prov., 1732. Cath. Pr. of Gloucester, 1733. Def. Reg., 1737. Consecrated Bp. of Niba, and Coadjutor to Western District, 1741. Succeeded, 1750. Retired in old age to S. Greg., and d. at Douai.

1770. Aug. 4th. D. GEORGE JAMES CROOK. b. Chorley, Lancas. Prof. St. Ed., 1739. Was Cellerarius, 1749-54. d. at Chateau Thierry.

1772. Oct. 3rd. D. JOSEPH JAMES LE GRAND.
b. Middlesex, 1611. Educ. Eng. Coll., Rome. Ord., 1734.
Prof. Lambs, 1737. Sent on the mission to the S.
Prov., 1743. Passed to the N. Prov. and stationed at
Holme, Yorks., then Standish. Was at Lawkland,
1744, and d. there.

1772. Nov. 8th. D. WILLIAM PLACID NAYLOR.
b. Scarisbrick, Lancas. Prof. St. Lau., 1711. Was
Cellerarius. Sent on the mission to the N. Prov.
Was at Brindle, 1722-69. Def. Prov., 1733. Def.
Reg., 1737. Prov. of York, 1741-66. Cath. Pr. of
Norwich, 1741, then Durham, 1745. Canterbury,
1769. Pres. Gen., 1766, till death at Dieulward.

1773. Jan. 30th. D. BERNARD BENEDICT BOLAS.
b. Preston Goballs, Shropshire. Prof. Lambs, 1744.
Sent on the mission to the N. Prov., 1755. Was at
Croxteth, Lancas., then Gilmoss, where he died.

1773. April 5th. D. MICHAEL EDWARD TEMPEST.
b. London. Prof. Lambs., 1719. Was Prior, 1740-6,
and d. there.

1773. June 16th. D. EDWARD AMBROSE ELLIOT.
b. Shropshire. Prof. St. Greg., 1719. Sent on the
mission to the S. Prov. Was at Acton Burnell till
1762. Cheame, Surrey, 1762. Ockendon Hall,
Essex, where he died. Was Def. Reg., 1765.

1774. Jan. 13th. D. FRANCIS AUSTIN SOUTHCOT.
b. Witham Place, Essex. Prof. St. Greg., 1708. Was
sent to St. Lau., and to St. Ed., 1718. Sent on the
mission to the S. Prov. Was at Salford, Warwicks.,
1727-30. Thorndon Hall, Essex, 1732-60. Sec. to

Pres., 1733. Proc. Prov., 1745. Def. Prov., 1749. Cath. Pr. of Norwich, 1757. Def. Reg., 1764. Went to Cambray, and d. there.

1774. May 13th. D. EVANS ANSELM EASTHAM.
b. Walton-le-Dale, Lancas. Prof. St. Ed., 1731. Sent on the mission to the N. Prov. Was at Whitehaven, 1750. Capheaton, 1751-4. Passed to the S. Prov., and was at Coughton, Warwicks., till 1758. Again to the N. Prov., and was at Low, Strangways, Lancas., retired to St. Ed., 1773, and d. at La Celle.

1774. July 2nd. D. THOS. BENED. SHUTTLEWORTH.
b. Middlesex. Prof. Lambs., 1723. Sent on the mission to the N. Prov. Was at Woolstan, Lancas., 1735-71. Warrington, 1771, till death there. Was Def. Prov., 1754.

1774. July 10th. D. WM. MAURUS WESTBROOK, OR DARELL.
b. Kent. Prof. Lambs., 1726. Was Prior, 1736-9. Sent on the mission in the N. Prov., 1740. Was at Wyton, Yorks., 1740. Gilling Castle, 1743-50. Passed to the S. Prov., and was at Flixton, Suffolk, 1752. Was Sec, to Pres., 1745. Cath. Pr. of Bath, 1757. Def. Reg., 1757-72. Retired to Lambspring, and d. there.

1774. Aug. 19th. D. BERNARD BRADSHAW.
b. Preston Goballs, Shrops. Prof. Lambs., 1723. Was Prior, 1731-4. Sent to the mission to the N. Prov., 1734. Was at Little Mosna, Lancas., 1740. Passed to the S. Prov., and was at Bath, 1747. Was Def. Reg., 1749. Cath. Pr. of Ely, 1753. Returned to Lambspring, 1757, and was Prior. Again in the S.

Prov., 1760, and was at Acton Burnell, 1762, till death there. Was Prov. of Canterbury, 1769, till death.

1775. June 15th. D. JAMES AUGUSTINE MOORE.
b. Fawley, Berks., 1724. Prof. St. Greg., 1740. Sent on the mission to the S. Prov., 1750. Pr. of St. Greg., 1755-75. Cath. Pr. of Durham, 1769. d. at Douai.

1775. July 10th. D. JOHN BENEDICT DANIEL, OR SIMPSON.
b. Lancas. Prof. St. Lau., 1773. Sent on the mission to the N. Prov. Was at Capheaton, 1743. Passed to the S. Prov., and was at Weston, Bucks., 1747-67, Def. Prov., 1761-9. Vicar of nuns at Cambray, 1769, till death there.

1775. Sep. 6th. D. LEWIS JOHN BARNES.
b. London, 1730. Prof. St. Ed., 1746. Sent on the mission to the S. Prov. Was at Witham Place, Essex, 1754-74. Went to the nuns at Liege, 1774, and d. there.

1776. Feb. 2nd. D. AMBROSE WAREING.
b. Brindle, Lancas. Prof. St. Lau., 1761. Sent on the mission in the N. Prov. Was at Lawkland, 1773-5. Whitehaven, 1775, and d. there.

1776. Mar. 11th. D. PETER WILCOCK.
b. Lancas. Prof. St. Lau., 1737. Confessor to nuns at Lisbon, 1742-68. Returned to St. Lau., and d. at Dieulward.

1776. Oct. 29th. D. PHILIP JEFFERSON.
b. Hexham, 1732. Prof. St. Ed., 1750. Sent on the

mission to the N. Prov. Was at Whitehaven, 1761-4.
Warwick Bridge, 1764-5. Returned to St. Ed., 1765,
and d. in Paris.

1777. Feb. 27th. D. LANCELOT BEDE NEWTON.
b. Stocksfield Hall, Northumb., 1714. Prof. Lambs,
1732, Ord., 1737. Was Prior, 1748. Sent on the
mission to the S. Prov., 1750. Was at Witham
Place, Essex. Passed to the N. Prov. Was at Gilling
Castle till 1761. Brandsby. Plompton. Beaufront,
1766-74. Whitehaven, 1774-5, and d. at Birtley.
Was Def. Prov., 1773.

1777. Mar. 31st. D. FRANCIS ANSELM LYNCH.
b. London, 1693. Prof. St. Greg., 1714. Was Cellerarius, 1723. Sub-prior, 1726-31. Vicar of nuns at
Cambray, 1731, till death there. Was Cath. Pr. of
Rochester, 1753.

1777. June 30th. D. JAMES AMBROSE KAYE.
b. Lancas. Prof. St. Lau., 1735. Sent on the mission
to the N. Prov., and was at Sefton, Lancas., 1742.
Pr. of St. Lau., 1753-65. Again in the N. Prov. and
at Warwick Hall, Cumb., 1765, till death there. Was
Def. Prov, 1766, till death.

**1777. Oct. 9th. D. EDWARD ALEXIUS POPE. OR
FISHER.**
b. Lancas. Prof. St. Lau., 1749. Sent on the mission
to the S. Prov. Was at Welshpool, 166–, till death
there.

1778. Jan. 5th. D. JOHN GREGORY MACKAY.
b. Northumberland. Prof. St. Greg., 1726. Was Sec.
to Pres., 1737. Sent on the mission to the N. Prov.
Was at Alderley, Cheshire, 1739, till death there.

1779. July 5th. D. FRANCIS BEDE ANDERTON.
b. Euxton, Lancas., 1740. Prof. St. Greg., 1757. Sent on the mission to the S. Prov. Was at Lindley, Shrops., 1772, and d. there.

1779. July 17th. D, AUGUSTINE GREGSON.
b. Lancas. Prof. St. Lau., 1725, and d. at Dieulward.

1779. Nov. 27th. D. ANSELM BROMLEY.
b. Liverpool. Prof. St. Lau., 1766. Sent on the mission to the N. Prov. and d. in Liverpool.

1780. Jan. 18th. D. ROBERT BENEDICT STEARE.
b. London. Prof. St. Greg., 1720. Pr. of St. Greg., 1737-45. Cath. Pr. of Peterboro', 1745. Sent on the mission to the N. Prov. Was at Parlington, Yorks., 1746, till death there. Was Def. Prov., 1757. Prov. of York, 1766-77.

1780. Mar. 19th. D. CHARLES SMITH.
b. London, 1727. Prof. St. Greg., 1746. Sent on the mission to the N. Prov. Was at Swinburne, 1759-61. Gilling Castle, 1761. Returned to St. Greg., 1761. Again on the mission in the S. Prov. and at Cossey Hall, 1767-9. Returned to St. Greg., 1769, and d. at Douai.

1780. July 5th. D. WILLIAM PLACID FONTAINE.
b. Lapwick, Northamptons. Prof. St. Greg., 1731, and d. at Douai.

1780. Sep. 9th. D. WILLIAM PLACID MELCALFE.
b. Lincolns., 1723. Prof. Lambs., 1740. Sent on the mission to the S. Prov. Was at Winchester, 1758-69. Weston, Bucks., 1769. Kelvedon Hall, 1769-76. d. in Sussex.

1781.   Sep. 9th.   D. EDWARD BERNARD CATTERAL.
b. Samsbury, Lancas. Prof. St. Lau., 1725. Pr. of St. Lau., 1733-53. Cath. Pr. of Gloucester, 1745. Sent on the mission to the N. Prov. and was at Woolton, 1753, till death there. Was Def. Prov., 1755-73. Def. Reg., 1773.

1781.   Sep. 12th.   D. ROBERT DANIEL.
b. Whittingham, Lancas. Prof. St. Lau., 1735. Sent on the mission to the N. Prov. Was at Capheaton, 1750. Whitehaven, 1751-9. Birtley, 1759, till death there.

1782.   June 25th.   D. PET. DUNSTAN HOLDERNESS.
Prof. St. Lau., 1741. Sent on the mission to the N. Prov. Was at Capheaton, 1753-73. Pr. of St, Lau., 1773-81, and d. at Dieulward.

1782.   Dec 5th.   D. JOHN WILFRID STRUTT, OR BRIDGEMAN.
b. Middlesex, 1710. Educ. Eng. Coll., Rome. Ord. sec. priest and came on the mission. Prof. Lambs., 1743. Sent on the mission to the S. Prov. Was at Leigh-land, Somerset, 1759-62. Lanherne, 1762-71. Re-tired to Lambspring and d. there.

1783.   Sep. 3rd.   D. FRANCIS JOSEPH CARTERET.
b. London. Prof. St. Greg., 1723. Sent on the mission to the S. Prov. Was at Bromley Hall, Kent, 1737-8. Returned to St. Greg. and was Cellerarius, 1739-41. Again in the S. Prov. Was at Coughton, 1744-54. Confessor to nuns at Lisbon, 1754-61. Again on the mission in London, 1761-80. Retired to St. Greg., blind, and d. at Douai. Was Proc. Prov., 1749. Cath. Pr. of Chester, 1757. Def. Prov., 1761-72. Def. Reg., 1772. Prov. of Canterbury, 1774-7.

1784. Dec. 30th. D. MICHAEL ANSELM CHAPLIN.
b. Middlesex, 1754. Prof. Lambs., 1771. Was Novice
Master, 1783. Sent on the mission in the N. Prov.
to St. Mary's Liverpool, 1784, and d. there.

1785. April 29th. D. BASIL EYSTON.
b. Brecknock. Prof. St. Greg., 1733, and d. at Douai.

1785. Nov. 1st. D. JOHN CUTHBERT SIMPSON.
b. Preston, 1724. Prof. St. Ed., 1746. Sent on the
mission to the S. Prov. Was at Coughton, 1758-84.
Bath, 1784, and d. there.

1786. Feb. 2nd. D. JOHN CUTHBERT GRIME.
b. Essex, 1743. Prof. St. Greg., 1764. Ord., 1784,
and d. at Douai.

1786. Feb. 25th. D. EDWARD HUSSEY.
b. Marnhull, Dorset. Prof. St. Greg., 1731. Was Sec.
to Chapter, 1741-45. Sub-prior. Sent on the mission
to the S. Prov. Was at Witham Place, Essex, 1749.
Flixton, 1750-2. Kirkham House, Exeter, 1752-5.
Coughton, 1758. Marlboro', Wilts., 1758-85. Marnhull, 1785, till death there.

1786. Oct. 4th. D. ROGER JOSEPH WHITTEL.
b, London, 1707. Prof. St. Ed., 1726. Sent on the
mission to the S. Prov. Was at Bath, 1752. Returned to St. Ed. and d. in Paris.

1786. Nov. 4th. D. JAMES BERRY.
b. Wigan, 1758. Prof. St. Ed., 1779. Sent on the
mission to the N. Prov. and was at Cowley Hall,
Lancas., 1786, and d. there.

1786. Dec. 7th. D. JOHN CHARLTON.
b. Reedsmouth, Northumb., 1710. Prof. St. Greg., 1736.
Sent on the mission to the N. Prov. Was at
Plompton, 1745-62. Follyfoot, 1762-4. Returned
to St. Greg., 1764. Was Novice Master and Sub-
prior and d. at Douai.

1787. Jan. 6th. D. JAMES DUNSTAN KNIGHT.
b. Reasby, Lincolns., 1714. Prof. Lambs., 1732. Sent
on the mission to the S. Prov. Was at Little
Malvern, 1766, till death there. Was Cath. Pr. of
Rochester, 1777.

1787. Feb. 18th. D. WM. LAURÈNCE HARDISTY.
b. Middlesex, 1714. Prof. Lambs., 1732. Ord., 1738.
Sent on the mission to the N. Prov. Was at Easingwold, 1743-54. Grantham, Lincolns. Everingham,
till 1761. Passed to the S. Prov. Was at Spetchley,
1761. Returned to Lambs. and d. there.

1787. June 4th. D. THOMAS PATTEN.
b. Lancas., 1727. Prof. St. Greg., 1746. Sent on the
mission to the N. Prov., 1758. Was at Standish, 1767.
Returned to St. Greg. Went to St. Ed., 1779. Returned to St. Greg., 1786, and d. at Douai.

1788. July 2nd. D. JOHN CYPRIAN BARNEWELL.
b. London, 1761. Prof. Lambs., 1783, and d. there.

1788. Sep. 10th. D. BERTRAM MAURUS BALMER.
b. 1714. Prof. St. Lau., 1724. Sent on the mission to
the N. Prov., 1732, and stationed at Ormskirk, and
d. there.

1789. Feb. 4th. D. ROBERT BEDE SCOTT.
b. Beaufront, 1743. Prof. Lambs., 1763, and d. there.

1789.   Feb. 26th.   D. JOHN BERNARD DAVIS, OR KIRKE.

b. Middlesex, 1714.   Prof. Lambs., 1733.   Ord., 1738. Was sent on the mission to the S. Prov.   Returned to Lambspring, and d. there.

1790.   Mar. 12th.   D. RICHARD PETER WALMSLEY, OR SHERBURNE.

b. Westwood Hall, Wigan, 1717.   Prof. St. Greg., 1736. Was Prefect of Students for fifty years.   Cath. Pr. of Durham, 1777.   d. at Douai.

1790.   Aug. 20th.   D. THOMAS WELCH.

b. Lancas.   Prof. St. Ed.   Sent on the mission to the N. Prov., 1752.   Was at Corby Castle.   Pr. of St. Ed., 1765-73.   Cath. Pr. of Winchester, 1773.   Def. Reg., 1775, till death.   Vicar of nuns at Cambray, 1775, till death there.

1790.   Oct. 19th.   D. RICHARD BEDE BARTON.

b. Wheaton, Lancas., 1738.   Prof. St. Ed., 1757, and d. at Paris.

1790.   Dec. 28th.   BR. PITT ROBERT COPSEY.

b. Middlesex, 1717.   Prof. Lambs., 1733.   d. at Tournai.

1791.   July 31st.   D. ALEX. BENEDICT CATTERAL.

b. Samsbury, Lancas., 1724.   Prof. St. Ed., 1743.   Sent on the mission to the N. Prov.   Was at Brandsby, Yorks., 1761-4.   Whitehaven, 1764-74.   Capheaton, 1774-83.   Confessor to nuns at Paris, 1753, till death there.

1792.   Mar. 24th.   D. GEORGE EDMUND DUCKETT.

b. Claughton, Lancas.   Prof. St. Ed., 1760.   Sent on the mission to the N. Prov., 1773.   Was at Strangways, Lancas.   Hindley, 1789, and d. there.

1792. April 28th. D. HUGH JEROME HEATLEY.
b. Preston, 1757. Prof. Lambs., 1777. Sent on the mission to the S. Prov. to Bath, 1787, and d. there.

1792. June 16th. D. JNO. GREGORY WATKINSON.
b. London, 1727. Prof. St. Greg., 1746. Sent on the mission to the N. Prov. Was at Middleton Lodge, Yorks., 1759, till death there.

1792. Nov. 15th. D. JOHN JEROME BERRY, OR BUTLER.
b. Lancas., 1714. Prof. St. Lau., 1731. Went to St. Greg., 1740. Sent on the mission to the N. Prov., and was at Swinburne, 1747-59. Beaufront, 1759-67. Cheeseburne Grange, 1767. Passed to the S. Prov. Was at Hartbury Court, Gloucester, till 1773. Waterperry, Oxfords., 1773. Marlborough, till 1790. Bonham, 1790. d. in Lancashire.

1792. Dec. 6th. D. WILLIAM BERNARD NECHILLS.
b. London, 1711. Prof. St. Ed., 1729, and d. in Paris.

1793. Jan. 27th. D. JOHN FISHER.
b. Lancas., 1710. Prof. St. Lau., 1726. Sent on the mission to the N. Prov. Was at Standish, 1742-3. Holme Hall, 1743-88. Retired in old age to St. Lau., 1788, and d. at Dieulward. Was Sec. to Chapter, 1753-7. Proc. Prov., 1753-72. Def. Prov., 1753-61. Def. Reg., 1761-72. Pres.-Gen., 1772-77. Def. Reg., 1777. Cath. Pr. of Canterbury, 1773.

1793. Oct. 15th. D. OSWALD EAVES.
b. Lancas., 1739. Prof. St. Lau., 1755. Was Sub-prior. Sent on the mission to the N. Prov. Was at Cuerdon, Lancas., 1764-80. Brownedge, 1780, till death there.

Was Proc. Prov., 1773, till death. Cath. Pr. of Rochester, 1789.

1793. Oct. 19th. D. FRANCIS BESWICK.
b. St. Helens, 1765. Prof. at S. Greg. for St. Ed., 1786. d. in Paris in prison on account of the Revolution.

1794. Jan. 9th. D. BENEDICT CAWSER.
b. Ormskirk. Prof. St. Ed., 1764. d. in Paris in prison,

1794. Jan. 13th. D. GEO. AUGUSTINE WALKER.
b. Hindley, 1720. Prof. St. Ed., 1743. Sent on the mission to the N. Prov., 1750, and was at Tanfield. Durham, till 1753. Pr. of St. Ed., 1753-7. Procurator at Rome, 1757-77. Pres. Gen., 1777, till death. Cath. Pr. of Worcester, 1765. Vicar of nuns at Cambray, 1790. d. at Compèigne in prison on account of the Revolution.

1794. June 1st. D. EDMUND PENNINGTON.
b. Lancas., 1757. Prof. St. Lau., 1778. Confessor to nuns at Paris, 1782-7. Sent on the mission to the S. Prov. and was at Swinnerton, Staffords., 1787. Passed to the N. Prov. to St. Mary's Liverpool, 1787, and d. there.

1794. Oct. 23rd. D. DANIEL SPENCER.
b. Crosby, Lancas., 1766. Prof. at St. Greg. for St. Ed., 1788. Was Sub-prior. Sent to the mission in the N. Prov, 1793, to St. Mary's, Liverpool, and d. there.

1794. Dec. 3rd. D. RICHARD MAURUS BARRET.
b. Lancas., 1735. Prof. St. Lau.. 1753. Sent on the mission in the S. Prov., 1764. Was at Leighland, Somerset till 1767. Returned to St. Lau. and d. in prison at Pont-a-Mousson on account of Revolution.

1795.　Jan. 16th.　D.　John Placid Naylor.
b. Lancas.　Prof. St. Lau., 1741.　Sent on the mission to the S. Prov.　Was at Bath, 1757-76.　Cheame, Surrey, 1776-85.　London, 1785-7.　Confessor to nuns at Paris, 1787.　Imprisoned at Revolution, and d. on release in Paris.

1795.　Mar. 1st.　D.　John Placid Bennet.
b. 1741.　Prof. St. Lau., 1757.　Was Sub-prior.　Sent on the mission to the N. Prov., 1771.　Was at Evering-ham till 1780.　Confessor to nuns at Paris, 1780-1.　Passed to the S. Prov.　Was at Lanherne, 1781-3.　Lindley.　Beckford, Gloucester.　Then to the N. Prov.　Was at Hindley, 1792-3, and d. at Liverpool.

1795.　Mar. 23rd.　D.　John Anselm Geary.
b. Middlesex, 1714.　Prof. Lambs., 1732.　Ord., 1738.　Was at Novice Master, 1743.　Sent on the mission to the S. Prov., 1744.　Was at Coughton.　Leighland, Somerset till 1748.　Bath, 1749-52.　Leighland, 1752-3.　London, 1753-73.　Waterperry, Oxfords., 1773-4, then to Wiltshire.　Retired in old age to Bath, and d. there.　Was Proc. Prov., 1753-61.　Def. Reg., 1781-5.　Cath. Pr. of Chester, 1785.　Def. Prov., 1789.

1795.　Aug. 6th.　D.　Thomas Ballyman.
b. Devon., 1737.　Was a convert.　Prof. Lambs., 1756.　Sent on the mission to the S. Prov., 1768.　Was at Salford, Warwicks., till 1774.　Acton Burnell, 1774, till death at Bath.

1795.　Oct. 27th.　Br. Richard Benedict Marsh.
b. 1767.　Prof. St. Lau., 1793.　Escaped at the Revolu-tion.　Went to Acton Burnell, then Birkenhead, and there d.　Was Ord. Sub-deacon.

1796. Jan. 29th. D. Thomas Benedict Garner.
b. Lancas., 1736. Prof. Lambs., 1758, and d. there.

1797. April 8th. D. Goderic Joach. Swinburne.
b. Co. of Durham, 1754. Prof. Lambs., 1776. Was
Novice Master, 1792. Prior for three years, and
d. there.

1797. Sep. 30th. D. Thomas Anselm Bolas.
b. Preston Goballs, Shrops., 1732. Prof. Lambs., 1751.
Sent on the mission to the N. Prov., 1760. Was at
Whitehaven. Hesleyside, 1761-77. Warwick Bridge,
1777, till death there. Was Prov. of York, 1777-85.
Cath. Pr. of Bath, 1777. Def. Reg., 1785.

1797. Oct. 8th. Br. William Maurus Eastham.
b. Bamberbridge, Lancas., 1774. Prof. St. Lau., 1794.
Went to Acton Burnell. d. at Bamberbridge.

1797. Nov. 25th. D. Charles Walmsley.
b. Westwood Hall, Wigan, 1722. Prof. St. Ed., 1739.
Took degree of D.D. at Sorbonne. Elected F.R.S.
Pr. of St. Ed., 1749-53. Procurator at Rome, 1754.
Consecrated Bp. of Rama and Coadjutor of Western
District, 1756. Succeeded, 1764. d. at Bath and
buried at Bristol.

1798. Feb. 13th. D. Robert Goolde.
b. London, 1734. Prof. St. Ed., 1755. Sent on the
mission to the N. Prov., 1774. Passed to the S.
Prov., 1776, was at Marlboro'. Kelvedon Hall.
London, 1778-82. Chaplain to the Duke of Norfolk.
Again in London till death there.

1798. Feb. 16th. D. Thomas Jerome Marsh.
b. Lancas., 1743. Prof. St. Lau., 1761. Was Sub-prior.

Sent on the mission to the N. Prov. Was at Aberford, 1780. Everingham, 1781. Pr. of St. Lau., 1781-5. Again in the N. Prov. at Tone Hall. Northumb., 1785-7. Beaufront, 1787-8. Stockeld, 1788. Lawkland, 1789. Swinburne Castle, 1790-5, Holme Hall, 1795, till death there.

1798.   Mar. 5th.   D. THOMAS BARKER.
b. Cambridgsh., 1768.   Prof. St. Greg., 1760.   In prison at Revolution, escaped to Acton Burnell.   Ord., and and d. there.

1799.   Jan. 20th.   D. BERNARD ANSELM BRADSHAW.
b. Esk, Durham, 1742.   Prof. Lambs., 1760.   Sent on the mission to the N. Prov., 1769.   Was at Standish till 1770.   Angram, 1770-3.   Warrington, 1773, till death there.   Was Def. Prov., 1781-99.

1799.   June 19th.   D. WILLIAM GREGORY COWLEY.
b. Lancas., 1732.   Prof. St. Lau., 1749.   Pr. of St. Lau., 1765-73.   Cath. Pr. of Coventry, 1773.   Pr. of St. Ed., 1773-89.   Sent on the mission to the S. Prov. Was at Marlboro', 1790.   Pres. Gen., 1794-9.   Cath. Pr. of Canterbury, 1794.   Was at Vernon Hall with St. Lau., 1794.   And d. there and was buried at Liverpool.

1799.   July 22nd.   D. JAMES ADRIAN HORSMAN.
b. Knaresboro', 1765.   Prof. Lambs., 1787, and d. there.

1799.   Dec. 19th.   D JOHN JOSEPH STOREY.
b. Northumberland.   Prof. Lambs., 1751.   Sent on the mission to the N. Prov.   Was at Follyfoot, 1765-87. Aberford, 1787-92.   Holme Hall, 1792-5.   Retired to Lambspring, and d. there.

1800.　Jan. 10th.　D, GEORGE JOSEPH CROOK.
b. Chorley, 1754.　Prof. Lambs., 1771.　Was Novice
Master, 1778.　Sent on the mission to the N. Prov.
1780 to Whitehaven.　Was at Ormskirk, 1781, till
death there.　Was Proc. Prov., 1794, till death, and
Sec. Chapter, 1794.

1800.　Sep. 10th.　D. RICHARD VINCENT GREGSON.
b. Lancas., 1721.　Prof. St. Lau., 1741.　Was Sub-prior.
Sent on the mission to the N. Prov.　Was at Sefton,
1754, till death.　He founded the mission at Netherton.
Was Def. Prov., 1775.　Cath Pr. of Chester, 1798.

1800.　Oct. 14th.　D. THOMAS BEDE BENNET.
b. Bath, 1723.　Prof. St. Greg., 1741.　Was Cellerarius,
1754-6.　Sent to the mission to the S. Prov.　Was at
Leighland, Somerset, till 1759.　London 1759, till
death there.　Was Proc. Prov., 1761, till death.　Def.
Prov., 1769.　Cath. Pr. of Peterboro', 1781.　Def.
Reg., 1791-8.

1800.　Oct. 18th.　D. WILLIAM GREGORY GREGSON.
b. Samsbury, Lancas., 1728.　Prof. St. Ed., 1751.　Was
Sub-prior.　Sent on the mission to the S. Prov.　Was
at Kelvedon Hall, 1764.　Weston, Bucks., 1769, till
death there.　Was Def. Prov., 1789.

1801.　May 2nd.　D. RICHARD BENEDICT SIMPSON.
b. Preston.　Prof. St. Lau., 1753.　Was at St. Greg.,
1771.　St. Ed., 1777-90.　Sent on the mission to the
N. Prov.　Was at Stockeld, 1790-3.　Beaufront,
1793-6.　Retired to St. Lau., and d. at Vernon Hall.

1801.　July 10th.　D. JOHN VINCENT WEARDEN.
b. Walton, Lancas., 1769.　Prof. Lambs., 1787.　Sent on
the mission to the N. Prov. to Warrington, and d. there.

1801. Aug. 31. D. THOMAS SLATER.
b. Shivington, Standish, 1756. Prof. St. Lau., 1777. Sent on the mission to the N. Prov., 1786. Was at Swinburne, 1786. Beaufront, 1787. Houghton, Yorks., 1788, till death there.

1801. Sep. 6th. D. DANIEL BERNARD YOUNG.
b. Ormskirk, 1741. Prof. Lambs., 1760. Sent on the mission to the S. Prov., 1772. Was at Waterperry, Oxfords. Hartbury Court, Gloucesters., 1773--8. Welshpool till death there.

1802. Aug. 1st. D. JOHN THOMAS TURNER.
b. Walton, Lancas., 1743. Prof. St. Lau., 1759. Sent on the mission to the N. Prov. Was at Woolstan, 1771-9. Morpeth, 1779, till death there. Was Proc. Prov.

1802. Aug. 15th. D. WM. MAURUS HEATLEY.
b. Dunkenhall, Lancas., 1722. Prof. Lambs., 1740. Ord., 1746. Was at St. Greg., 1750. Sent on the mission to the S. Prov., 1753, and was at Cheame, Surrey. Def. Prov., 1757. Abbot of Lambspring, 1762-1802, and d. there.

1802. Dec. 12th. D. JOHN BASIL BRINDLE.
b. Clayton, Lancas., 1746. Prof. St. Lau., 1765. Was Sub-prior. Confessor to nuns at Paris, 1779-82. Sent on the mission in the S. Prov. Was at Kelvedon Hall, Essex. Lanherne, 1783-90. Bonham, 1790-1801. d. at Clayton.

1803. May 31st. D. JOHN LAURENCE BARNES.
b. Dorset, 1748. Prof. St. Greg., 1768. Went to St. Ed., 1785. Returned to St. Greg., 1786. Sent on the mission to the N. Prov. Was at St. Peter's, Liverpool, 1790-7. d. at Shaftesbury.

1803.   Oct. 16th.   D. ROGER BONIFACE HALL.

b. Lancas., 1737.   Prof. Lambs., 1756.   Sent on the
mission to the S. Prov., 1768.   Was at Cossey Hall,
1769-71.   Lanherne, 1771-81.   Plymouth.   Returned
to Lambspring and d. there.

1803.   Dec. 15th.   D. WILLIAM JOSEPH COLLINS.

b. London, 1758.   Prof. Lambs., 1783.   Sent on the
mission to the N. Prov., 1791.   Was at St. Mary's,
Liverpool, 1794-6.   Retired to Lambs. and d. there

1803.   Dec. 18th.   D. GEORGE JOHNSON.

b. Warwicks., 1748.   Prof. St. Greg., 1768.   Was Sub-
prior, 1784-8.   Cellerarius, 1788-92.   Sent on the
mission to the S. Prov. and was at Lindley, Shrops.,
1792, till death there.

1805.   Jan. 11th.   D. JOHN BONIFACE TAYLOR.

b. Altcar, Lancas., 1775.   Prof. Lambs., 1792, and d.
there.

1805.   May 9th.   D. JOHN LEWIS HEATLEY.

b. Samsbury, Lancas., 1752.   Prof. Lambs., 1776, and
d. there.

1805.   May 30th.   D. JOSEPH LAURENCE HADLEY.

b. London, 1739.   Prof. St. Greg., 1757.   Sent on the
mission to the N. Prov., 1764.   Was at Biddleston,
1764-7.   Brindle, 1767-1802.   Retired in ill health
to Netherton, Samesfield, Hereford, and Liverpool,
and d. there.

1805.   Dec. 22nd.   D. JOHN ANSELM BOLTON.

b. Brindle, 1735.   Prof. St. Lau., 1753.   Sent on the
mission to the S. Prov., 1763, and was at Leighland,

Somerset. Passed to the N. Prov. Was at Biddle-ston, 1764. Gilling Castle, 1764-93. Removed to Ampleforth, 1793. Handed it over to St. Lau., 1802, and retired to Birtley and d. there. Cath. Pr. of Peterboro', 1802.

1806. Nov. 20th. D. MICHAEL BENED. PEMBRIDGE.
b. London, 1725. Prof. St. Greg., 1741. Sent on the mission to the N. Prov., 1755. Was at Greystock, Cumberland, 1755-71. Passed to the S. Prov. Was at Holme Lacy, Herefords., 1771-81 Bath, 1781-6. Dorking, Surrey, 1786-91. Bath, 1791-2. Dorking, 1792. Tixall, Staffords., 1792-8. Bath, 1798, till death there. Was Cath. Pr. of Gloucester, 1785. Winchester, 1794. Def. Reg., 1794-1806.

1807. Feb. 8th. D. ROWLAND MICHAEL LACON.
b. Lindley, Shrops., 1744. Prof. St. Greg., 1761. Sent on the mission to the N. Prov., 1771. Was at Brandsby, 1771-92. Aberford, 1792-1806. Retired to Lindley, and d. there. Was Prov. of York, 1785-1806.

1807. Mar. 8th. D. JOHN AUSTIN ATKINSON.
b. Brampton, Yorks., 1785. Prof. St. Greg., 1802. d. at Acton Burnell.

1807. Mar. 24th. D. JOHN EDMUND HADLEY.
b. London, 1744. Prof. St. Greg., 1761. Sent on the mission to the S. Prov., 1763, to London. Was at Waterperry, Oxfords., 1773-4. Coughton, 1774-7. Trismore, Oxfords., 1777, London, 1778-85. Passed to the N. Prov. Was at Stourton House, Yorks., 1785-1803. Pocklington, 1803, till death there.

1807. Mar. 25th. D. THOMAS PLACID HARSNIP.
b. Ormskirk, 1753. Prof. Lambs., 1770. Was at
Fulda, 1772-4. Ord., 1777. Sec. to Pres., 1785. Cath.
Pr. of Bath, 1798. Superior, 1802. d. at Lambspring.

1807. April 27th. D. JOHN BERNARD WARMOLL.
b. Norfolk, 1719. Prof. St. Greg., 1737. Was Cellera-
rius, 1751-4. Sent on the mission to the S. Prov.
Was at Leighland, Somerset. Bidwell, Exeter, 1755.
Brise Norton, Oxfords., 1755-69. Woolters Hill,
Worcestershire, 1769-99. Pershore, 1799-1805. Re-
tired to St. Greg., and d. at Acton Burnell. Was Def.
Prov., 1774. Prov. of Canterbury, 1777-1805. Cath.
Pr. of Norwich, 1781.

1807. Aug. 25th. D. Jos. PAUL GRIMBALDESTONE.
b. Alston, Lancas., 1756. Prof. Lambs., 1776, and d.
there.

1807. Oct. 1st. D. JOHN JOSEPH BURDEN.
b. Canterbury, 1777. Prof. St. Greg., 1797. Ord.,
1802. d. in London, and was buried at St. Pancras.

1808. April 1st. D. JAMES JEROME SHARROCK.
b. Walton-le-Dale, 1750. Prof. St. Greg., 1768. Pr.
of St. Greg., 1785-1808. Was in prison for thirteen
months at the Revolution. Came with St. Gregory's
to Acton Burnell, and d. there. Cath. Pr. of Gloucester, 1794. Durham, 1806.

1808. April 22nd. D. JAMES MAURUS CHAPLIN.
b. Norfolk, 1745. Prof. Lambs., 1763. Sent on the
mission to the N. Prov., 1776. Was at Whitehaven,
1776-9. Woolstan, 1779-83. Standish, 1783-6.

Lawkland, 1786-8. Returned to Lambspring, 1788-1801. Again in the N. Prov at Woolton, Lancas., 1801, and d. there.

1808. Dec. 7th. D. JAMES PLACID DUVIVIERS, OR WATERS.

b. Middlesex, 1740. Prof. St. Greg., 1757. Was sent on the mission to the S. Prov., 1772. Horton, Gloucester, 1772-7. Was Procurator in Rome, 1777, till death in Rome. Cath. Pr. of Peterboro', 1806.

1809. June 8th. D. ROBERT AUGUSTINE KELLET.

b. Plumpton, Lancas., 1732. Prof. St. Ed., 1751. Was Cellerarius many years. Sec. to Pres., 1769. Cath. Pr. of Ely, 1777. Was in prison at the Revolution, and lived in Paris after release, and d. there.

1809. Oct. 17th. D. WM. GREGORY SHARROCK.

b. Walton-le-Dale, 1742. Prof. St. Greg., 1758. Ord., 1766. Took degree of D.D. Was Cellerarius, 1766-75. Pr. of St. Greg., 1775-81. Consecrated Bishop of Tolmessus and Coadjutor to Western District, 1781. Succeeded, 1797. d. at Bath, and buried at Bristol.

1810. Mar. 13th. D. JOHN BERNARD SLATER.

b. Shivington, Standish, 1744. Prof. St. Lau., 1761. Sent on the mission to the N. Prov. Was at Birtley, 1782, till death there.

1810. June 7th. D. JOHN DAWBER.

b. Standish, 1769. Prof. St. Lau., 1791. Was in prison at the Revolution. Sent on the mission to the S. Prov., and was at Coventry, 1803, till death there.

1810. June 9th. D. RICHARD HARRIS.

b. Winchester. Prof. St. Ed., 1755. Was Sub-prior.

Sent on the mission to the S. Prov., 1765. Was at Clytha, 1769-72. Cheame, 1772-6. Returned to St. Ed. Was in prison at the Revolution. Released, and d. in Paris.

1811. Jan. 5th. D. THOMAS ADRIAN GURNAL.
b. London, 1742. Prof. Lambs., 1763. Ord., 1767. Sent on the mission to the N. Prov., 1774. Was at Capheaton, 1774. Beaufront, 1774-80. Hesley-side, 1780-1. Everingham, 1781, till death there. Was Def. Prov., 1800. Cath. Pr. of Worcester, 1802.

1811, July 23rd. D. JNO. GREGORY BALLYMAN.
b. Devon., 1734. Was a convert. Prof. Lambs., 1754. Was Prior, 1768-92. Cath. Pr. of Worcester, 1798. d. at Lambspring.

1812. Mar. 12th. D. JAMES CYRIL MATHER.
b. Goosnargh, 1769. Prof. Lambs., 1790. d. at Hildes-heim.

1812. April 27th. D. CHAS. BONIFACE TAYLOR.
b. Goosnargh, 1752. Prof. Lambs., 1772. Sent on the mission to the N. Prov. Was at Whitehaven, 1780. Aberford, 1780-6. Beaufront, 1786. Crosby, Lancas., 1786, till death there.

1812. Sep. 5th. D. WILLIAM AMBROSE ALLAM.
b. London. Prof. St. Greg., 1768. Was at St. Ed., 1779, and returned to St. Greg. Sent on the mission to the S. Prov., and was at Bonham, 1785-96. London. Lawkland. Stratford-on-Avon for eight or ten years. Coventry, 1810, and d. there.

1814. Jan. 12th. D. WM. DUNSTAN GARSTANG.
b. Brindle, 1736. Prof. St. Ed., 1753. Sent on the

mission to the S. Prov., 1762.   Was at London, 1767,
till death there.   Was Def. Prov., 1798-1805.   Prov.
of Canterbury, 1805-6.

1814.   Jan. 29th.   D. RALPH MAURUS SHAW.

b. Rothbury, Northumb.   Prof. St. Ed., 1757.   Was
Sub-prior.   In prison at the Revolution.   Released
and remained in Paris.   Was Confessor to nuns at
Woolton, and then Salford, where he died.   Was
Cath. Pr. of Ely, 1806.   Def. Reg., 1810.

1814.   Feb. 5th.   D. RALPH AINSWORTH.

b. Liverpool, 1763.   Prof. at St. Lau. for St. Greg., 1784.
Went to St. Greg., 1787.   Ord., 1788.   Sent on the
mission to the N. Prov., 1791.   Was at Follyfoot,
1791-5.   Lawkland, 1798-1800.   Netherton, 1800-4.
Passed to the S. Prov.   Was at Foxcote, 1804-11.
Again to the N. Prov. and was at Everingham,
1811-3, and d. at Woolton.

1814.   Mar. 26th.   D. RICHARD PETER KENDAL.

b. Bath, 1758.   Prof. St. Greg., 1779.   Ord., 1782.
Was Cellerarius.   Escaped at the Revolution, to
Acton Burnell, 1793.   Pr. of St. Greg., 1808-14.
d. at Wootton, Warwicks.   Was Cath. Pr. of Coventry,
1810.

**1814.   July   29th.   D. ARCHIBALD BENEDICT
MACDONALD.**

b. Lochaber, Scotland, 1739.   Prof. St. Greg., 1757.
Sent on the mission to the N. Prov.   Was at
Houghton Hall, 1766-70.   Standish, 1770-83.   The
first Benedictine at St. Mary's, Liverpool, 1783.
Founded St. Peter's, Liverpool, 1788, and d. there.
Was Def. Reg., 1806, till death.   Cath. Pr. of
Rochester, 1810.

1815. Jan. 8th. D. WM. AUGUSTINE CALDWELL,
OR WALMESLEY.

b. Lancas., 1735. Prof. St. Greg., 1757. Sent on the mission to the S. Prov. Was at Brambridge, Hants., 1764, till death there. Def. Prov., 1806. Cath. Pr. of Ely, 1814.

1815. July 16th. D. EDWARD ALBAN CLARKSON.

b. Goosnargh, 1766. Prof. Lambs., 1787. Sent on the mission to the N. Prov., 1798. Was at Holme Hall, 1798, till death there. Was Def. Prov., 1811-5.

1815. Dec. 15th. JOHN LAURENCE FORSHAW.

b. Ormskirk, 1769. Prof. Lambs., 1788. Was Novice Master, 1795. Sent on the mission to the N. Prov., 1801. Was at Hindley, 1801-5. Ellingham, 1805-10. Birtley, 1810, till death there.

1816. April 9th. D. STEPHEN HODGSON.

b. Pontops, Durham, 1763. Prof. St. Greg. for St. Lau., 1784. Went to St. Lau., 1787. Ord., 1788. Sent on the mission to the N. Prov., 1791. Was at Follyfoot, 1791-5. Lawkland, 1798-1800. Netherton, 1800-4. Passed to the S. Prov. Was at Foxcote, 1804-11. Again to the N. Prov. Was at Everingham, 1811-3. d. at Woolton.

1816. May 6th. D. SAMUEL AUSTIN MITCHELL.

b. 1767. Prof. St. Lau., 1788. Ord., 1791. Escaped to Acton Burnell at the Revolution. Sent on the mission to the S. Prov., 1793. Was at Plowden Hall, Staffords., 1793-1802. Returned to St. Lau. at Parbold. Then to the N. Prov. Was at Lawkland, 1803-12. Standish, 1813, till death there.

1816. June 12th. D. WM. DUNSTAN TARLETON.

b. Lancas., 1772. Prof. S. Lau., 1794. Sent to the mission to the N. Prov. Was at St. Mary's, Liverpool, 1802-9. St. Peter's, Liverpool, 1809, till death there.

1816. Aug. 17th. BR. WM. BASIL KNAPP.

b. Portsea, Hants., 1796. Prof. St. Greg., 1814. d. at Downside.

1817. June 1st. D. WM. JEROME ALCOCK.

b. Warrington, 1775. Prof. Lambs., 1792, and died there.

1817. July 8th. D. HENRY PARKER.

b. Kirkham, 1752. Prof. St. Ed., 1773. Was at St. Greg, 1779. St. Ed., 1686. Sub-prior. Pr. of St. Ed., 1789-1817. Was in prison at the Revolution. d. in Paris.

1818. Nov. 9th. D. JAMES OSWALD JOHNSON.

b. Wrightington, 1750. Prof. Lambs., 1772. Sent on the mission to the N. Prov. Was at Whitehaven, 1781, till death there.

1821. April 9th. D. JAMES CALDERBANK.

b. Liverpool, 1770. Prof. St. Lau., 1792. Escaped at the Revolution to Treves. Ord., there 1793. Accompanied St. Lau. to Acton Burnell, Birkenhead, Parbold, and Vernon Hall. Sent on the mission to the S. Prov. Was at Bath, 1800-5. Weston, Bucks., 1805-6. London, 1806-8. Passed to the N. Prov., and was at St. Peter's, Liverpool, 1808-9. Again to the S. Prov., and was at Bath, 1809-17. Crosby,

1817-9. Woolton, 1819, till death there. He was b. at St. Peter's, Liverpool. Was Cath. Pr. of Peterboro', 1810.

1821. Nov. 10th. D. JOHN AMBROSE NAYLOR.
b. Lancas., 1738. Prof. St. Greg., 1757. Sent on the mission to the N. Prov., 1767. Was at Biddleston, Northumb., 1767, till death there. Was Def. Prov., 1799, till death.

1822. April 5th. D. JOHN ATKINSON.
b. Ashton, Lancas., 1760. Prof., St. Ed., 1781. Ord., 1785. Sent on the mission to the N. Prov., 1790. Was at St. Mary's, Liverpool, 1790-3. Brownedge, 1793, till death there.

1822. April 18th. D. JOHN BEDE BREWER.
b. Preston, 1742. Prof. St. Lau., 1758. Was confessor to nuns at Paris., 1771-6. Took degree of D.D. at Sorbonne. Sent on the mission to the S. Prov., and was at Cheame, Surrey, 1776. Bath, 1776-81. Passed to the N. Prov., and was at Woolton 1781-1818. Retired to Ampleforth, 1818, and d. at Woolton, and was buried at St. Peter's, Liverpool. Was Cath. Pr. of Rochester, 1794. Def. Prov., 1785-9. Def. Reg., 1798. Pres.-Gen., 1799, till death. Cath. Pr. of Canterbury, 1802.

1823. April 6th. D. CLARE AUGUSTINE HATTON.
b. Norfolk, 1738. Prof. Lambs., 1758. Was Prior, 1766-8. Cellerarius, 1769-1808. Superior, 1810. Cath. Pr. of Coventry, 1814. d. at Lambspring.

1823. May 20th. D. THOS. BERNARD BARR.
b. Hants., 1739. Prof. St. Greg., 1757. Sent on the mission to the S. Prov. and was at Foxcote, 1767-84.

Coughton, 1784, till death there. Was Def. Prov., 1791-8, also 1805-10. Def. Reg., 1810-4. Cath. Pr. of Bath, 1810. Prov. of Canterbury, 1814-22.

1823. Aug. 28th. D. GEORGE CYPRIAN KEARTON. b. Ormskirk, 1778. Prof. Lambs., 1796, and d. there.

1824. Jan. 15th. D. RICH. EDWARD FISHER. b. Lancas., 1748. Prof. St. Lau., 1766. Was at St. Ed., 1771. Ord., 1772. Returned to St. Lau., 1772. Sent on the mission to the N. Prov. Was at Hesley-side, 1777-80. Beaufront, 1780-6. Standish, 1786-1812. Lawkland. 1812, till death there. Was Proc. Prov., 1802-10.

1824. Oct. 17th. D. WILLIAM CLEMENT GRIMBALDESTONE. b. Alston, Lancas., 1752. Prof. Lambs., 1774. Sent on the mission to the N. Prov. Was at Woolstan, 1783, till death there.

1825. April 7th. D. WM. JEROME DIGBY. b. Middlesex, 1744. Prof. St. Greg., 1761. Was at St. Ed., 1767. Returned to St. Greg., 1771. Sent on the mission to the N. Prov. Was at Etal, Northumb., 1783. St. Mary's, Liverpool, 1784. Passed to the S. Prov. Was at Bath, 1785. London till 1794. Again to the N. Prov. and was at St. Mary's, Liverpool, 1794-6. St. Peter's, Liverpool, 1796-1808. Warrington, 1808-16. Saltwell, Durham, 1816-22. Retired to St. Greg. and d. at Downside.

1825. July 2nd. D. RICHARD BERNARD BUTLER. b. Lancas., 1748. Prof. St. Greg., 1776. Was Cellerarius. Sent on the mission to the N. Prov. Was at St. Mary's, Liverpool, 1785-7, Follyfoot, 1787-91. Westby, Lancas., 1791-182-. Retired to St. Greg. and d. there.

1826. Oct. 14th. BR. WM. GREGORY PHILIPSON.
b. Swinburne, Northumb., 1808. Prof. St. Greg., 1825. d. at Little Malvern.

1826. Oct. 14th. D. JOS. DUNSTAN SCOTT.
b. Beaufront, 1740. Prof. Lambs., 1760. Sent on the mission to the S. Prov. Was at Flixton, 1772, till death there. Was Cath. Pr. of Chester, 1802. Def. Prov., 1810-8.

1827. May 22nd. D. THOMAS JEROME COUPE.
b. South Hill, Chorley, 1754. Prof. S. Lau., 1775. Was Sub-prior. Pr. of St. Lau., 1785-9. Sub-prior, 1789-91. Sent on the mission to the N. Prov. Was at Brandsby, 1791-4. Craike and Oulston, 1794-1826. Retired to St. Lau., and d. at Ampleforth.

1828. June 3rd. D. JOS. MARTIN LEVAUX.
b. 1746. A Maurist monk and priest. Prof. St. Greg., 1798. Was Sub-prior. Novice Master. Died at Campiegne.

1828. July 24th. D. RICHARD POPE.
b. 1760. Prof. at St. Greg. for St. Lau., 1781. Sent on the mission to the N. Prov. Was at St. Peter's, Liverpool, 1789-90. Lawkland, 1790-4. Lytham. Netherton, 1804, till death there.

1829. Jan. 27th. BR. JOHN ALBAN BANKS.
b. Preston, 1797. Prof. St. Greg., 1816. Ord. Sub.-deacon. d. at Downside.

1829. May 19th. D. Jos. CUTHBERT WILKS.
b. Coughton, 1743. Prof. St. Ed., 1764. Ord., 1772.
Sent on the mission to the S. Prov. Was at Swinnerton, Staffords., 1782-6. Bath, 1786-92. Italy, 1792,
Hetherop, Oxfords., 1794-6. Newport, Shrops., 1796-1800. Resided on the Continent, and d. at Douai.
Was Def. Prov., 1787-9. Def. Reg., 1789-92. Cath.
Pr. of Durham, 1794.

1829. July 21st. D. HENRY LAWSON.
b. York, 1763. Prof. St. Greg., 1785. Ord., 1788. Sent
on the mission to the S. Prov., 1793. Was at Bath,
1793-1800. Passed to the N. Prov., and was at
Brindle, 1800-2. Morpeth, 1802, till death there.
Prov. of York, 1822.

1829. Aug. 13th. BR. JOHN RAYMUND ELDRIDGE.
b. London. Prof. St. Greg., 1792. Was in prison at
the Revolution, and after release at Acton Burnell.
Ord. Sub-deacon. d. at Froidmont.

1829. Aug. 26th. D. MATT. DENIS ALLERTON.
b. Ormskirk, 1754. Prof. Lambs., 1771. Sent on the
mission to the N. Prov. Was at Knaresboro', 1802-8.
Allerton Park, 1808-24. Aberford, 1824-7. d. at
Liverpool.

1829. Dec. 10th. D. JOHN BERNARD CLARKSON.
b. Lancas. Prof. St. Lau., 1817. Ord., 1823. Sent on
the mission to the N. Prov. Was at Lawkland,
1824-5. Craike, 1825-6. Went to Cheltenham and
Bath. Retired to St. Lau., and d. at Ampleforth.

1830. April 23rd. D. Thos. AUSTIN LAWSON.
b. York, 1768. Prof. St. Greg., 1779. Ord., 1783.
Sent on the mission to the N. Prov. Was at Danby,

Yorks., 1793-4. Richmond, 1794-1814. Pr. of St.
Greg., 1814-8.   Again in the N. Prov. at Kilvington,
1818-22. Vicar of nuns at Salford, 1822, till death
there. Was Cath. Pr. of Gloucester, 1818.

1831. May 7th. D. JOHN DUNSTAN SHARROCK.
  b. Walton, Lancas., 1754. Prof. St. Lau., 1775. Sent
  on the mission to the N. Prov. Was at Danby,
  Yorks., 1787-93. Hesleyside, 1793-4. Long Horsley,
  1794, till death there.

1832. Feb. 2nd. D. MICHAEL ANSELM LORYMER.
  b. Monmouthsh., 1751. Prof. St. Greg., 1768. Was
  Cellerarius. Sub-prior, 1792. In prison at the
  Revolution, then at Acton Burnell. Sent on the
  mission to the S. Prov., and was in London, 1797-
  1830. Retired to St. Greg., and d. at Downside. Was
  Proc. Prov., 1802-26. Def. Reg., 1814-22. Cath. Pr.
  of Norwich, 1810. Durham, 1822.

1832. Feb. 25th. D. WM. ALEXIUS CHEW.
  b. Fulford, Lancas., 1771. Prof. St. Lau., 1792.
  Escaped at the Revolution to Acton Burnell. Ord.,
  1795. Sent on the mission to the N. Prov., 1802,
  Was at Lawkland, 1803-4. Passed to the S. Prov. to
  Lindley, 1804-6. Again to the N. Prov. to Aberford,
  1806-7. Hazlewood, 1807, till death there.

1832. May 31st. D. WM. MAURUS ROBINSON.
  b. Barstwick, Yorks., 1777. Prof. Lambs, 1792, and d.
  there.

1832. July 15th. D. EDWARD BEDE SLATER.
  b. Liverpool, 1774. Prof. St. Lau., 1794. Ord., 1798.
  Sent on the mission to the N. Prov. Was at Croston,
  Lancas., 1804-14. Germany, 1814-7. Rome, 1817.

Consecrated Bishop of Ruspa and V.A. of the
Mauritius, 1818. d. at sea.

1834. Mar. 17th. Br. Jos. Maurus Grafton.
b. Alcester, Warwicks., 1813. Prof. St. Ed., 1833. d. at
Douai.

1834. May 14th. D. Edward Benedict Glover.
b. Prescot, 1787. Prof. St. Lau., 1804. Ord., 1811.
Sent on the mission to the N. Prov. Was at St.
Mary's, Liverpool, 1814-19. Crosby, 1819, till death
there. Was Def. Reg., 1822. Cath. Pr of Gloucester,
1826.

1835. Oct. 14th. D. Thos. Francis Fairclough.
b. Lancas., Prof. St. Lau., 1817. Ord., 1822. Sent on
the mission to the N. Prov. Was at St. Mary's,
Liverpool, 1822, till death there.

1835. Dec. 13th. D. James Higginson.
b. Wrightington, 1764. Prof. St. Greg., 1785. Was
with the nuns at Cambray, 1792. In prison at the
Revolution. Sent on the mission to the N. Prov.
Was at Swinburne, 1795-1828. Birtley, 1828, till
death there. Was Def. Prov., 1830. Cath. Pr. of
Norwich, 1830.

1836. Aug. 8th. D. Henry Gregory Flinn.
b. Liverpool. Prof. St. Lau., 1824. Ord., 1830. Sent
on the mission to the N. Prov. Was at Morpeth,
1831, till death there.

1836. Dec. 9th. D. Thos. Clement Rishton.
b. Calcutta. Prof. St. Lau., 1803. Ord., 1805. Was
Sub-prior, 1805. Sent on the mission to the N.
Prov. Was at Workington, 1810-14. Passed to the
S. Prov., and was at Bath, 1814-5. Pr. of St. Lau.,

1815-7. Again to the S. Prov. At Bungay, 1818.
Then to the N. Prov. At Workington, 1819-20. At
St. Ed., 1822-7. Then at the Cape of Good Hope,
1827-35. Returned to St. Lau., and d. at Ampleforth.

1837. Jan. 15th. JOHN BEDE RIGBY.
b. Warrington, 1774. Prof. Lambs., 1798. Sent on the
mission to the N. Prov., and was at Houghton Hall,
1803-5. Passed to the S. Prov. At Bath, 1805-6.
Weston, Bucks., 1806-9. Again to the N. Prov. At
Liverpool, 1810-4. Workington, 1814-6. Was at
St. Lau., 1816-9. Again to the N. Prov. At Birtley,
1819-27. Then to St. Greg., 1827-35. Broadway,
1835-6. Then to Lamspring, and d. there.

1837. Feb. 19th. D. JAMES ALEXIUS POPE.
b. Lancas., 1755. Prof. St. Lau., 1776. Sent on the
mission to the N. Prov., and was at Beaufront,
1788-93. Hesleyside, 1793-7. St. Mary's, Liverpool, 1797-1802. Lawkland, 1802. Brindle, 1802-30.
Retired to Southport, and d. there.

1837. Mar. 12th. D. ROB. BASIL BRETHERTON.
b. Lancas. Educ. at Ushaw. Prof. St. Lau., 1820.
Was at St. Ed., 1822. Ord., 1824. Sent on the
mission to the S. Prov. Was at Coventry, 1824-7.
Returned to St. Lau., 1827-8. Then to the N. Prov.
At Knaresboro', 1828-30. Again at St. Lau., 1830-2.
In France, 1832, till death at Amiens.

1837. May 2nd. D. THOS. GREGORY ROBINSON.
b. 1779. Was surgeon in the Navy. Prof. St. Lau.,
1804. Ord., 1807. Pr. of S. Lau., 1810-5. Sent on
the mission to the N. Prov., and was at St. Peter's,

Liverpool, 1815, till death there. Was Sec. to Pres., 1818. Prov. of York, 1822, till death. Cath. Pr. of Peterboro', 1820.

1837. Aug. 2nd. D. JOHN AUSTIN BIRDSALL.
b. Liverpool, 1775. Prof. Lambs., 1796. Ord., 1801. Sent on the mission to the S. Prov. Was at Bath, 1806-9. Cheltenham, 1809-34. Broadway, 1834, till death there. Was Def. Prov., 1814. Prov. of Canterbury, 1822-6. Pres. Gen., 1826, till death. Cath. Pr. of Winchester, 1826. Abb. of Westminster, 1830.

1837. Aug. 22nd. D. JAMES BEDE BURGESS.
b. Clayton, Lancas., 1768. Prof. St. Lau., 1789. Ord., 1792. Escaped at the Revolution to Acton Burnell. Sent on the mission to the N. Prov., and was at Middleton Lodge, 1797, till death there. Was Cath. Pr. of Peterboro', 1822.

1840. May 26th. D. JAS. IGNATIUS GREENOUGH.
b. Lancashire. Prof. St. Ed., 1827. Ord., 1829. Sent on the mission to the N. Prov. Was at Standish, 1831-40, and d. there.

1840. Aug. 6th. D. VINCENT JOSEPH GLOVER.
b. Prescot, 1791. Prof. St. Lau., 1807. Ord., 1814. Sent on the mission to the N. Prov. Was at Knaresboro', 1815. St. Peter's, Liverpool, 1815-1838. Brownedge, 1838, till death there. Was Def. Prov., 1834.

1841. July 3rd. D. ROBERT ALEXIUS POPE.
b. Wigan, 1795. Prof. St. Greg., 1814. Ord., 1820. Sent on the mission to the S. Prov. Was at Coughton, 1823-34. Redditch, 1834-40. Coventry, 1840. d. at Scarisbrick.

1841.   Sept. 26th.   D. ANDREW BERNARD RYDING.
b. Wigan, 1752. Prof. at St. Greg. for St. Ed., 1769. Ord.,
1776.   Sent on the mission to the N. Prov. Was at
Capheaton, 1783-7. Warwick Bridge, 1787-8. Holme
Hall, 1788-92. Hindley, 1792-7. Warwick Bridge,
1797-1834. Retired to St. Lau., 1834, and d. there.
Was Cath. Pr. of Rochester, 1818. Def. Prov., 1822-6.

1842.   Jan. 4th.   D. RALPH RADCLIFFE.
b. Brandsby, Yorks., 1772. Prof. St. Greg., 1797. Ord.,
1802. Was Missioner at Acton Burnell, 1808. Novice
Master, 1809-14. Remained on the mission at Acton
Burnell after St. Greg. left in 1814, till death there.
Was Def. Prov., 1834, till death.

1842.   June 1st.   D. THOMAS ANSELM APPLETON.
b. Lancas., 1766. Prof. St. Lau., 1788.   Ord., 1790.
Escaped at the Revolution. Sent on the mission to
the N. Prov. Was at Lawkland, 1794-5.   Follyfoot,
1795-7. Knaresboro', 1797-1802. Pr. of St. Lau.,
1802-6.   Again in the N. Prov. At Hindley, 1806-36.
Was at S. Lau., 1836-40. Went to Liverpool, 1840,
and d. at Wigan.

1843.   Feb. 23rd.   D. RICHARD MARSH.
b. Hindley, 1762. Prof. at St. Greg. for St. Lau., 1783.
Went to St. Lau., 1785. Ord., 1786. Was Pr. of St.
Lau., 1789-1802. Escaped at the Revolution, and
accompanied St. Lau. to Acton Burnell, Birkenhead,
Scoles, Vernon Hall, and Parbold.   Kept up a school
at Parbold, 1802-3.   Passed to the mission to the N.
Prov. Was at Hindley, 1805-7. Aberford, 1807.
Was Prov. of York., 1806-22. Pr. of St. Lau.,
1806-10. Pres.-Gen., 1822-6 and 1837-42.   Cath.

Pr. of Winchester, 1810. Canterbury, 1822. Was made D.D. in Rome. He was at Woolstan, 1826-9. Rome. Rixton, 1831, till death there. Was Abbot of Westminster, 1838.

1843. July 6th. D. Peter Austin Baines.
b. Kirkby, Lancashire, 1787. Prof. St. Lau., 1804. Sent on the mission to the S. Prov., and stationed at Bath., 1817. Consecrated Bishop of Siga, 1823. Became V.A. of the Western District, 1829, and d. at Prior Park, Bath.

1843. Oct. 22nd. D. Edward Austin Clifford.
b. Chudleigh, 1803. Prof. St. Lau.. 1823. Ord., 1827. Sent on the mission to the S. Prov. Was at Bungay, 1827-8. Passed to the N. Prov. Was at Netherton, 1828-30. Was at St. Lau., 1830. Then St. Greg., and to the Mauritius, 1832, and was at Port Louis, and then Mahebourg Station, where he died.

1844. Mar. 5th. D. Richard Adrian Towers.
b. Preston, 1781. Prof. Lambs., 1802. Ord., 1805. Was at St. Lau., 1817. Sent on the mission to the N. Prov., and was at Workington, 1820-1. Germany, 1821-2. Workington, 1822. Passed to the S. Prov., and was at Taunton, 1822-30. Pr. of St. Lau., 1830-4. Again to the S. Prov. At Taunton, 1834-41. Poole Dorset, 1841, till death there. Was Sec. to Chapter, 1822. Def. S. Prov., 1926-30.

1844. July 13th. D. John Turner.
b. Woolstan, Lancas., 1764. Prof. at St. Greg. for St. Ed., 1786. Went to St. Ed. Ord., 1790. In prison at the Revolution. Released and remained in Paris. Sent on the mission to the N. Prov. Was at Croston,

1814. Holme Hall, 1815-43. Retired to St. Lau., 1843, and d. at Ampleforth. Cath. Pr. of Worcester, 1822.

1844. Sep. 18th. D. JAMES BERNARD GORE.
b. Liverpool, 1817. Prof. St. Ed., 1838. Ord., 1842, and d. at Douai.

1845. Jan. 29th. D. JOSEPH OSWALD ORRELL.
b. Liverpool, 1799. Prof. St. Lau., 1819. Ord., 1823. Sent on the mission to the N. Prov. Was at Kilvington, 1824-7. Felton, 1827, till death there.

1845. Nov. 7th. D. JAMES BENEDICT DEDAY.
b. Norwich, 1771. Prof. St. Greg., 1794. Ord., 1800. Sent on the mission to the S. Prov. Was at Woolters Hill, 1805-6. Wootton, 1806, till death there. Was Def. Prov., 1818-26. Prov. of Canterbury, 1826-34. Def. Prov., 1834-45. Cath. Pr. of Rochester, 1842.

1846. Mar. 6th. D. JOHN AUGUSTINE HARRISON.
b. Brough, Yorks., 1770. Prof. St. Greg., 1792. Escaped at the Revolution. Was at Acton Burnell, 1793. Ord., 1800. Sent on the mission to the S. Prov. Was at Wootton, 1803-7. Returned to St. Greg., 1807. Was Sub-prior, 1814. Again to the S. Prov. at Kenilworth. Shrewsbury, 1822-4. Tywisog, Denbigh, 1824. Talacre. Shottery, Stratford-on-Avon, 1831. Beckford till 1835. Returned to St. Greg. and d. at Downside.

1846. Oct. 23rd. Br. ROBERT CLEMENT GIBSON.
b. 1823. Prof. St. Lau., 1844, and d. at Ampleforth.

1847. Feb. 18th. D. CHARLES AMBROSE FERAUD.
b. Wootton, Warwicks., 1786. Prof. St. Greg., 1802. Ord., 1810. Sent on the mission to the S. Prov.

Was at Coventry, 1812-24. Sawston Hall, Cambridgesh., 1824-6. Returned to St. Greg., 1826. Was at Tournai, Rome, and other places on the Continent till 1833, when he returned to St. Greg. and d. at Downside.

1847. April 12th. D. THOMAS WILFRID FISHER.
b. Cheadle, 1767. Prof. Lambs., 1787. Ord., 1790. Was Prior, 1797. Sent on the mission to the N. Prov. Was at St. Mary's, Liverpool, 1800, till death there. Was Sec. to Pres., 1810. Sec. to Chapter, 1814. Def. Prov., 1815-8. Def. Reg., 1818, till death. Cath. Pr. of Bath, 1818. Durham, 1834. Abbot of St. Alban's, 1838. Glastonbury, 1842. St. Alban's again, 1846.

1847. April 21st. D. JAMES OSWALD TALBOT.
b. Lancas., 1768. Prof. St. Lau., 1789. Ord., 1792, Escaped at the Revolution to Acton Burnell, 1793. Sent on the mission to the N. Prov. Was at St. Mary's, Liverpool, 1797-1800. Ormskirk, 1800-45. d. at Southport. Was Def. Prov., 1834-46. Cath. Pr. of Coventry, 1826.

1847. May 26th. D. JAMES FRANCIS APPLETON.
b. Preston, 1807. Prof. St. Ed., 1827. Ord. 1830. Pr. of St. Ed., 1833-41. Sent on the mission to the N. Prov. Was at St. Peter's, Liverpool, 1841-7. d. at Stanbrook. Was D.D., 1841. Cath. Pr. of Norwich, 1842.

1847. May 31st. D. JOHN AUGUSTINE GILBERT.
b. 1820. Prof. St. Ed., 1840. Ord., 1845. Sent on the mission to the N. Prov. Was at St. Mary's, Liverpool, 1846, till death there.

1847.   June 26th.   D. WILLIAM VINCENT DALE.
b. Lancas., 1800.   Prof. St. Ed., 1829.   Ord., 1833. Sent on the mission to the N. Prov.   Was at Warwick Bridge, 1834-1838.   St. Mary's, Liverpool, 1838, till death there.

1847.   Sep. 2nd.   D. SAMUEL STEPHEN BARBER.
b. Macclesfield, 1784.   Prof. St. Greg., 1802.   Ord., 1809.   Confessor to nuns at Salford, 1813-4.   Sent on the mission to the N. Prov. and was at Workington, 1814.   Vicar of nuns at Salford, 1814-7.   Went to St. Lau., 1817.   Again to the N. Prov. at Aberford. 1819-24.   Lawkland, 1823-32.   Passed to the S. Prov,, and was at Salford, 1838-43.   Bonham, 1843-5. Spetisbury, 1845-7.   d. at Salisbury.

1848.   May 8th.   D. WM. HENRY DUNSTAN WEBB.
b. Birmingham, 1764.   Prof. Lambs., 1784.   Ord., 1789. Sent on the mission to the N. Prov.   Was at Middleton Lodge, 1792-7.   Hindley, 1797-1801.   Warrington 1801-8.   d. at Hindley.

1848.   Sep. 18th.   D. JAMES AMBROSE DUCK.
b. Thornboro', Yorks., 1797.   Prof. St. Greg., 1816. Ord., 1824.   Sent on the mission to the N. Prov. Was at Standish, 1824-31.   Passed to the S. Prov. Was at Cheltenham, 1831-5.   Returned to S. Greg., 1835-6.   Again in the S. Prov. at Weobly, 1836-40. Bungay, 1840-6.   Chipping Sodbury, 1846.   Westbury, 1847-8.   Returned to St. Greg., 1848, and d. at Brislington, Bristol.

1850.   May 9th.   D. LEWIS FRANCIS COOPER.
b. Walton, Lancas., 1771.   Prof. St. Lau., 1792.   Escaped at the Revolution to Acton Burnell, 1793.

Ord., 1795. Went with St. Lau. to Birkenhead, Vernon Hall, Parbold. Sent on the mission to the N. Prov. Was at Liverpool, 1803-6. Wrightington, 1806, till death there. Was Proc. Prov., 1814-42. Cath. Pr. of Bath, 1834.

1850. July 28th. D. THOS. ANSELM KENYON.
b. Warrington, 1770. Prof. Lambs., 1787. Ord., 1794. Sent on the mission to the N. Prov., 1801. Returned to Lambspring, 1803. Returned to England, 1826. Was Confessor to nuns at Orrell Mount, 1827-34. Passed to the S. Prov. Was at Cheltenham. 1834. Beckford till 1840. Stanbrook, 1840, till death there.

1850. Nov. 22nd. D. HENRY LEO SPAIN.
b. London, 1790. Prof. St. Greg., 1808. Sent on the mission to the N. Prov. and stationed at St. Peter's, Liverpool, 1814-5. Returned to St. Greg., 1815. Again in the N. Prov. at Birtley, 1815-6. d. at Lommelet, Lisle.

1850. Dec. 29th. D. LUKE BERNARD BARBER.
b. Macclesfield, 1790. Prof. St. Greg., 1808. Ord., 1814. Pr. of St. Greg., 1818-30. Vicar of nuns at Salford, 1830, and at Stanbrook till death. Prov. of Canterbury, 1834-42. Pres. Gen., 1842, till death. Cath. Pr. of Chester, 1830. Winchester, 1842. Canterbury, 1846. Abbot of St. Alban's, 1842. Westminster, 1846.

1851. May 21st. D. JAMES AUSTIN WILKINSON.
b. near Preston, 1811. Prof. St. Ed., 1828. Ord., 1837. Sent on the mission to the N. Prov. Was at St. Mary's, Liverpool, 1837-50. Wrightington, 1850-1, and d. at Scarisbrick.

1851. Oct. 9th. D. JOHN BERNARD ROBINSON.

   b. 1766. Prof. St. Lau., 1788. Ord., 1791. Sent on the mission to the N. Prov. Was at Aberford, 1827-43. Rixton, 1843-51, and d. there. Cath. Pr. of Ely, 1818.

1852. Feb. 8th. D. JOHN EDMUND MARSH.

   b. Hindley, 1802. Prof. St. Ed., 1824. Ord., 1826, Sent on the mission to the N. Prov. Was at Middleton Lodge, 1837-49. Passed to the S. Prov. and was at Aston - le - Walls, 1849-52, and d. at Wappenbury.

1852. Sep. 7th. D. JOHN BASIL THOMAS.

   b. London, 1814. Prof. St. Lau., 1836. Ord., 1838. Sent on the mission to the N. Prov. Was at Cowpen, 1838-45. St. Peter's, Liverpool, 1845. Returned to Ampleforth, 1846-50. Again on the mission at Lawkland, 1850. Passed to the S. Prov. and was Chideock, 1853, and d. there.

1854. Feb. 15th. D. GEORGE TURNER.

   b. Broughton, Lancas., 1770. Prof. St. Greg., 1790. Ord., 1800. Sent on the mission to the N. Prov. Was at Hesleyside and Bellingham, 1800-30. Pr. of St. Greg., 1830-4. Again on the mission to the S. Prov., and was at Princethorpe, 1834-54, and there d.

1854. May 17th. D. CHARLES HENRY DAVIS.

   b. Usk, 1815. Prof. St. Greg., 1834. Ord., 1840. Was Prefect of Studies. Cellerarius. Consecrated Bishop of Maitland, Australia, 1848, and d. at Sydney.

1854. Sep. 12th. BR. FRANCIS DUNSTAN
ARKWRIGHT.

   b. Blackburn, 1830. Prof. St. Lau., 1852. Was ordained Sub-deacon. d. at Ampleforth.

1855. April 3rd. D. SAMUEL MAURUS PHILIPS.
b. Bristol, 1794. Prof. St. Greg., 1811. Ord., 1819.
Sent on the mission to the N. Prov., 1820. Was at
Standish, 1822. Woolton, 1824-55, and d. there.
Was Sec. Pres., 1842-54. Sec. Gen. Chap, 1846.

1855. May 14th. D. CAMILLE ROMUALD
DEMONCHY.
b. Clermont, 1810. Prof. St. Ed., 1846. Ord., 1849.
Sent on the mission to the N. Prov., 1851., and was at
St. Augustine's, Liverpool, 1851-4. Returned to St.
Ed., and d. at Douai.

1856. Aug. 20th. D. JOHN ANSELM BRADLEY.
b. near Preston, 1819. Prof. St. Ed., 1840. Ord., 1846.
Sent on the mission to the N. Prov., 1854. Was at
Seaton Delaval, 1854. St. Augustine's, Liverpool,
1854-5. Aberford, 1855-6, and there d.

1856. Oct. 15th. BR. WILLIAM PLACID STYLES.
b. Liverpool, 1833. Prof. St. Lau., 1855, and d. at
Ampleforth.

1856. Dec. 15th. D. RICHARD AUSTIN MARSH.
b. Hindley, 1794. Prof. St. Ed., 1824. Ord., 1826.
Sent on the mission to the N. Prov., 1833. Was at
Lawkland, 1833-8. Passed to the S. Prov., and was
at Wappenbury, 1838-56, and d. at Hindley.

1858. April 3rd. D. CHARLES FRANCIS COOK.
b. Coughton, 1815. Prof. St. Ed., 1840. Ord., 1845.
Sent on the mission to the N. Prov. Was at St.
Mary's, Liverpool, 1848-9. St. Augustine's, Liverpool, 1849-58, and d. there.

1858. Oct. 1st. BR. EDMUND WOLSTAN ROWLEY.
b. Netherton, 1836. Prof. St. Lau., 1856. d. at Liverpool.

1859. Jan. 8th. D. WM. GREGORY HOLDEN.
b. Eccles, Lancas., 1791. Prof. St. Greg., 1809. Ord., 1816. Sent on the mission to the N. Prov., 1818. Was at Whitehaven, 1818-54. Cleator, 1854-9, and d. there.

1859. Mar. 31st. D. PATRICK IGNATIUS CALLAGHAN.
b. Gormanstown, Co. Meath, 1830. Prof. St. Lau., 1849. Ord., 1854. Sent on the mission to the N. Prov. Was at St. Mary's, Liverpool, 1854, and d. there.

1860. April 25th. D. CHRIS. AUSTIN SHANN.
b. Knaresboro', 1801. Prov. S. Lau., 1819. Ord., 1824. Sent on the mission to the N. Prov., 1824. Was at Scarisbrick, 1824-6. Returned to Ampleforth, 1826-9. Again on the mission in the N. Prov., and was at Morpeth, 1829-31. Brandsby, 1833-4. Passed to the S. Prov., and was at Cheltenham, 1835-40. Bath, 1840-2. Returned to the N. Prov., and was at Aigburth, 1842-3. Little Crosby, 1843-50. Aigburth, 1850-3. St. Anne's, Liverpool, 1853-4. Brandsby, 1854. Ormskirk, 1854-8. Little Crosby, 1858-60, and d. there. Was Def. Prov., 1846-54. Cath. Pr. Norwich, 1854.

1860. Oct. 8th. D. JAMES JOSEPH SHERIDAN.
b. Navan, Ireland, 1801. Prof. St. Lau., 1836. Ord., 1838. Sent on the mission to the N. Prov., 1841, and was at Birtley, 1841-50. St. Mary's, Liverpool, 1850-60., and d. there.

1860. Oct. 13th. JOHN ALBAN MOLYNEUX.

b. Liverpool, 1782. Prof. St. Lau., 1804. Ord., 1806. Sent on the mission to the N. Prov., 1806. Was at Knaresboro', 1806-16. Warrington, 1816-60., and d. there. Was Prov. of York, 1846-50. Pres. Gen., 1850-4. Def. Reg., 1854-8. Cath. Pr. Gloucester, 1846. Durham, 1850. Canterbury, 1854. Abbot of St. Alban's, 1850.

1860. Dec. 5th. D. RICHARD AMBROSE PREST.

b. Yorks., 1800. Prof. St. Lau., 1819. Ord., 1824. Sent on the mission to the N. Prov., 1824. Was at Knaresboro', 1824-8. Swinburne, 1828. St. Peter's, Liverpool, 1828-32. Returned to Ampleforth, 1832-7. Again on the mission in the N. Prov., and was at Aigburth, 1837-41. Went to Rome, 1841-2. Was at Stockeld, Wetherby, 1844-6. Prior of Ampleforth, 1846-50. Again on the mission in the N. Prov., and was at Aberford, 1850. Rixton, 1851-2. Waterloo, Liverpool, 1852. Aigburth, 1853-9. Passed to the S. Prov., and was at Abergavenny, 1858-9. Hereford, 1859. Retired to Ampleforth, 1860, and d. at Aberford. Was Proc. in Rome, 1838-42. Cath. Pr. of Gloucester, 1850.

1861. Nov. 1st. D. BERNARD COLLYER.

b. Manchester, 1792. Prof. St. Greg., 1816. Went to the Mauritius, 1819. Ord., 1820. Came to England, 1851. Returned to the Mauritius, and d. there.

1862. Aug. 13th. D. CELESTINE MAURUS FRANCOMME.

b. Calonne-sur-Lys, 1823. Prof. St. Ed., 1854. Ord., 1857. Sent on the mission to the N. Prov., and was at St. Augustine's, Liverpool, 1858-62, and d. there.

1862. Dec. 5th. D. NICHOLAS MAURUS HODGSON.
b. Newcastle-on-Tyne, 1815. Prof. St. Greg., 1834.
Ord., 1840. Was Sub-prior. Sent on the mission
to the S. Prov., 1850. Was at Princethorpe, 1850
Bath, 1850-5, Studley, 1855-8. Passed to the N.
Prov. and was at Holme, 1858. Went to Belmont,
1859-60, again on the mission in the S. Prov. and
was at Blackmore Park, 1860-2, and d. at Redditch,
Was Sec. Gen. Chap., 1850-62. Proc. in Rome,
1850-8.

1863. April 2nd. D. JAMES BASIL DUCK.
b. Low House, Borwick, Northumb., 1813. Prof. St.
Greg., 1831. Ord., 1839. Sent on the mission to
the S. Prov., 1839. Was at Spetisbury, 1839.
Weobly, 1839-40. Passed to the N. Prov. and was
at Whitehaven, 1840-52. Returned to the S. Prov.
and was at Cheltenham, 1852-3. Studley, 1853-5.
Again to the N. Prov. and was at St. Augustine's,
Liverpool, 1855-6. St. Anne's, Liverpool, 1856-63,
and d. there.

1863. Nov. 12th. D. JAMES BENEDICT (OR AUSTIN)
DULLARD.
b. Kilkenny, 1795. Ord. sec. priest, 1823. Prof. St.
Ed., for SS. Adrian and Denis, 1832. Went to
Ampleforth, 1833-7. Broadway, 1837. Sent on
the mission to the S. Prov. Was at Bungay, 1837-40.
Weobly, 1840-1. Rugely, 1841-63, and d. there.

1864. May 2nd. D. THOS. BENEDICT BONNEY.
b. Standish, 1814. Prof. Broadway, 1835. Ord., 1839.
After the community broke up, he remained on the
mission at Broadway, 1841-4. Passed to N. Prov.

and was at St. Peter's, Liverpool, 1844-64, and d. at Little Malvern. Was Def. Prov., 1854-64.

1864. July 9th. D. JOHN ATHANASIUS CLARKSON.
b. Birmingham, 1816. Prof. St. Ed., 1837. Ord., 1840. Sent on the mission to the S. Prov., 1842. Was at Coventry, 1842-50. Passed to the N. Prov. Was at St. Anne's, Liverpool, 1850-4. Returned to the S. Prov., and was at Pontypool, 1855-61. Returned to St. Ed., 1861-2. Again on the mission in the S. Prov. Was at Merthyr Tydvil, 1862-3. Rhymney, 1863-4. where he d.

1864. Sep. 28th. D. THOMAS AUSTIN ROLLING.
b. Yorkshire, 1789. Prof. St. Greg., 1808. Ord., 1815. Sent on the mission to the S. Prov., 1815. Was at Bath, 1815-7. Passed to the N. Prov., and was at Knaresboro', 1817-24. Allerton Park, 1824-34. Again to the S. Prov. Was at Cannington, 1834-6. Colwich, 1836-8. Chipping Sodbury, 1838-40. Little Malvern, 1840-2. Acton Burnell, 1842-6. Bungay, 1846-50, Coventry, 1850-1. Weobly, 1851-5. Longworth, 1855-63. Retired to Downside, 1863, and there d. Was Def. Prov., 1845-50. Def. Reg., 1850-4. Cath. Pr. of Peterboro', 1838.

1864. Dec. 15th. D. JAMES HILARY DOWDING.
b. Bath. Prof. St. Lau., 1833. Ord., 1834. Was Sub-prior. Sent on the mission to the N. Prov. Was at Little Crosby, 1840-3. Passed to the S. Prov., and was at Cheltenham, 1843-50. Again to the N. Prov., and was at Little Crosby, 1850-6. Ormskirk, 1856-8. Aigburth, 1858-64, and d. there.

1865. Feb. 12th. D. HENRY BENEDICT BLOUNT.
b. London, 1821. Prof. St. Greg., 1841. Ord., 1849.
Was Prefect of Studies. Master of the Novices. Sent
on the mission to the S. Prov. Was at Cheltenham,
1854-61. Belmont, 1861. Rotherwas, 1861-5, and
d. there. Was Canon of Newport and Menevia,
1862-5.

1865. Mar. 4th. D. RICHARD BENEDICT HOOLE.
b. Pemberton, near Wigan, 1799. Prof. St. Ed., 1824.
Ord., 1825. Sent on the mission to the N. Prov., and
was at Scarisbrick, 1826-65, and d. there. Was Def.
Prov., 1854-65. Cath. Pr. of Chester, 1850.

1865. Mar. 14th. D. CHAS. FRANCIS KERSHAW.
b. Burscough, 1811. Prof. Broadway, 1834. Ord., 1836.
Sent on the mission to the N. Prov. Was at Workington, 1838-41. Lawkland, 1841-50. Leyland, 1850-5.
Woolton, 1855-8. Ormskirk, 1858-65, and d. there.

1865. April 11th. D. WM. BERNARD O'SULLIVAN.
b. Cork, 1823. Prof. St. Greg., 1841. Ord., 1850. Sent
on the mission to the N. Prov. Was at St. Mary's,
Liverpool, 1851-4. St. Anne's, Liverpool, 1854-65,
and d. there.

1865. Aug. 13th. BR. THOMAS CYPRIAN
HUBBERSTY.
b. Radburn, Lancas. Prof. St. Lau., 1844. Went to
Australia, and d. at Melbourne.

1866. June 9th. D. CHAS. OSWALD TINDALL.
b. Carlton, Yorks., 1834. Prof. St. Lau., 1855. Ord.,
1862, and d. at Ampleforth.

1866. June 27th. D. JAMES WILFRID BURCHALL.
b. Aspull, near Wigan, 1818. Prof. St. Ed., 1839. Ord.,

1843. Sent on the mission to the N. Prov. Was at Cowpen, 1845-66, and d. there.

1867. May 15th. D. JAMES WOLSTAN BARTON. b. Warrington, 1842. Simply Prof. at Belmont, 1862. Solemn. at St. Lau., 1865. Ord. Deacon. d. at Ampleforth.

1867. Aug. 29th. D. WM. JEROME HAMPSON. b. Ashton, Lancas., 1802. Prof. St. Lau., 1819. Ord., 1826. Was Cellerarius. Sent on the mission to the N. Prov. Was at Brandsby, 1834-5. Keighley, 1835-6. Little Crosby, 1836-8. Knaresboro', 1838-56. Lawkland, 1856-62. Woolton, 1862-7. Retired to St. Lau., 1867, and d. at Ampleforth.

1867. Dec. 17th. D. ABRAHAM IGNATIUS ABRAM. b. Liverpool, 1796. Prof. St. Greg., 1814. Ord., 1820. Sent on the mission to the N. Prov. Was at Workington, 1822-30. Netherton, 1830-67, and d. there. Was Proc. Prov., 1844-62. Cath. Pr. of Worcester, 1862.

1868. Feb. 4th. D. RICHARD CLEMENT CROFT. b. Liverpool, 1805. Prof. St. Lau., 1823. Ord., 1830. Sent on the mission to the N. Prov. Was at St. Mary's, Liverpool, 1831-8. Brownedge, 1838-9. St. Anne's Cemetery, Liverpool, 1842-4. Brindle, 1844. Cowpen, 1845. Went to Belgium, and d. at Courtrai.

1868. Dec. 14th. D. JAMES BEDE JOLLEY. b. Wigan, 1826. Prof. St. Ed., 1847. Ord., 1855. Sent on the mission to the N. Prov. Was at St. Mary's, Liverpool, 1855-9. Whitehaven, 1859-63. St. Mary's, Liverpool, 1863-8, and d. there.

1869. Jan. 1st. D. RALPH MAURUS COOPER.
b. Bamberbridge, 1799. Prof. St. Lau., 1817. Ord.,
1823. Sent on the mission to the S. Prov. Was at
Bath, 1823-46. Chipping Sodbury, 1846-69, and d.
there.

1869. Jan. 18th. D. LEWIS CUTHBERT SPAIN.
b. London, 1797. Prof. St. Greg., 1814. Ord., 1819.
Left for the Mauritius, 1819. Was at Port Louis and
Flacq. Returned to St. Greg., 1846. Was on the
mission at Stanbrook, 1847. Retired to St. Greg.,
1855, and d. at Downside.

1869. Feb. 5th. D. GEORGE AUSTIN LOWE.
b. Stainton, Yorks., 1806. Prof. St. Lau., 1831. Ord.,
1835. Sent on the mission to the N. Prov. Was at
St. Mary's, Liverpool, 1835-6. Morpeth, 1836-69,
and d. there.

1769. Mar. 11th. D. PETER JOSEPH HEWITT.
b. Marston, Lincolns., 1812. Was a Convert. Prof. St.
Greg., 1841. Ord., 1846. Sent on the mission to the
S. Prov. Was at Acton, London, 1846. Weobly,
1847-51. Wootton, 1851-69, and d. there. Was
Proc. Prov., 1854-69.

1869. April 6th. D. JOSEPH AUSTIN KITCHEN.
b. Hathersage, 1824. Prof. St. Ed., 1851. Ord., 1859.
Sent on the mission to the N. Prov., 1866. Was at
St. Augustine's, Liverpool, 1866-8. Went to Belmont,
1868-9, and d. at Chesterfield. Was Canon of Newport
Menevia, 1868-9.

1869. June 7th. D. THOMAS PAULINUS
HEPTONSTALL.
b Tadcaster, 1798. Prof. St. Greg., 1816. Ord., 1827.

Sent on the mission to the S. Prov., 1831. Was at
Acton, London, 1831-50. Coventry, 1850-3. Stanbrook, 1853-67. Blackmore Park, 1867-9, and d.
there. Was Proc. Prov., 1842-52. Prov. Cant., 1852-
66. Def. Reg., 1866-9. Cath. Pr. of Durham, 1854.
D.D. and Abbot of St. Edmundsbury, 1862.

1869. Sep. 2nd. D PAULINUS KIRTTAN.
   b. Yarme, Yorks., 1840. Simply Prof. at Belmont,
1861. Returned to St. Ed., 1863, and Solemn Prof.,
1864. Ord., 1867. Was Cellerarius. d. at Cheltenham.

1870. Jan. 15th. D. GEORGE ALBAN CALDWELL.
   b. Warrington, 1804. Prof. St. Lau., 1826. Ord., 1830.
Send on the mission to the N. Prov. Was at St.
Peter's, Liverpool, 1832-4. Clayton Green, 1834-9.
St. Peter's, Liverpool, 1839-44. Ormskirk, 1844-56.
Little Crosby, 1856-9. Lee House, 1859-68, Nether-
ton, 1868-70, and d. in Liverpool.

1870. Feb. 5th. D. EDWARD BERNARD PAILLET.
   b. Bath, 1810. Prof. St. Greg., 1834. Ord., 1839.
Sent on the mission to the S. Prov., 1840. Was at
Cheltenham, Chipping Sodbury, and Acton Burnell,
and then lost his sight. Returned to St. Greg., 1842,
and left in 1847. Was at Whitehaven, 1847-54.
Cleator, 1854-62. Stratford-on-Avon, 1862-4. Wol-
verhampton, 1864-5. Rhymney, 1865-6. Bungay,
1867. Abergavenny, 1868-70, and d. there.

1870. Feb. 16th. D. SAMUEL BEDE DAY.
   b. Welton, Somerset, 1791. Prof. St. Lau., 1807. Sent
on the mission to the N. Prov. Was at Standish,
1816-22. Clayton Green, 1822-34. Pr. of St. Lau.,

1834-8. Again on the mission to the S. Prov. Was at Coventry, 1838-40, Kemerton, 1842-4. Passed to the N. Prov. Was at Brownedge, 1844-5. Aigburth, 1845-50. Felton, 1850-69. Retired to S. Lau., 1869, and d. at Ampleforth.

1870. Sep. 19th. Br. CUTHBERT COLLINS.
b. Holme, Yorks., 1841. Simply Prof. at Belmont for St. Ed., 1868. d. at Holme.

1870. Sep. 21st. D. MICHAEL ADRIAN HANKINSON.
b. Warrington, 1817. Prof. Broadway, 1836. Went to S. Ed., 1838. Ord., 1841. Was Sub-prior. Sent on the mission to the N. Prov., 1851. Was at St. Peter's, Liverpool, 1851-4. Pr. of St. Ed., 1854-63. Consecrated Bp. of Port Louis, 1863. d. at Douai. Was Cath. Pr. of Gloucester, 1862-3.

1870. Oct. 26th. D. PETER IGNATIUS GREENOUGH.
b. Wigan, 1801. Prof. St. Lau., 1819. Ord., 1825. Sent on the mission to the N. Prov. and was at Ince, Lancas., 1826-65. Scarisbrick, 1865-70, and d. there. Was Def. Prov., 1846-50. Prov. of York, 1850-8. Def. Reg., 1858-66. Cath. Pr. of Coventry, 1850.

1871. Mar 13th. Br. PETER HILARY TAYLOR.
b. 1847. Simply Prof. at Belmont for St. Lau., 1868. d. at Standish.

1871. July 1st. D. THOS. BENEDICT WASSELL.
b. Stourbridge, 1791. Prof. St. Greg., 1808. Ord., 1816. Sent on the mission to the S. Prov., 1817. Was vicar to the nuns at Salford, 1818-22. Shrewsbury, 1822-4. Bonham, Wilts., 1824-70. Retired to St. Greg., 1870, and d. at Downside. Was Cath. Pr. of Norwich, 1850-4.

1871. July 6th. D. Richard Cyprian Tyrer,

b. near Preston, 1799. Prof. St. Lau., 1822. Ord., 1828. Sent on the mission to the N. Prov. Was at Easingwold, 1828-36. Birtley, 1836-7. Lawkland, 1837-40. Standish, 1840-62. Hindley, 1862-4. St. Anne's, Liverpool, 1864-70. Lee House, 1870-1, and d. there.

1871. Oct. 17th. D. Joseph Bede Sumner.

b. Sambourne, 1803. Prof. St. Greg., 1833. Went to Australia, 1834. Ord., 1836. d. in Australia.

1871. Nov. 18th. D. Henry Gregory Lane.

b. Wardour, Wilts., 1818. Prof. St. Greg., 1840. Ord., 1846. Sent on the mission to the N. Prov. Was at Mary's, Liverpool, 1847-9. Bath, 1849. Returned to St. Greg. Was Prefect of Studies. Again on the mission in the S. Prov. Was at Wootton, 1857-9. Stratford-on-Avon, 1859-64. Old Longworth, 1864-5. Bartestree, 1866. Mechlin, 1866-71, and d. there.

1872. Jan. 25th. Br. Robert Maurus M'Kenna.

b. Dublin, 1834. Prof. St. Greg., 1856. Ord. Subdeacon, 1861. Was at Belmont, 1862-3. Gheel, Belgium, 1863-72, and d. there.

1872. Feb. 18th. D. Wm. Placid Morris.

b. London, 1794. Prof. St. Greg., 1811. Ord., 1818. Sent on the mission to the S. Prov. and was in London, 1819 in South Street, and in 1830 at Chelsea. Consecrated Bp. of Troy and Vicar Apostolic of the Mauritius, 1832. Returned from the Mauritius, 1840, and was at Roehampton, 1841-72, and d. there.

1872. Feb. 20th. D. Thos. Anselm Cockshoot.

b. 1805. Prof. St. Lau., 1823. Ord., 1830. Sent on the mission to the S. Prov. Was at Coventry, 1830-8. Pr. of St. Lau., 1838-46. Again on the mission in the N. Prov. and was at Holme, 1846-58. Was at Belmont, 1858-62. Again on the mission in the S. Prov. Was at Cheltenham, 1862-3. Longworth, 1863-4. Old Longworth, 1864-6. Bartestree, 1866-72, and d. there. Was Def. Reg., 1850-66. Cath. Pr. of Chester, 1846. Canon of Newport Menevia, 1863-72. Vic. Gen., 1864-72.

1872. May 31st. D. Patrick Alban Dunn.

b. Ireland, 1797. Prof. St. Lau., 1845. Ord., 1847. Sent on the mission to the N. Prov. Was at Brandsby, 1850-1. Sickling Hall, Wetherby, 1851-2. Rixton, 1852-72, and d. there.

1872. Sep. 8th. D. William Placid Corlett.

b. Isle of Man, 1807. Prof. St. Lau., 1826. Ord., 1834. Sent on the mission to the N. Prov. Was at St. Peter's, Liverpool, 1834-6. Hindley, 1836-63. Standish, 1863-72. Retired, and d. at Brindle.

1872. Oct. 12th. D. Wm. Dunstan Scott.

b. Swinburne, 1791. Prof. St. Greg., 1816. Ord., 1824. Was Cellerarius. Sent on the mission to the S. Prov., Was at Acton, London, 1825-34. Returned to Downside, 1834-41. Again on the mission at Little Malvern, 1841-72, and d. there. Was Proc. Prov., 1826-42. Def. Prov., 1830-4. Prov. of Cant., 1842-6. Def. Reg., 1846-72. Cath. Pr. of Worcester, 1846. Winchester, 1862. Abbot of Glastonbury, 1850.

1873.   Sept. 27th,   D. THOMAS BEDE ALMOND.
b. Liverpool, 1821.   Prof. St. Lau., 1838.   Ord., 1845.
Sent on the mission to the N. Prov.   Was at St.
Mary's, Liverpool, 1847-73, and d. at Ampleforth.
Was Proc. Prov., 1862-73.

1873.   Oct. 10th,   D. WM. ALPHONSUS FLEMING.
b. Liverpool, 1828.   Prof. St. Ed., 1850.   Ord., 1856.
Sent on the mission to the N. Prov., 1863.   Was at
St. Aug., Liverpool, 1863-5,   Walton-le-Dale, 1865-6.
Cleator, 1866-7.   Warrington, 1867-9.   St. Anne's,
Liverpool, 1870-1.   St. Mary's, Liverpool, 1871-2.
Standish, 1872-3.   Whitehaven, 1873, and d. there.

1873.   Dec. 12th.   D. FRANCIS PLACID DE PAIVA.
b. Macao, 1836.   Prof. St. Greg., 1856.   Ord., 1864.
Was Cellerarius, and d. at Downside.

1874.   Jan. 29th.   D. JOSEPH BEDE SMITH.
b. Wrax Abbey, Yorkshire, 1801.   Prof. St. Lau., 1819
Ord., 1825.   Sent on the mission to the N. Prov.
Was at St. Mary's, Liverpool, 1827-9.   Brindle,
1829-74, and d. there.

1874.   Oct. 5th.   D. GEORGE AMBROSE GILLETT.
b. Preston, 1820.   Prof. St. Ed., 1840.   Ord., 1845.   Sent
on the mission to the N. Prov.   Was at St. Mary's,
Liverpool, 1849.   Brandsby Hall, 1852,   Lawkland,
1852-6.   Knaresboro', 1856-73.   Retired to St. Ed.,
1873, and d. at Douai.

1875.   Mar. 25th.   BR. CHAS. FRANCIS McELROY.
b. Liverpool, 1854.   Simp. Prof. at Belmont for St.
Lau., 1874, and d. at Belmont.

1875. April 27th. D. JAMES AELRED KEARNS.
b. Birmingham, 1842. Simp. Prof. at Belmont, 1864. Solemn. at St. Greg., 1867. Ord., 1871. Was Cellerarius, and d. at Downside.

1875. May 18th. D. RALPH EPHREM PRATT.
b. Richmond, Yorks., 1802. Prof. St. Greg., 1820. Ord., 1827. Sent on the mission to the N. Prov. Was at at Knaresboro', 1830-8. St. Peter's, Liverpool, 1838-40. Passed to the S. Prov., and was at Redditch, 1840-50. Coventry, 1850-70. Retired to St. Greg., 1870, and d. at Downside.

1875. Oct. 22nd. D. FRAN. BERNARD WILLIAMS.
b. Caerwent, Monmouths., 1799. Prof. Broadway, 1837. Went to Downside, 1841. Ampleforth, 1842. Ord. 1843. Sent on the mission to the N. Prov. Was at Maryport, 1844-59. Cleator, 1859-68. Aberford, 1868-75, and d. there.

1875. Nov. 17th. D. JOSEPH BERNARD SHORT.
b. Bath, 1800. Prof. St. Greg., 1820. Ord., 1827. Sent on the mission to the S. Prov. Was at Little Malvern, 1830-40. Woolton, 1840-51. Vicar of nuns at Stanbrook, 1851-63. Retired to St. Greg., 1863-4. Was at Abbots Leigh, Devon, 1864-5. Dun Esk, Teignmouth, 1865-6. Bungay, 1866-7. Colwich, 1867-70. Retired to St. Greg., and d. at Downside. Was Def. Prov., 1846-50.

1876. Jan. 13th. D. PETER ATHANASIUS ALLANSON.
b. London, 1805. Prof. St. Lau., 1821. Ord., 1828. Sent on the mission to the N. Prov., and was at Swinburne, 1828-76, where he died. Was Prov. of

York, 1858-76. Cath. Pr. of Norwich, 1862. Abbot of Glastonbury, 1874.

1876. Mar. 26th. D. THOS. AUSTIN ATKINSON. b. Newcastle, 1815. Prof. St. Lau., 1838. Ord., 1842. Sent on the mission to the N. Prov. Was at Brownedge, 1842-3. Aberford, 1843-66. Whitehaven, 1866-72. Rixton, 1872-4. Lee House, 1874-6, and d. there.

1876. June 3rd. D. HENRY LAURENCE VRIGNON. b. Calcutta, 1822. Prof. St. Greg., 1845. Went to India, 1850. Returned to St. Greg., 1854. Ord., 1857, and d. at Downside.

1876. Aug. 23rd. D. JOSEPH BEDE CUMMINS. b. Liverpool, 1847. Simp. Prof. at Belmont, 1866. Solemn. at St. Lau., 1869. Ord., 1873. Sent on the mission to the S. Prov. Was at Swansea, 1874-6. Bath, 1876, and d. at Waterloo, Liverpool.

1877. Jan. 30th. D. RALPH WILFRID COOPER. b. Bamberbridge, 1819. Prof. St. Lau., 1836. Ord., 1844. Sent on the mission to the N. Prov. Was at St. Mary's, Liverpool, 1845-8. St. Anne's, Liverpool, 1848-50. Prior of St. Lau., 1850-63. Again on the mission in the N. Prov. Was at St. Peter's, Liverpool, 1863. St. Augustine's, Liverpool, 1863-75. Clayton Green, 1875-7, and d. there. Was Def. Prov., 1870-7. Cath. Pr. of Worcester, 1870.

1877. Feb. 5th. D. JOSEPH BENEDICT MURPHY. b. Ormskirk, 1834. Prof. St. Lau., 1855. Ord., 1862. Sent on the mission to the N. Prov. Was at St. Augustine's, Liverpool, 1862-3. St. Anne's, Liverpool, 1863-4. St. Peter's, Liverpool, 1864. Ormskirk,

1864-8. Lee House, 1868-70. Warrington, 1870-1
Lee House, 1871-4. Cowpen, 1874-6. Passed to the
S. Prov. Was at Rhymney, 1876-7, and d. in Liver-
pool.

1877. Mar. 16th. D. JOHN BEDE POLDING.
  b. Liverpool, 1794. Prof. St. Greg., 1811. Ord., 1819.
Was Novice Master, 1819-34. Sub-prior. Consecrated
Bishop of Hiero Cesarea, 1834. Went to Australia,
and became Archbishop of Sydney, 1851. d. at
Sydney.

1877. June 17th. D. JOHN AUGUSTINE DOWDING.
  b. London, 1806. Prof. St. Greg., 1825. Ord., 1831.
Sent on the mission to the N. Prov., 1835. Was at
Easingwold, 1835-77, and d. there.

1877. July 19th. D. HENRY GREGORY GREGORY.
  b. Cheltenham, 1813. Prof. Downside, 1834. Ord.,
1837. Went to Australia, 1834. Made D.D. Abbot
1841. Returned to England, and was on the mission
at Stanbrook, 1861-2. Bullingham, 1862-3. Brox-
wood, 1863-77, and d. there. Canon of Newport
Menevia, 1864-77.

1877. Oct. 24th. D. JAMES VINCENT DOWDING.
  b. Bath. 1809. Prof. St. Greg., 1830. Ord., 1836. Sent
on the mission to the N. Prov., 1839. Was at Clayton
Green, 1839-75. Passed to the S. Prov. Was at
Studley, 1875-7, and d. there.

1877. Oct. 26th D. WILLIAM WILFRID RYAN.
  b. Liverpool, 1802. Prof. St. Lau., 1823. Ord., 1826.
Sent on the mission to the S. Prov., and was at
Calehill, Kent, 1827-38. Passed to the N. Prov. Was
at Warwick Bridge, 1838-77, and d. there. Was

Def. Prov., 1866-70. Def. Reg., 1870-7. Cath. Pr. of Winchester, 1874.

1878. Feb. 12th. D. CHAS. LAURENCE WRIGHT. b. Wigan, 1849. Simp. Prof. at Belmont, 1868. Solemn. at St. Lau., 1871. Ord., 1875. Sent on the mission to the S. Prov. Was at Swansea, 1875-8, and d. there.

1878. Mar. 23rd. D. CHARLES WILFRID PRICE. b. Liverpool, 1819. Prof. Broadway, 1836. Went to St. Greg., 1841-2. St. Lau., 1846. Ord., 1849. Sent on the mission to the N. Prov. Was at St. Anne's, Liverpool, 1850-2. Passed to the S. Prov., and was at Coventry, 1852-3. Chidecock, 1853-4. Coventry, 1854. Chepstow, 1857-8. Abergavenny, 1858-9. Chidecock, 1859-64. Bridgend, 1864-73. Swansea, 1873-6. Retired to St. Lau. Again on the mission at Clytha, 1877-8, and d. there. Was Canon of Newport Menevia, 1872-76.

1878. Mar. 24th. D. JAMES VINCENT SPEARS. b. Liverpool, 1824. Prof. St. Ed., 1844. Ord., 1850. Was Novice Master. Sub-prior. Sent on the mission to the S. Prov., 1860. Was at Hereford, 1860-72. Bartestree, 1872-3. Stratford-on-Avon, 1873-8, and d. in Liverpool. Canon of Newport Menevia, 1862-72.

1878. July 19th. D. JAMES EDMUND POOLE. b. Liverpool, 1819. Prof. St. Lau., 1838. Ord., 1845. Sent on the mission to the N. Prov. Was at Warrington, 1846-57. Whitehaven, 1857-9. Maryport, 1859-68. Walton-le-Dale, 1868, and d. in Liverpool.

1878. July 24th. D. JOHN JEROME JENKINS. b. Sedgeley, Staffords., 1796. Prof. St. Greg., 1813. Ord., 1820. Sent on the mission to the N. Prov.

Was at Woolton, 1821-6. Standish, 1826. Passed
to the S. Prov. Was at Little Malvern, 1826-30.
Cheltenham, 1830-3. Bath, 1833-7. Bungay, 1837-8.
Broadway, 1838-40. Chipping Sodbury, 1840-1.
Cheltenham, 1842-3. Rome, 1843. Bath, 1846-50.
Redditch, 1850-2. Taunton, 1852-59 Coventry,
1859-78. d. at Ampleforth. Was Sec. Gen. Chapter,
1834-42. Sec. Pres., 1838-42. Proc. in Rome, 1842-6.
Prov. of Canterbury, 1846-52. Def. Reg., 1870-8.
Cath. Pr. of Bath, 1850, Durham, 1870. Abbot of St.
Alban's, 1870.

1879. July 21st. D. EDWARD VINCENT DINMORE.
b. Knaresboro', 1805. Prof. St. Lau., 1824. Ord., 1830.
Sent on the mission to the N. Prov. Was at
Goosnargh, 1833-79, and d. there.

1879. Aug. 22nd. D. RICHARD GREGORY KENDAL.
b. Bath, 1848. Simp. Prof. at Belmont, 1867. Solemn.
at St. Greg., 1870. Went to Australia, 1873. Ord.,
1874. Returned to St. Greg., and d. at Downside.

1879. Sep. 6th. D. PETER GERARD TIERNAN.
b. Liverpool, 1854. Simp. Prof. at Belmont, 1872.
Solemn. at St. Ed., 1875. Ord., 1878. d. at Douai.

1879. Oct. 6th. BR. JOHN BERNARD BELL.
b. Liverpool, 1860. Simp. Prof. for St. Ed., 1879. d. at
Douai.

1880. April 4th. D. MATTHEW CHARLES
FAIRCLOUGH.
b. Wigan, 1788. Prof. St. Lau., 1818. Went to Douai,
1818. Ord., 1820. Sent on the mission to the N.
Prov. Was at Biddleston, 1822. Passed to the S.

Prov. Was at Bungay, 1826-7. Went to St. Gery., Arras, and was there, 1828-78. Retired to St. Ed., 1878, and d. at Douai.

1880. April 12th. D. Thos. Joseph Brown.
b. Bath, 1796. Prof. St. Greg., 1814. Ord., 1823. Pr. of St. Greg., 1834-40. Consecrated Bishop of Appolonia, 1840, and V.A. of Western District. Became Bishop of Newport Menevia, 1850. d. at Bullingham. Was Cath. Pr. of Winchester, 1833-40. D.D. 1834.

1880. Sep. 20th. D. John Placid McAuliffe.
b. Bath, 1848. Simp. Prof. Belmont, 1866. Solemn. at St. Lau., 1869. Ord., 1874. d. at Ampleforth.

1880. Sep. 25th. D. Edwin Oswald Davis.
b. Usk, 1819. Prof. St. Greg., 1839. Ord., 1848. Was Cellerarius and Sub-prior. Sent on the mission to the S. Prov., 1869. Was at Blackmore Park, 1869-70. Bonham, 1870-9. Retired to St. Greg., 1879, and d. at Downside.

1880. Dec. 25th. D. John Jerome Lynch.
b. Wavertree, Liverpool, 1849. Simp. Prof. Belmont, 1868. Solemn. at St. Lau., 1872. Ord., 1875. Sent on the mission to the N. Prov., and was at St. Mary's, Liverpool, 1877-80, and d. there.

1881. Feb. 22nd. D. Thos. Bernard Jackson.
b. Liverpool, 1815. Prof. St. Lau., 1836. Ord., 1839. Was Sub-prior, 1846. Sent on the mission to the N. Prov. Was at Middleton Lodge, 1849-65. Aberford, 1866-8. Brownedge, 1869-81. d. at Leyland.

1881. Oct. 15th. D. John Carroll.
b. Liverpool, 1828. Prof. St. Ed., 1852. Ord., 1859. Sent on the mission to the N. Prov., 1864. Was at

Whitehaven, 1864-6. Walton-le-Dale, 1866-8. Maryport, 1868-81. Retired to St. Ed., and d. at Douai.

1882. May 1st. Br. Henry Celestine Froes.
b. Wakefield, 1860. Simp. Prof. at Belmont for St. Lau., 1879, and d. at Wellington, Shropshire.

1882. Aug. 30th. D. John Maurus Potter.
b. Liverpool, 1848. Simp. Prof. at Belmont, 1868. Solemn. at St. Lau., 1872. Ord., 1874. Sent on the mission to the N. Prov., and was at S. Augustine's, Liverpool, 1875-81. St. Anne's, Liverpool, 1881. Again at St. Augustine's, 1881, and d. at Ormskirk.

1883. Jan. 7th. D. Edward Benedict Lynass.
b. St. Helen's, 1823. Prof. St. Lau., 1843. Ord., 1850. Sent on the mission to the S. Prov. Was at Redditch and Cheltenham. Retired to Ampleforth. Again on the mission in the N. Prov. Was at Waterloo, Leyland, 1854-9. Whitehaven, 1859-73. Knaresboro', 1873-83, where he died.´

1883. April 16th. D. James Norbert Sweeney.
b. Bengalore, 1821. Prof. St. Greg., 1839. Ord., 1848. Was Professor of Theology. Sub-prior. Pr. of St. Greg., 1854-9. Pr. of St. Michael's, Belmont, 1859-62. Sent on the mission to the S. Prov. and was at Bath, 1862, till death there. Was Sec. to Chapter, 1866-78. Cath. Pr. of Gloucester, 1866. D.D., 1870. Def. Prov., 1874-8. Abbot of St. Alban's, 1878. Def. Reg., 1878-82. Prov. of Canterbury, 1882, till death.

1883. May 1st. D. James Ambrose Cotham.
b. Liverpool, 1810. Prof. St. Ed., 1830. Ord., 1834, at Prior Park, for the Tasmanian mission. Went to

Tasmania, 1835, and was at Launceston and Richmond, 1835-44. Hobart Town, 1844-51. Returned to England, 1851, and was sent to the S. Prov. and was at Cheltenham, 1852-73. Retired to St. Ed., 1873-6. Went to La Cava, Italy, 1876-8. Was at Belmont, 1879. Again on the mission at Bonham, 1879-81. Retired to Bath, 1881-2, and to Belmont, 1882, where he d.

'83 - June 12th. D. Anselm Glassbrook (E) - died at Preston aged 78. Religion 62. Priest 54.

'3. August 18th. Most Rev. Roger Bede Vaughan (G) Archbishop of Sydney died suddenly at Ince Blundell aged 50. Religion 38 - Bishop 10.

'3. December 4th. D. Nicholas Kendal (G) died at St Gregory's Downside aged 78 - rel. 58. Priest 53.

'4 - January 15th. Right Rev. Abbot Smith (G) died at St Gregory's Downside - aged 69. rel. 49 - Priest 40.

'4 - July 16th. D. Jerome Watmough (L) died at Kidlington aged 47 - rel. 28 Priest 20.

'4 - August 14th. D. Cuthbert Croton (L) died at St Lawrence's Ampleforth - aged 63 - rel. 39 - Priest 34.

'4 - December 15th. D. Paulinus Thomas (E) died at St Mary's Warrington - aged 36. rel. 15. Priest 8.

'5. January 30th. D. Laurence Shepherd (L) died at St Mary's Abbey - Stanbrook - aged 59 - rel. 41 - Priest 35.

'5. February 8th. Mr. Patrick McCarthy died at St Michael's Belmont - Oblate - aged 66 - rel 4.

'5. March 7th. Right Rev. Abbot Burchall (E) died at St Mary's Woolton - aged 75 - rel. 52. Priest 49.

'5. May 2nd. D. Clement Worsley (L) died at St John's Bath aged 73 - rel. 54 - Priest 48.

'6 - May 4th. D. Ignatius Dewhurst (H.B) died at Lee House aged 72 - rel. 52 - Priest 43.

'6 - August 28th. D. Ignatius Sutton (L) died at St Lawrence's Ampleforth aged 74 - rel 53 - Priest 49.

'7 - May 19th. D. Bede Searle (E) died at St Edmund's Douai aged 79 - rel. 60 - Priest 45.

'8 - March 8th. D. Anselm Gillett (L) died at Bullingham aged 64 - rel. 43 - Priest 38.

'8 - May 4th. D. Osmund Morris (E) died at St Edmund's Douai aged 40 - rel. 20 - Priest 13.

888 - October 2nd - D. Peter Wilson (Y) died at St Gregory's Downside aged 90 - rel. 69 - Priest 61 -

888 - November 21st Right Rev. Abbot Hickey (L) died at Ormskirk aged 60 - rel. 40 - Priest 33.

889. March 21st Most Rev. William Bernard Ullathorne (g) died at St Mary's Oscott - aged 83 - rel 65 - Epis - 43 -

889 - May 10th D. Placid Dillon (L) died at St Edmunds Douai aged 61 - rel 39. Priest 31

1889 - May 15th D. Francis Davis (Y) died at Coughton aged 84 - rel. 66 - Priest 58 -

1890 - April 19th D. Maurus Shepherd (L) died at an Asylum in France aged 72 - rel 52 - Priest 43.

89a May 28th D. Benedict Talbot (L) died at Little Malvern aged 57 - rel 28 - Priest 21

890 - June 30th D. Placid Hall (A.D) died at St Augustine's Liverpool - aged 71 - rel 56 - Priest 46 -

890 - November 21st Right Rev. William Bernard Allen Collier (died at St Osburg's Coventry aged 89 - rel 67 - Epis 57

891 - March 2nd Mr Benedict McEntee (L) - lay brother - died at St Lawrence's Ampleforth aged 81 - rel 54.

1891 - April 10th D. Cuthbert Murphy (Y) died at Easingwold aged 65 - rel 44. Priest 36 -

1891 - June 16th D. Edmund Roche (L) died at Clifton aged 65 rel 38 - Priest 30.

1891. June 27th D. Maurus Margison (L) died at Wrightington aged 77 - rel 59. Priest 54

891 - July 1st D. Lawrence Burge (L) died at Barton-on-Humber aged 81 - rel 60 - Priest 56.

1891 - August 26th D. Ambrose Brindle (L) died at St Augustine's Newton Abbot - aged 73 - rel 52 - Priest 47.

1891 - December 28th Right Rev. Abbot Clifton (L) died at Workington aged 73 - rel 50 - Priest 47.

1290 - December 8th - D. Vincent Murphy (L) - died at Charleville Ireland - aged 43 - rel. 16 - Priest 13.

'93 - April 6th - Br Joseph Bennett (E) lay brother died at St Edmund's Douai - aged 79 - rel 56 -

'93 - April 19th D. Stanislaus Holohan (E) died at Ormskirk aged 72 - rel 50 - Priest 44.

8.3 - July 8th D. Anselm Walker (L) died at Brownedge aged 72 - rel 56 - Priest 48.

'/4 - April 2nd D. Bernard Fazakerley (E) died at Stratford on Avon aged 65 - rel 42 - Priest 32 -

'/4 - June 29th D. Stanislaus Giles (E) - died at Warwick Bridge - aged 81 - rel 61 - Priest 56 -

3.5 - January 11th D. Maurus Wilson (E) died at Cheltenham aged 52 - rel 32 - Priest 25.

'5 - February 18th D. Stephen Grddy (E) died at St Edmunds Douai - aged 45 - rel 20 - Priest.

'5 - March 20th D. Dunstan Chambers (E) died at Kirtley aged 50 - Bed 31 - Priest 25 -

'5 - Aug 18th - D. Hildebrand Bradley (L) died at St Lawrence's Ampleforth aged 57 - rel 18 - Priest 11

'5 - Aug 29th D. Stanislaus Nugent (G) died at St Gregory's Downside - aged 28 - rel 10 - Priest 2.

'5 - Sept 18 - D. Aloysius Ridgway (E) died at Kemerton aged 81 - rel 61 - Priest 57

'6 - Jan 7 - D. Placid Sinnott (G) died at St Gregory's Downside aged 93 - rel 70 - Priest 65 -

'6. Jan 11 - Br Benedict White (E) lay brother died at St Edmunds Douai aged 78 - rel 57

'6 - March 10 - D. Gregory Smith (L) died at Knaresborough aged 59 - rel 38 - Priest 30

'6 - Nov 7 - D. Francis Mary (E) died at Penang Australia aged 61 - rel 39 - Priest 32

'7 - March 1 - D. Edmund Caldwell (E) died at Ilford aged 79 - rel 60 - Priest 50

'7 - March 3 - D. Ceolfrid Treharne (E) died at Cheltenham aged 35 - rel 15 - Priest 8

1897 - June 26 - D. Paul Pontony (S) died at Ceres in
South Africa - aged 27 - rel 8. Priest 1

1897 - July 23 - D Laurence Tarrant (S) died at Marypo[rt]
aged 55 - rel 34 - Priest 27

1897 - Sept 8 - Br Didacus Six (E) Lay brother, died at
St Edmund's Douai - aged 79 - rel 56.

1897 - Sept 19 - D Egbert Turner (S) died at Ramsgate
aged 45. rel 25 - Priest 18

1898 - March 4 - D. Benedict Rawley (E) died in London
aged 64 rel 44 - Priest 35

1898 - May 9 - D. Bernard Saunders (E) died at Bristol
aged 56 - rel 39 - Priest 29.

1898 - Oct 28. D. Placid O'Brien (S) died at Aighburth
aged 74 - rel 51 - Priest 46

1899 - Jan 2 - Dom. Ephrem Guy. (G) died at St
Gregory's Downside aged 66 - rel. 48 - Priest 40

1899 - Feb 6 - Dom. Aloysius Serg (E) - died at St Gregory's
Cheltenham - aged 80 - rel 55 - Priest 50

1899 - Feb 8. Dom. Bruno Kengellbacher (G) died at Bournem[outh]
aged 48

1899 - Feb 19. Dom. Edmund Moore - (G) died at St Mary's
Woolton - aged 74 - rel 55 - Priest 45.

1899 - Oct. 10. Br. Robert Adams (St Michael's) Lay brother, d[ied]
at Belmont - aged 84. rel 34

1900 - March 9 - Dom. Maurus Anderson (S) died at
St Peter's L'pool aged 72 - rel 52 - Priest 46

1900 - March 13 - Dom. Bernard Pozzi (S) died at
Llandudno - aged 70 - rel 50 - Priest 43

1900 - May 2 - Dom. Alexius Bayes (S) died in London
aged 48 - rel 29 - Priest 21

1900 - October 31 - Dom Joseph Davis (G) died. at
St John's Kath - aged 73 - rel 55 - Priest 46.

— February 7 - 18—. Anselm Barnewall (L) died at Downside Abbey
  aged 79 - rel 55.

— April 2 - Dom. Oswald Tavenhall (C) died at Cowpen.
  aged 67 - rel 43 - Priest 36.

1 - May 23 - Dom. Norbert Ward (C) died at Cleator
  aged 57 - rel 38 - Priest 30

1 - July 6 - Dom. Francis Penton (L) died at Grahamstown S. A
  aged 33 - rel. 15 - Priest 7.

1 - Oct 18 - Dom. Anselm O'Gorman (C) died at The
  Monastery Great Malvern aged 68 — rel 52 - Priest 45 —

— Nov 13 - Dom. Bernard Kulbeck (L) died at St
  Mary's Priory - Princethorpe aged 76 - rel 51 - Priest 42.

1 - Dec 19 - Dom Gregory Knowles (L) died at Maryport
  aged 71 - rel 51 - Priest 45 —

2 - May 25. Dom. Francis Kenron (C) -- aged 61 - rel 39 - Pr 32
2 - June 18 Dom. Bede Brady (C) -- aged 58 - rel 41 - C. 31
2 - Nov. 30 - Dom. Dunstan Ross (C) - aged 65 - rel 46 - C. 37
  - Dec 16 - Dom Wilfrid Drinkwater (C) -- 81 - rel 50 - P. 44
  - Dec 19. Dom Benedict Tidmarsh (L) .. 85 - '68 - 5-7
3 - Feb 18. Dom Anthony Kulbeck (L) --- 82 - 63 - 51
  Nov 25 Dom Werpedijck (Prior) (L) --- 68 - - 44 - 37
  " 30 Dom Bede Priest (L) -- 72 -- 54 - 48
  Jan 10 Dom Augustinus King (L) -- 77 -- 61 - 54
  June 9 Dom Wilfridus Raynal (L) -- 74 - 56 - 47
  Jan 17 Dom Benedict ——— (L) --- 66 - 1
  " - Nov 10 - Dom Romuald Magann (L) -- 61 - 46 - 33
  05 - Jan 17 - Dom Benedictus ——— (L) --- .. - 49 - 40
  " 21 - Dom Gregory Brown (L) --- 52 - 33 - 25
  " - May 2. Dom Wilfrid Brown (L) -- 73 - 54 - 47
  " - Nov 19 Dom Ignatius Stewart (L) -- 80 - 62 - 56
  " - Dec 2 - Dom Ambrose Turner (L) -- 51 - 32 - 25
  " " 25 Dom Willibrord Van Valckenisson (L) - 61 - 31 - 24
  Jan 9 - Dom Benedict Malley (L) --- 60 - 41 - 34
       died at San Anselmo - Rome.
  April 21 - Dom Adrian Beaumont (L) 54 - 35 - 28
       died at Wynnmaur - S W
  " 30 - Dom Richard O'Hare (L) -- -- 62 - 47 - 36
       died at St John's P.

'906 – May 10 – Dom Aloysius O'Leary (B) – 44 – 24 – 17
    died at Kingstown
    May 26 Dom Romuald Turner (B) 72 – 50 – 43
    died at Trigington
'907 – Jan 13 Dom. Aloysius Wilkinson (B) 71 – 51 – 44
    died at Cheltenham
" – Feb 12. Dom Basil Heyworth (S) – 71 – 51 – 43
    died at Belmont
" May 11 – Dom. Joseph Davies (J) – – 62 – 44 – 34
    died at Clayton Green suddenly
" Dec 27. Dom. Romuald Woods (S) – 75 – 57 – 43
    died suddenly at Cardiff
1908 – March 1 – Dom Joseph Fitzgerald (J) – 44 – 24 – ..
" – May 9 Dom. Bernard Caldwell (B) – 82 – 64 – 5
" – " 7 – Most Rev. Benedict Snow Bishop N. (B) – 80 – 64 – 5
'909 – March 6 Dom Placid Wray (S) – – Bishop – 36 / 43 – 25 –
    June 27 Dom Aidan Howlett (J) – – 53 – 34
(200) + July 6 – Dom Bernard Davey (S) .. 81 – 46
    9 Dom Stephen Wade (S) – – 63 – 49
    Sept 2. Dom Wilfrid Sumner (S) – 68 – 46
1910. – June 6. Dom Oswald O'Neill (B) – – 66 – 48
    9 Dom Wulstan Perkins (B) – 67 – 40
    Sept 1. Dom Conrad Vanheart (J) – 67 – 3
1911 – Feb 19. Dom Alphonsus Morrall (J) – 85 – 6
" – Oct 17 Dom Gregory Nathe (B) – – 54 – 3
" – Nov 6, Right Rev. Peter Augustine O'Neill (B) 69 –
" – Dec 2. Dom Dunstan Breen (J) – – – 70 –
1912 – Aug 17. Dom Hildebrand Sanbon Fox (St N) – – 41 –
" – Sept 30. Dom Placid Corlett (S) – – 58 –
" – Oct 7. Dom Meinrad Fulton (J) – – 53 –
" – Nov 5 – Dom Isidor Green (J) – – 76 –
1913 – Jan 8 – Dom Jerome Pearson (S) – – 69 –

CHRONOLOGICAL LIST

OF THE

DECEASED LAY BROTHERS

OF THE

ENGLISH CONGREGATION

OF THE

Order of Saint Benedict.

1631.   Feb. 12th.

R. Anselm Hamoy.
  b. St. Malo.   Prof. St. Malo, 1620.

1633.   May 27th.   Br. Edmund
Arrowsmith.

  b. Lancashire.   Prof. St. Greg., 1614.

1647.   Sep. 2nd.   Br. Dominic Taylor.
  Prof. St. Malo, 1615.

1649.   ——— Br. Edmund Ward.
  b. Norfolk.   Prof. St. Ed., 1639.

16—   Dec. 5th.   Br. Benedict Galli.
  Prof. St. Malo.

1653. June 19th. BR. CLAUDE MOLINER.
Prof. St. Lau., 1620.

1656. Feb. 25th. BR. JOHN GRATIAN.
Prof. St. Lau., 1631.

1658. May 9th. BR. ANTHONY TENANT.

1658. May 15th. BR. WILLIAM TAHON.

1658. May 20th. BR. JOHN BRADSTOCK.

16— ——— BR. JAMES MEUNIER.
Prof. St. Malo, 1614.

16— May 13th. BR. JOHN BARBIERRE.
Prof. St. Malo.

1662. Mar. 25th. BR. ANTHONY LOVEL.
Prof. St. Lau., 1620.

1664. Aug. 13th. BR. PETER HUITSON.
b. Ashburne, Derbyshire. Prof. St. Greg., 1610.

1669. June 17th. BR. FRANCIS CHAMBERLAIN.
Prof. St. Malo.

1669. July 19th. BR. PAUL WATY.
Prof. St. Lau., 1639.

1669. Nov. 2nd. BR JOHN SHERWOOD.
b. Somerset. Prof. Lambs., 1656.

1674. Oct. 26th. BR. PETER HOLMES.
Prof. St. Greg.

1679. May 19th. BR. THOMAS PICKERING.
b. 1621. Prof. St. Greg., 1660. Sent to Somerset House,
1665. Hanged at Tyburne.

1682. Nov. 21st. BR. BAUL LAURENCE BROCAST.
b. Dieulwart. Prof. St. Lau., 1640.

1684.   Aug. 15th.   BR. PETER STREET.
Prof. Lambs., 1656.

1689.   Sep. 21st.   BR. JOHN LOCKERS.
Prof. St. Lau., 1663.

1690.   Mar. 5th.   BR. RANDAL BENEDICT
                    HANKINSON.
Prof. St. Ed., 1648.

1691.   Sept. 2nd.   BR. JOSEPH BLAKEY.
b. Newcastle-on-Tyne.   Prof. Lambs., 1666.

1695.   Nov. 21st.   BR. BEDE BARNES.
b. County of Durham.   Prof. Lambs., 1665.

1698.   Aug. 6th.   BR. GREGORY WILKINSON.
b. London.   Prof. St. Ed., 1650.

1699.   Oct. 20th.   BR. JOHN GREEN.
Prof. St. Greg., 1685.

17—   ———   BR. ALEXIUS HIGGS.
b. London.   Prof. St. Greg., 1699.

1702.   Sep. 8th.   BR. JOSEPH MOSSE.
b. Lancashire, 1625.   Prof. St. Ed., 1657.

1704.   July 16th.   BR. ANTHONY DANDY.
Prof. St. Greg., 1700.

1705.   July 10th.   BR. THOMAS BRABANT.
Prof. St. Greg., 1685.

1706.   Sep. 5th.   BR. THOMAS TUCKER.
b Bradford, Wilts.   Prof. Lambs., 1663.

1711.   June 1st.   BR. WM. ANDREW TOWNSON.
Prof. St. Greg., 1695.

1712.   May 17th.   BR. PETER GREGSON.
b. Lancashire.   Prof. St. Lau., 1701.

1714. Jan. 18th. BR. FRANCIS WEST.
b. Lancashire. Prof. St. Lau., 1664.

1714. May 24th. BR. BERNARD HUNTLEY.
b. Shadsford, Durham. Prof. S. Lau., 1673.

1715. June 5th. BR. ROBERT RICHARDSON.
b. Lancashire. Prof. St. Lau., 1661.

1715. Dec. 20th. BR. JOHN ARMSTON.
Prof. St. Greg., 1705.

1717. Sep. 8th. BR. WM. AUSTIN RUMLEY.
b. Lancashire. Prof. St. Lau., 1672. Sent to London.
Tried and acquitted for Oates' Plot. d. at Lambspring.

1720. April 8th. BR. ANTHONY DOUTCH.
b. Lambspring. Prof. Lambs., 1715.

1723. Dec. 31st. BR. PETER MONCY.
Prof. St. Greg., 1684.

1724. Feb. — BR. CHAS. MAURUS MIDDLETON.
Prof. St. Ed., 1698.

1726. Nov. 4th. BR. ROBERT ROWSTON.
Prof. St. Lau., 1719.

1728. Feb. 5th. BR. JEROME SIX.
b. Antwerp. Prof. Lambs., 1685.

1733. Jan. 29th. BR. PETER DEVAL.
Prof. St. Greg.

1733. Mar, 10th. BR. JOSEPH BATESON.
Prof. St. Lau., 1690.

1737. Feb. 7th. BR. MICHAEL GABRIEL BOCQUET.
Prof. St. Greg., 1704.

1738. Dec. 20th. BR. MAURUS GRAINCOURT.
Prof. St. Greg., 1727.

1738. Dec. 21st. BR. MARK LE DOUX.
Prof. St. Greg.

1739. Aug. 31st. BR. JAMES DRAPER.
Prof. St. Lau., 1719.

1740. April 20th. BR. HENRY LAWSON.
b. 1660. Prof. St. Greg., 1685.

1744. Mar. 9th. BR. ADRIAN MULLER.
b. Lambspring. Prof. Lambs., 1715.

1745. Feb. 28th. BR. LAURENCE DELATTRE.
Prof. St. Ed., 1699.

1755. Mar. 25th. BR. BEDE HOUGHTON.
b. Lancashire. Prof. St. Lau., 1729.

1767. May 1st. BR. DOMINIC BENEDICT MONPAS.
b. Douai. Prof. St. Greg., 1756.

1769. July 27th. BR. GEORGE JEROME CLARKSON.
b. Brindle. Prof. Lambs., 1748.

1776. Feb. 20th. BR. NICHOLAS ANDREW
BARGUET.
b. Champagne, 1703. Prof. St. Greg., 1738.

1777. April 17th. BR. CHRISTOPHER OSBALDSTONE.
Prof. St. Lau.

1780. July 20th. BR. ANTHONY PARKINSON.
b. Lancashire, 1699. Prof. St. Greg., 1736.

1782. ——— BR. JOSEPH BARKER.
Prof. St. Greg.

1782. May 11th. BR. JOHN JANSEN.
b. Lambspring. Prof. Lambs., 1744.

1782. July 14th. BR. ANDREW BURN.
Prof. St. Lau.

1786. Sep. 19th. BR. JOSEPH JOHNSON.
Prof. St. Lau.

1787. April 15th. BR. JOHN DUNSTAN OSBALDESTONE.
Prof. St. Greg., 1738.

1792. Dec. 18th. BR. JOSEPH BERNARD BECKMAN.
b. Lambspring. Prof. Lambs., 1735.

1794. Nov. 13th. BR. WILLIAM JOSEPH SHARROCK.
Prof. St. Greg., 1738.

1797. Nov. 17th. BR. ROBERT JAMES JOHNSON.
b. Lancashire, 1714. Prof. St. Lau., 1740.

1798. March 1st. BR. JOSEPH VALENTINE.
b. Samsbury, 1733. Prof. St. Ed., 1750.

1802. April 8th. BR. SYLVESTER QUINCE.
b Kent. Prof. St. Greg., 1778.

1819. Oct. 3rd. BR. PAUL WILSON.
Prof. St. Greg., 1781.

1820. April 12th. BR. FRANCIS HOLDERNESS.
b. Preston. Prof. St. Greg., 1777.

1822. April 15th. BR. FRANCIS AMBROSE PAPE.
b. Lambspring. Prof. Lambs., 1777.

1824. April 3rd. BR. FRANCIS TEGETMEYER.
b. Lambspring. Prof. Lambs., 1779.

1824. Aug. 14th. BR. JAMES MINNS.
b. Hants. Prof. St. Ed., 1773.

1824.   Dec. 26th.   Br. JOHN KNACKSTERDT.
Prof. Lambs., 1786.

1827.   Mar. 18th.   Br. JOSEPH LOUGHRY.
Prof. St. Greg.

1828.   July 4th.   Br. WALTER WM. SHARROCK.
b. Lancashire, 1756.   Prof. St. Greg.

1867.   Oct. 31st.   Br. CUTHBERT HEPTONSTALL.
b. 1804.   Prof. St. Lau., 1830.   d. in the Mauritius.

1876.   Feb. 4th.   Br. NICHOLAS FRANCIS REA.
b. 1805.   Prof. St. Greg., 1831.

1876.   Nov. 13th.   Br. PAUL CORDONNIER.
b. 1814.   Oblate of St. Ed.

1881.   July 24th.   Br. JOSEPH LAWSON.
b. 1816.   Prof. St. Lau., 1841.

CHRONOLOGICAL LIST

OF THE

DECEASED NUNS

OF THE

Abbey of Our Lady of Consolation, Cambray.

HE same spirit that guided the Benedictine Missionaries in England, and the success that attended the rapid development of the English Congregation, induced many ladies to whom God had given a vocation for a cloistered life, to desire the restoration of the Benedictine convents that had studded the land before the Reformation. The erection of a Convent in England was impossible, and hence emulating the zeal of the Benedictine monks, they were anxious to establish a community in a foreign clime, so that in more propitious times they might return to their native land, and continue the old Benedictine life. The result was the formation of the Abbey of Cambray,

the origin of which is narrated in Weldon's Chronological Notes recently published. Nine young English ladies were gathered together by the Benedictine fathers to form the nucleus of a community: a great granddaughter of Sir Thomas More with two of her cousins, a daughter of the Vavasours of Hazlewood, of the Morgans of Weston, Warwicks., of the Gascoignes of Barnelow, Yorks., of the Watsons of Parke, Beds., with two to serve as lay sisters, formed the little band. They crossed the sea and took possession of a ruined monastery near the town of Cambray, a desolate place, with four dilapidated walls standing without a roof, and requiring the expenditure of five hundred pounds, a large sum in those days, to render it habitable. It was a dependency of the Abbey of Femy, and was lent to them free of rent, on condition that they were to leave after six months' notice on reimbursement of their expenses over repairs. On Dec. 31st, 1623, the Archbishop of Cambray said the first mass in the new chapel, and assisted by the President General, F. Rudesind Barlow, solemnly clothed the nine postulants with the Benedictine habit. Three English nuns came from the Benedictine Convent at Brussels to superintend the rising community, and on January 1st, 1625, the nine novices made their solemn vows, and this is considered the foundation day of the Abbey of Our Lady of Consolation.

In 1638 they obtained the donation of the building, and the gift was ratified by a special Bull of Urban viii., another signal proof of his fostering care of the English Benedictines. The building was now their own: extensions and improvements were undertaken, gardens and houses were purchased to enlarge the enclosure, and in a short time the establishment was not unworthy of the name of an Abbey. There these English Dames secured the calm and peaceful life of the cloister: they rose at mid-night for the Divine office, and carried out the Holy Rule of St. Benedict as modified by the Constitutions delivered to them by the General Chapter. They were exiles in a foreign land with an exile's hope and longing to return, they watched with eager interest the workings of God's grace in their own country, and by their intercession and good works helped their brothers who were toiling and suffering in their beloved England: many a grace, many a conversion was due to the earnest silent prayers of the nuns before the altar at Cambray. In peace they lived their days and in peace they died, and as each one calmly passed away in her Convent cell she was laid in her more lasting cell within the Abbey walls: and as time rolled on there was a community in the convent and a community in the cemetery. Into their convent home was received a limited number of the daughters of English families for education: it was not a boarding-school or academy, with its trim line of demarkation where school ends and convent begins, but the girls lived in the enclosure as true "alumnæ," a part of the Benedictine family, growing up in traditions of piety, and combining the training of the heart with the culture of the mind. The staunch old Catholic families of England loved the old Benedictine tradition and the old Benedictine method, for on the roll of the alumnæ of Cambray occur again and again the names of the Widdringtons, the Plumptons, the Constables, the Stourtons, the Radcliffes, the Middletons, the Howards, the Meynells, the Jenisons, the Gascoignes whose daughters left the Cambray cloister to perpetuate Catholic life in England, to be examples of Catholic principle in the family homestead and in the midst of the Court, to be the mothers of sons and daughters whose fidelity to the old faith and the old piety has kept for us the old religion in the land.

For one hundred and seventy years the peaceful convent life continued in monastic observance, until the upheaving of the French Revolution shook the framework of society. The Republic was established, the war against order, society, and religion had commenced : nobles and ladies, priests and nuns, were hurried indiscriminately to the guillotine : religion was proscribed, the churches closed, the religious garb declared illegal, and to add to the difficulty of the situation the allied army was approaching Cambray. In anxious terror the sisters knew not what was to come, each day brought its sinister rumours, and each day increased the fervour of their prayers for the safety of their convent home: as a precaution the alumnæ were dismissed to their families. On the evening of Sunday, Oct. 13th, 1793, the twenty nuns who then formed the community, retired at 8.30 for the first sleep before the mid-night office, when a thundering at the enclosure door aroused the whole convent. The Lady Abbess, Mother Lucy Blyde, after a little delay opened the door, and four commissioners of the local authority at Cambray, roughly announced that they had come to take possession of the convent, and to declare them prisoners of the Republic. The trembling nuns assembled before the commissioners, who by the light of a lamp read a long official document, and forthwith went officially through the whole enclosure from room to room to affix their seal on all papers and documents, threatening the direst punishment if the least article of property were concealed. Aroused by the noise and confusion their chaplain, the Venerable F. Augustine Walker, hastened from his little house close by, to render assistance and inspire courage, but his entreaties and expostulations were sternly silenced. A long process was drawn up, to which was added the desire of the sisters to be allowed to remain prisoners in their own convent.

Placing a guard, they left the enclosure at eleven o'clock, and proceeded to the Chaplain's house, where after taking possession, and fixing their seal on all property, they arrested F. Walker and his socius F. James Higginson, and the nuns from their windows saw them at mid-night marched off to prison.

Five fearful days of terror and uncertainty followed, during which the gates were strictly guarded: no intimation of their fate was given, whether death, exile, or imprisonment, and day after day they expected to be summoned to hear their doom. On Friday, Oct. 18th, a troop of Hussars surrounded the Abbey, and a company entered the enclosure, headed by a brutal swaggering official of Cambray. In savage and insulting terms he ordered that all should clear out of the house within a quarter of an hour; he would allow no trunk or box, but each might take what clothes could be carried in a small bundle. He stamped about the room and, brandishing his stick, hurried the weeping and terrified nuns in their preparations for departure, so that some in their grief and stupor could not even gather together a change of clothes. In less than half-an-hour, with oaths and threats, they were hustled down to the entrance ignorant of what was to happen, and when the door was opened they saw a troop of Hussars with naked swords guarding some rude open country carts, into which, without ceremony, they were hurried. In tears and mute agony they thus were parted from their loved Abbey, their peaceful convent life was roughly crushed, they were torn from their quiet home, their beloved altar, their cells, their treasured garden and enclosure, their departed sisters sleeping tranquilly in the little cemetery, and huddled together in these rude carts they took their last look at their dear Cambray. Surrounded by soldiers, exposed to the gaze of the people, insulted by the jeers of the mob, with little rest and scant food, these ladies whose days had been spent in total seclusion behind the grille, were for five days jolted along the public road for about sixteen miles each day.

The Hussars were not told their destination, but each night received orders for the next day. Friday night was spent in a ruin at Bapaume, Saturday in the citadel at Peronne, Sunday in the prison at Ham, Monday, in an inn at Noyon, and on Tuesday they arrived at Compiègne, the place fixed upon for their incarceration. The building that served for a prison was an old convent of the Order of the Visitation in which the prisoners from Cambray, fifty-two in number, were lodged that night, the old infirmary of the convent being assigned to the twenty-one sisters who formed the community. The number of prisoners increased day by day: some died, some lost their reason, some were led to the guillotine, but the vacancies were speedily filled by fresh arrivals of prisoners in every rank of life. On November 25th the community had the sad consolation of welcoming the aged F. Augustine Walker, F. James Higginson, and the Hon. Thomas Roper, who had been sent from Cambray to share their lot: their delight was immediately mitigated by a prohibition of all communication, lest they might assist at any religious service.

The horrors of a French prison at the time of the Revolution are well known from published histories and memoirs, and from these we can imagine the trials and hardships that the daughters of St. Benedict endured, during the eighteen months of their imprisonment. Confined in one room with the windows nailed up, with one mattress and one blanket for each, without change of clothes, living on the gaol allowance of one pound of bread a day and a meal at the expense of the prisoners jointly, having their names called over twice each day to prevent escape, the sisters passed eighteen long months without mass, and not daring to say their prayers aloud. Sickness was inevitable: in January, 1794, fever broke out, and one by one the nuns were stretched helpless on their prison bed, and became so weak that the living were scarcely able to assist the dying. On January 13th, the venerable F. Walker at the age of 73 breathed his last after an illness of but 24 hours: on January 14th, died D.

Anselma Ann, aged 79; on the 21st, D. Teresa Walmesley, aged 55; on February 6th, S. Ann Pennington, a lay sister in her 60th year, and on April 3rd, D. Margaret Burgess, aged 72. Thus four of the little band, their lamps prepared, their hearts chastened by suffering, unconscious of the prison bed, calmly went forth to meet the Bridegroom as if from their dear cells at Cambray, and their bodies were laid in a prison grave far away from their sisters in their own little cemetery. Slowly the rest recovered; weak and emaciated they rose from their bed of sickness to meet greater privations and hardships. The rigour of the discipline and the harshness of the gaolers increased: they were subjected to a rigid examination by coarse officials, their persons searched by rude hands, their crosses, reliquaries, even their silver thimbles seized, their scanty pittance of food was reduced, and sometimes limited to coarse brown bread and water. In the middle of June sixteen Carmelite nuns were brought to the prison, and a short time after their arrival they received a letter of encouragement from an emigrant priest, their former confessor: this was a crime unpardonable, they were ordered to Paris, took an affectionate leave of the Cambray nuns by signs and gestures, and were all guillotined at Paris on July 16th, the Feast of Our Lady of Mount Carmel. Shortly after their departure the Mayor insisted on the Cambray nuns putting off the religious habit which was proscribed by law: they had no other clothes, and the Mayor gave them some old ones left by the Carmelites, precious but ominous relics; one of the sandals is still preserved at Stanbrook.

At the beginning of 1795 the rigour of the prison life relaxed: F. James Higginson and the Hon. Thos. Roper were allowed to go on parole into the town, and they were indefatigable in their efforts to relieve the necessities of the sisters. In April the Mayor advised them to petition for their passports to England, he forwarded the memorial to Paris, and it was granted. As an act of thanksgiving for their deliverance they managed to procure the sacred vessels and vestments, and had the consolation of hearing the first mass and only mass during the eighteen months. By the forethought and generosity of Edward Constable, Esq., of Burton, they were able to draw money from Hamburg to provide for the journey. Two carts were obtained and they left Compiègne on April 24th, 1795, were conveyed to Calais, crossed the sea to Dover, and arrived in London on Monday, May 4th, where they were charitably received in a house prepared for them by the Marchioness of Buckingham, who, although a Protestant, had compassion on these innocent victims of the Revolution. Destitute and penniless they came to London, but found warm and generous friends who were eager to supply their wants: Mr. Coghlan, the

Catholic bookseller of those days, Edward Constable,
Esq., of Burton, Francis Sheldon, Esq., of Wycliffe,
were the most active in the work of charity. As
soon as their arrival was notified, the President General,
F. Gregory Cowley, at once made arrangements for
their establishment, and Dr. Brewer secured for their
lodging and maintenance a ladies' school attached to the
mission at Woolton, Lancashire, where they arrived on
May 21st, 1795. They resumed conventual life and
monastic observance as far as practicable, and remained until the generosity of Francis Berkely, Esq.,
of Spetchley, offered them rent free his manor of
Salford, near Evesham, Worcestershire, and in 1807
they took possession of their new home. Their numbers
increased and their fortunes prospered, and before his
death they were able to purchase Stanbrook Hall,
Worcester, where they removed in 1838. Here they
have built a beautiful church, dedicated in 1871, and
commenced their new Abbey in 1878, one wing of
which is now completed, and thus Providence through
suffering and trial has firmly established the daughters
of St. Benedict in their native land, and the Abbey
of Stanbrook is a fit representative of the convents of
the old Benedictine times.

In 1652 the Congregation established another convent
in Paris under the title of Our Lady of Good Hope,
to which six nuns from Cambray were transferred to

assist at the foundation, but as this convent was under the jurisdiction of the Bishop, it did not form part of the English Congregation: it is now perpetuated at Colwich, Staffordshire.

In the following list D. signifies Dame, S. Sister, M. Mother. The first Christian name is the Baptismal, the second the Religious name, if only one it is the Religious name; where the Religious name is known to be the same as the baptismal it is repeated. The year of profession is in some cases approximate only as the Profession book was not preserved at the Revolution.

CHRONOLOGICAL LIST

OF THE

DECEASED NUNS

OF THE

Abbey of Our Lady of Consolation,

Cambray.

1631. April 1st.

JANE MARTHA MARTIN, Lay S.
b. 1588. Prof., 1625. One of the first nine professed.

1631. Sep. 22nd. D. FRANCES EBBA BROWN.

b. 1609, at Kiddrington, Oxfordshire. Prof., 1629.

1633. Aug. 17th. D. HELEN GERTRUDE MORE.

b. 1603. Daughter of Sir Thomas More. Prof 1625
One of the first nine professed.

1635. Feb. 24th. S. ELIZABETH BARBARA SMITH, NOVICE.

d. 1617. Clothed, 1634. Prof. on her death bed.

1637. Aug. 16th. D. MARGARET MARGARET
GASCOIQNE.

b. 1608, at Barnbow, Yorkshire. Prof., 1631.

1640. April 18th. D. ANNE BENEDICTA MORGAN.

b. 1604, at Weston, Warwicks. Prof., 1625. One of the
first nine professed.

1640. May 7th. M. MARY FRANCES GAWEN.

b. 1576. Prof. at Brussels, 1602. Was Abbess, 1625-9.

1640. June 13th. D. ANNE SCHOLASTICA
TIMPERLEY.

b. 1605, at Timperley, Suffolk. Prof., 1626.

1640. Oct. 24th. D. MARY LUCY CAPE.

1641. Jan. 25th. D. MARY FRANCES LUCY.

b. 1621. Prof., 1640.

1641. Dec. 6th. S. ISETTE ANGELA MULLINS,
Lay S.

b. 1616. Prof., 1640.

1645. May 14th. S. MARGARET MARGARET
KENYON, LAY S.

b. 1604-10. Prof., 1632.

1645. Dec. 21st. D. PUDENTIANA DEACONS.

b. 1581. Prof., 1610, at Brussels.

1648. Mar. 6th. S. ELIZABETH BENEDICTA ROPER,
NOVICE.

b. 1631. Clothed, 1647. Prof., on her death bed.

1650. April 18th. D. CATHERINE SHELDON.

b. 1618, at Beoly, Warwicks. Prof., 1642.

1650. Nov. 1st.. D. LUCY MAGDALEN CARY.

b. 1619. Daughter of Viscount Falkland. Prof., 1640.

1651.   Mar. 13th.   D. CECILY CECILY HALL.
b. 1627, at High Meadows, Gloucestershire.   Prof., 1650.

1652.   Oct. 7th.   S. ELIZABETH GERTRUDE HODSON,
Lay S.
b. 1626.   Prof., 1649.   Sent to found the Convent at Paris in 1652, and d. in Paris.

1654.   Aug. 8th.   S.   ELIZABETH GERTRUDE SHAFTOE.
b. 1632.   Prof., 1653.

1655.   Mar 4th.   D. GRACE AGNES MORE.
b. 1594.   Prof., 1625.   One of the first nine professed.

16—   ——— S. TERESA L'ESTRANGE.

1656.   Feb. 18th.   D. MARGARET VIVIANA YAXLEY.
b. 1603.   Prof. at Brussels, 1620.

1657.   Nov. 10th.   S. HELEN HELEN KENYON,
LAY S.
b. 1604.   Prof., 1632.

1659.   Oct. 10th.   S. MARY BENEDICTA BOULT,
LAY S.
b. 1606.   Prof., 1633.

1660.   Jan. 1st.   D. ELIZABETH ELIZABETH BRENT.
b. 1607, at Sloake, Oxfordshire.   Prof., 1630.   Sent to found the Convent in Paris 1652, and d. in Paris.

1660.   April 1st.   D. GERTRUDE SWINBURNE.

1660.   June 10th.   D. FRANCES MARY WATSON.
b. 1608, at Parke, Beds. Prof. 1625.   One of the first nine professed.

1661.   Jan. 5th.   S. ANNE ANNE TAVERN, LAY S.
b. 1603.   Prof., 1640.

1662.   June 4th.   S. MARY AGNES ERRINGTON.
b. 1642.   Prof., 1661.

1662.   Nov. 5th.   D. MARGARET WINEFRID COLTON.
b. 1607, at Bedhampton, Hants.   Prof., 1625.

1662.   Nov. 9th.   D. ANN ANN MORE.
b. 1600.   Prof., 1625.   One of the first nine professed.

1662.   Nov. 9th.   D. ANNE MAGDALEN ENVE.
b. 1610, at Malton, Yorks.   Daughter of Baron Enve.
Prof., 1625.

1663.   April 18th.   D. ANTHOES MILDRED
LATCHMORE.
b. 1595.   Prof., 1627.

1665.   Feb. 2nd.   S. REBECCA FLAVIA BROWN,
Lay S.
b. 1604.   Prof., 1626.

1666.   Nov. 25th.   D. PLACIDA YAXLEY.

1667.   Mar. 4th.   S. MARY MARY HOSKINS, LAY S.
b. 1603.   Prof., 1625.   One of the first nine professed.

1668.   Aug. 6th.   S. MARY ETHELDREDA
STAPLETON.
b. 1625, at Carlton, Yorks.   Prof., 1650.

1670.   Feb. 6th.   S. MARY HILDA PERCY, LAY S.
b. 1596, of the family of the last Earl of Derwentwater.   Prof., 1631.

1671.   Mar. 23rd.   D. ELINOR TERESA TIMPERLEY.
b. 1606, at Timperley, Suffolk.   Prof., 1630.

1671.   April 26th.   D. ANNE CLEMENTINA CARY.
b. 1615.   Daughter of Viscount Falkland.   Prof., 1640.
Sent to found the Convent at Paris, and d. in Paris.

1675.   Jan. 26th.   D. JOAN GERTRUDE WRISDEN.
b. 1609.   Prof., 1635.

1676.   Jan. 26th.   D. ANNE MECHTILDIS FRERE.
b. 1612.   Prof., 1628.

1676.   May 21st.   M. CATHERINE CATHERINE
GASCOIGNE.

b. 1600 ,at Barnbow, Yorks.   Prof., 1625.   One of the
first nine professed.   Was Abbess, 1629-41, and
1645-73.

1676.   Aug. 18th.   D. CATHERINE CATHERINE
VAVASOUR.

b. 1610, at Hazlewood, Yorksh.   Prof. 1628.

1678.   Jan. 22nd.   S. ISABELLA TERESA GURNEY.
LAY S.
b. 1615.   Prof., 1641.

1680.   Jan. 20th.   D. WINEFRID CONSTABLE.

1680.   Aug. 14th.   D. MARGARET SMITH.
b. 1636.

1681.   Aug. 11th.   D. CLARE BRIDGET RADCLIFFE.
b. Divulston, Northumb.

1682.   July 3rd.   S. JOAN CATHERINE TREVELYAN.
LAY S.
b. 1623, in Cornwall.   Prof., 1656.

1682.   Nov. 17th.   D. ELIZABETH AUGUSTINA
CARY.
b. 1617.   Daughter of Viscount Falkland.   Prof., 1640.

1683. April 11th. S. Jane Jane Celler, Lay S.
b. 1603. Prof. 1630.

1684. Jan. 26th. D. Barbara Barbara Constable.
b. 1627, at Everingham, Yorks. Prof. 1640.

1684. May 7th. S. Elizabeth Lusher, Lay S.
b. 1629. Prof., 1651.

1685. Aug. 25th. D. Margaret Lucy Vavasour.
b. 1612, at Hazlewood, Yorks. Prof., 1625. One of the first nine professed.

1685. Sep. 21st. D. Jane Clare Cooke.
b. 1611. Prof., 1627.

1686. Nov. 19th. D. Mary Benedicta Conquest.
b. 1659. Prof., 1677.

1687. July 28th. S. Mary Frances Lusher, Lay S.
b. 1624. Prof., 1644.

1688, May 5th. D. Elinor Helen Brent.
b. 1611, at Sloake, Oxfordsh. Prof., 1635.

1688. Aug. 5th. D. Anne Benedicta Middleton.
b. 1631, at Stockeld, Yorks. Prof., 1650.

1689. Feb. 14th. D. Mary Euphrasia Tempest.
b. 1622, at Broughton, Yorks. Prof., 1640.

1689. June 29th. S. Dorothy Alexia Fenwick.
b. Northumberland.

1689. Sep. 28th. D. Mary Barbara Breton.
b. 1636.

1689. Oct. 30th. D. TOMLA URSULA RADCLIFFE.
b. 1683, at Divulston, Northumberland. Sister of the
Earl of Derwentwater. Prof., 1655.

1690. Mar. 12th. S. BRIDGET LUSHER, LAY S.
b. 1633. Prof. 1653.

1690. Mar. 17th. D. CATHERINE MAURA HALL.
b. 1634. Prof., 1651. Was Abbess, 1673-77.

1690. May 11th. D. ANN SCHOLASTICA HODSON.
b. 1621. Prof., 1642. Sent to Paris to found the convent
in 1652, and d. in Paris.

1690. May. 17th. D. JUSTINA GASCOIGNE.
b. 1623, at Barnbow, Yorksh. Prof., 1639. Sent to
Paris to found the convent in 1652. Was Prioress
there 1665-90, and d. in Paris.

1691. June 22nd. D. ELIZABETH MARY LEGGE.
b. 1643. Niece to Lord Dartmouth. Prof. 1669.

1692. Feb. 1st. D. ANNE ANNE GILL.
b. 1640. Prof., 1668.

1692. Oct. 12th. D BRIDGET BRIDGET MORE.
b. 1609. Daughter of grandson of Sir Thomas More
Sent to Paris in 1652, to found the convent. Was
Prioress there, 1652-65, and d. in Paris.

1693. Sep. 22nd. D. MARY MARY CARY.
b. 1621. Daughter of Viscount Falkland. Prof., 1640.

16— Feb 6th. S. ANNE JOSEPHA SOUTNEZ.

16— May 22nd. D. TERESA MANSFIELD.

16— Dec. 10th. D. TERESA CONQUEST.

1694. Jan. 29th. M. MARY MARINA APPLETON.
b. 1624, in Essex. Prof., 1646. Was Abbess, 1681-94.

1697. July 4th. D. BRIDGET TERESA MEYNELL.
b. 1672, at Kilvington, Yorks. Prof., 1689.

1700. May 5th. D. CATHERINE CATHERINE
KENNET.
b. 1651, at Coxhow-in-Bishoprick. Prof., 1683.

1700. Sep. 14th. M. CATHERINE CHRISTINA
BRENT.
b. 1601, at Sloake, Oxfordsh. Prof., 1630. Was
Abbess, 1641-45 and 1677-81.

1700. Dec. 27th. D. PLACIDA SHELDON.

1701. Feb. 1st. S. ANNE ANNE BATEMANSON,
Lay S.
b. 1648. Prof., 1680.

1701. Mar. 12th. D. MARY EUGENIA HOUGHTON.
b. 1621, at Parke Hall, Lancas. Prof., 1641.

1705. Dec. 4th. D. SUSANNA SUSANNA PHILIPS.
b. 1648, at Stoke Charity. Prof., 1673.

1707. Nov. 11th. S. ELIZABETH ELIZABETH
COMPLIN, Lay S.
Prof., 1778.

1707. Feb. 10th. S. ELIZABETH BENEDICTA
TAYLOR, Lay S.
b. 1664. Prof., 1693.

1708. Sep. 21st. D. FRANCES FRANCES
GASCOIGNE.
b. 1637, at Barnbow, Yorks. Prof., 1687.

1713. April 20th. D. MARY ANNA AYVAY.
b. 1654. Prof., 1672.

1715. Dec. 8th. S. MARY JOSEPHA DODD, Lay S.
b. 1652.

1719. Dec. 12th. D. MARY MAGDALEN MOORE.
b. 1658, at Fawley, Berks. Prof., 1675.

1720. Jan. 16th. S. FRANCES PLACIDA PULLEYNE.
b. 1653. Prof., 1677.

1720. Feb. 6th. D. MARGARET MAURA
HARRINGTON.
b. 1684, at Egbourth. Prof., 1701.

1720. Aug. 7th. D. ELIZABETH MARY JOSEPHA
O'MORE.
b. 1674. Prof., 1708.

.1721. April 9th. M. CECILY CECILY HUSSEY.
b. 1652, at Marnhull, Dorset. Prof., 1672. Was
Abbess, 1694-97 and 1705-10.

1722. Aug. 30th. S. ELIZABETH SCHOLASTICA
RYDER.
b. 1669. Prof., 1700.

1723. Oct. 23rd. D. ELIZABETH AGNES KENNET.
b. 1685, at Coxhow-in-Bishoprick. Prof., 1702.

1725. July 3rd. D. DOROTHY BENEDICTA
ENGLEFIELD.
b. 1676, at White Knights, Berks. Prof., 1695.

1726. Jan. 6th. M. DOROTHY SCHOLASTICA
HOUGHTON.
b. 1656, at Parke Hall, Lancas. Prof., 1674. Was
Abbess, 1697-1701 and 1710-13.

1726. Aug. 17th. D. DOROTHY MORE.

1726 Sep. 20th. D. CATHERINE AGATHA FAZAKERLEY.

b. 1658. Prof., 1683.

1726. Oct. 26th. S. MARY JOSEPHA DWERIHOUSE. Lay S.

b. 1701. Prof., 1720.

1727. Feb. 18th. S. MARY MARY GAUDELIER, Lay S.

b. 1671. Prof., 1693. Out-sister for six years.

1732. July 28th. D. MARY EVES.

1733. Feb. 18th. D. DOROTHY AGNES WIDDRINGTON.

b. 1666, at Widdrington Castle, Northumb. Prof., 1687.

1733. Feb. 21st. D. ISABELLA ISABELLA KENNET.
b. 1654, at Coxhow-in-Bishoprick. Prof., 1683.

1733. April 10th. D. MARGARET GERTRUDE CHILTON.

b. 1671. Prof., 1694.

17— Mar. 8th. D. MICHELLE ETHELDREDA DELATTRE.

Prof., 1697.

1734. Nov. 10th. S. ANNE ASTON, Lay S.
b. 1688. Prof., 1716.

1734. Dec. 4th. D. FRANCES MARY WINEFRID HOWET.

b. 1685. Prof., 1702.

1737. Sep. 7th. S. MARTHA SMITH.

1739. Mar. 10th. D. CATHERINE TERESA CHILTON.
b. 1672. Prof., 1696.

17—   April 20th.   D. Margaret Swinburne.
Was Abbess, 1701-5 and 1713-41.

1741.   Aug. 4th.   D. Benedicta Fairclough.

17—   May 18th.   D. Mary Gertrude Mansfield.
b. 1682.   Prof., 1704.

1744.   April 4th.   D. Scholastica Addison.

1744.   Dec. 9th.   S. Elizabeth Elizabeth Fairclough, Lay S.
b. 1698.   Prof., 1720.

1746.   Jan. 17th.   D. Mary Paula Gascoigne.
b. 1690, at Parlington, Yorksh.   Prof., 1714.

1747.   April 5th.   D. Monica Augustina Jenison.
b. 1703, at Walworth-in-Bishoprick.   Prof., 1723.

1749.   Jan. 31st.   S. Mary Magdalen Tolderwine, Lay S.
b. 1675.   Prof., 1701.

1749.   July 22nd.   S. Amanda Barrister.

1750.   Oct. 12th.   S. Gertrude Belerby.

17—   S. Ellen Teresa Naylor, Out Sister.
b. 1677.   Received, 1700.   Date of death uncertain.

1753.   Jan. 29th.   S. Margaret Lee.

1753.   Nov. 27th.   S. Alathea Clifton.

1754.   Mar. 15th.   D. Anne Benedicta Warwick.
b. 1678, at Warwick, Cumberland.   Prof., 1711.

1755.   Jan. 21st.   S. Anne Moody, Lay S.

1758.   April 23rd.   D. Anne Josepha Bate.

1758. April 24th. D. Bridget Bridget Coffin.
b. 1678. Prof., 1704.

1758. Sep. 14th. D. Anne Teresa Young.

1760. Jan. 28th. D. Dorothy Constance
Langdale.
b. 1677. Prof., 1695.

1760. April 29th. S. Olivia Darell, Novice.

1762. May 24th. D. Alathea Mary Teresa
Swinburne.
b. 1688, at Capheaton. Prof., 1707.

1763. April 22nd. D. Anne Benedicta Reeves.

1763. May 7th. S. Agnes Batchell, Lay S.

1764. Feb. 4th. D. Mary Benedicta Meynell.
b. 1677, at Kilvington, Yorksh. Prof., 1695.

1768. April 28th. D. Bernarda Plompton.
b. 1700, at Plompton. Prof., 1717.

1770. April 11th. S. Catherine Palliser.

1770. Sep. 16th. D. Scholastica Burgess.

1770. Sep. 29th. D. Mary Coffin.

1772. Feb. 12th. S. Josepha Tookey, Lay S.

1773. Oct. 20th. S. Bathildis Du Pery.
Prof., 1725.

1774. Jan. 25th. M. Cath. Josepha Gascoigne.
b. 1699, at Parlington, Yorksh. Prof., 1717. Abbess,
1741-73.

1774. Oct. 27th. S. Winefrid Ball.

1774. Dec. 12th. S. Alexia Elerby, Lay S.

1775. Jan. 19th. D. Teresa Wilks.
b. 1746. Prof., 1763.

1775. Aug. 24th. D. Augustina Widdrington.
b. 1705. Prof., 1726.

1776. July 6th. D. Mary Anne Rigby.
b. 1720. Prof., 1745.

1776. Sep. 4th. S. Helen Placida Wilson.

1778. Aug. 20th. D. Mary Mooney.

1779. Dec. 20th. D. Angela Plompton.
b. 1696, at Plompton. Prof., 1713.

1783. Nov. 21st. S. Benedicta Walker.

1786. July 6th. D. Placida Pullen.

1788. Nov. 3rd. D. Josepha Carrington.

1789. Mar. 1st. M. Agnes Ingleby.
b. 1708. Prof., 1727. Was Abbess, 1773-89.

1792. Aug. 2nd. D. Catherine Throckmorton.
b. 1695. An Augustinian residing at Cambray.

1792. Aug. 3rd. M. Christina Hooke.
b. 1715. Prof., 1734. Was Abbess, 1789-92.

1792. Oct. 30th. M. Clare Knight.
b. 1740. Was Abbess, 1792.

1794. Jan. 14th. D. Mary Anselma Ann.
b. 1715. Died in prison at Compiègne.

1794. Jan. 21st. D. Teresa Teresa Walmesley.
b. 1739. Died in prison at Compiègne.

1794.   Feb. 6th.   S. Anna Anne Pennington.
Lay S.
b. 1734.   Died in prison at Compiègne.

1794.   April 3rd.   D. Margaret Burgess.
b. 1721.   Died in prison at Compiègne.

1795.- 1807.   D. Elizabeth Haggerstone.
b. 1725.   Imprisoned at Compiègne.   Date of death uncertain.

1796.   July 15th.   S. Jane Josepha Miller.
Lay S.
b. 1766.   Prof., 1796.   Imprisoned at Compiègne.   d. at Woolton.

1799.   June 17th.   D. Jane Alexander.
b. 1715.   Imprisoned at Compiègne.   d. at Woolton.

1802.   June 17th.   S. Magdalen Kimberly, Lay S.
b. 1745.   Prof., 1767.   Imprisoned at Compiègne.   d. at Woolton.

1807.   Jan. 31st.   S. Louisa Mary Anne Le Feure, Lay S.
b. 1735.   Prof., 1757.   Imprisoned at Compiègne.   d. at Woolton.

1808.   July 14th.   D. Eliz. Frances Sheldon.
b. 1720.   Prof., 1740.   Imprisoned at Compiègne.   d. at Salford.

1809.   June 12th.   D. Anne Mary Teresa Shepherd.
b. 1762.   Imprisoned at Compiègne.   Was Abbess, 1802-6.

1811.   June 6th.   D. Louisa Hagan.
b. 1740.   Prof., 1762.   Imprisoned at Compiègne.

1812. Jan. 29th. S. Mary Anne Francis Helme, Lay S.

Prof., 1807.

1813. Mar. 2nd. D. Elizabeth Anne Josepha Knight.

b. 1742. Prof., 1765. Imprisoned at Compiègne.

1816. Aug. 12th. M. Mary Lucy Blyde.

b. 1729. Was Abbess, 1792-1802. Imprisoned at Compiègne.

1818. Feb. 12th. D. Helen Augustina Shepherd.

b. 1764. Imprisoned at Compiègne. Was Abbess, 1814-18.

1820. Sep. 4th. D. Elizabeth Anne Teresa Partington.

b. 1744. Imprisoned at Compiègne.

1825. Jan. 2nd. S. Martha Martha Fryar, Lay S.

b. 1761. Imprisoned at Compiègne.

1826. Dec. 28th. D. Mary Benedicta Partington.

b. 1751. Imprisoned at Compiègne.

1830. Feb. 13th. S. Anne Scholastica Caton, Lay S.

b. 1749. Imprisoned at Compiègne.

1830. April 14th. M. Christina Chare.

b. 1778. Prof., 1801. Was Abbess, 1822-30.

1830. June 11th. D. Agnes Robinson.

b. 1761. Imprisoned at Compiègne. Was Abbess, 1806-14, 1818-22.

1831.   Dec. 21st.   S. EDITH BREEN, Novice.

1832.   June 30th.   S. AUGUSTINA SPENCER.
b. 1813.   Prof., 1830.

1833.   Nov. 12th.   S. ELIZABETH MONICA
                        CROOKALL. Lay S.
b. 1777.   Prof., 1799.

1835. ——— D. MARG. BERNARDA BARNEWALL.
b. 1756.   Imprisoned at Compiègne.   Obtained per-
mission to join the Trappistines and d. at Stapehill.

1837.   May 20th.   S. AUGUSTINA SINNOT. Novice.
Prof., 1837, on her death bed.

1839.   Sep. 27th.   S. ANNE BENEDICTA FOLEY,
                        Lay S.
b. 1803.   Prof., 1825.   d. at Stanbrook.

1843.   Oct. 22nd.   D. APOLLONIA PLACIDA LE
                        CLERC.
b. 1801.   Prof., 1820.

1846.   Nov. 17th.   M. ANNE GERTRUDE WESTHEAD.
b. 1781.   Prof., 1806.   Was Abbess, 1830-46.   Brought
the community to Stanbrook.

1848.   May 8th.   S. ANNE BENEDICTA CHAPMAN.
b. 1820.   Prof., 1845.

1848.   Aug. 25th.   D. BRIDGET EUPHRASIA
                        WEETMAN.
b. 1806.   Prof., 1835.

1848,   Sep. 26th.   D. LETITIA MAURA RAYMENT
                        (née Houghton)
b. 1804.   Prof., 1835.

1851. Jan. 7th. M. Teresa Clare Crilly.
b. 1772. Prof., 1799.

1851. Jan. 16th. M. Jane Juliana Horsman.
b. 1769. Prof., 1800.

1853. Mar. 29th. S. Mary Felicitas Daniel,
Lay S.
b. 1818. Prof., 1842.

1855. Sep. 25th. Mary Cath. Crookall, Lay S.
b. 1781. Prof., 1816.

1855. Oct. 26th. D. Anne Edith Saul.
b. 1814. Prof., 1840.

1857. Feb. 23rd. S. Sarah Aloysia Bridge,
Lay S.
b. 1783. Prof., 1816.

1865. Jan. 23rd. D. Teresa Frances Sayles.
b. 1796. Prof., 1818.

1871. July 28th. D. Eliz. Teresa Sumner.
b. 1809. Prof., 1830.

1874. June 6th. D. Mary Winefrid Morrall.
b. 1809. Prof., 1834.

1875. Mar. 16th. M. Esther Scholastica
Gregson.
b. 1806. Prof., 1826. Was Abbess, 1846-62, 1870-72.

1876. July 27th. M. Isabella Josepha Spencer.
b. 1801. Prof., 1818.

1877. Aug. 12th. D. Cecily Edith Palmer.
b. 1826. Prof., 1864

1878.   Mar. 28th.   M. CONSTANCE MAGDALEN LE CLERC.

Prof., 1816. Went in 1847 to found the Convent at Subiaco, Paramatta, Sydney, N.S. Wales.   d. at Sydney.

1878.   Oct. 14th. S. MARY MARTHA CHEW, Lay S.
b. 1810.   Prof., 1833.

1878.   Dec. 6th.   D. MARY ANNE MONICA MORDLE.

b. 1813.   Prof., 1834.

1878.   Dec. 20th.   S. HELEN MARY AGNES LUCY, Lay S.

b. 1806.   Prof., 1826.

1880.   Nov. 11th.   S. MARINA ANASTASIA RICHARDSON (née BUCKLAND). Out-sister.

b. 1821.   Received, 1874.

1882.   July 17th.   D. WINEFRID EVANGELISTA WEETMAN.

b. 1806.   Prof., 1840.

1883 – Nov 16th – D. Marcella Plowden aged 84 – rel 7
1885 – Jan 15th – D. M. Ignatia Bower æt 76 . rel 49
1886 – April 30th – D. M. Theresa Styles æt 84 – rel 61
1887 – Dec 16th – S. M. Margaret Swarbrick æt 70 rel 48
          Lay S.

1888 – Feb. 25 – D. M. Ursula Winckfield æt 65 – rel 46
  „   Sept 5 – S. M. Anne McArdle æt 87 – rel 66 –
          Lay S.
1892 – Jan 13 – D. M. Magdalene Kirk æt 65 – rel 48
  „   May 15. S. M. Catharine Crosser æt 57 – rel 28
          Lay S.

'92 . Dec 29 _ D. M. Agnes St Leger Clarke _ cet 45. rel 22
'93 _ Ap 29 _ M. M. Justina Day cet 77 _ rel 55
. _ Aug 6 _ M. M. Augustine Tidmarsh cet 77 _ rel 54
'95 _ June 23 _ S. M. Veronica Mozan cet 75 _ rel 47
'97 _ April 1 _ D. M. Placid Duggan _ cet 75 _ rel 53
. _ Oct 19 _ R. R. D. D. Gertrude D' Aurillac Dubois Albers _
,00 _ Jan 18 _ S. Elizabeth Talbot cet 56. rel 33. Abt 26
                                  _ cet 56 _ rel 33 _

CALENDAR

OF THE

DECEASED RELIGIOUS

OF THE

ENGLISH CONGREGATION

OF THE

Order of Saint Benedict.

M.—signifies monastery of profession.   A.—age at death.
R.—years in religion.   P.—years of priesthood.
G.—the Monastery of St. Gregory.   L.—the Monastery of St. Laurence.
E.—the Monastery of St. Edmund.   A.D.—the Abbey of SS. Adrian and Denis.
B.—the Monastery of St. Benedict at St. Malo.
Cass.—professed in the Cassinese Congregation.   Sp.—the Spanish Congregation.
Miss.—professed on the mission.   B.V.M.—the Abbey of our Lady of Consolation.
The offices affixed are those held at death.

January.

—‹ 1 ›—

		M.	A.	R.	P.
1660.					

Year	Name	M.	A.	R.	P.
	Elizabeth Brent	B.V.M.	52	37	
1723.	D. Benedict Gibbon	A.D.	51		
1754.	D. Cuthbert Farnworth	L.	74	54	
1869.	D. Maurus Cooper	L.	70	53	46

January.

—‹2›—

		M.	A.	R.	P.
1704.	D. PLACID SCUDAMORE	A.D.		10	
1672.	D. AUGUSTINE HUNGATE	Sp.	88		
1742.	D. WILFRID HELME	E.		44	
1825.	LAY S. MARTHA FRYAR	B.V.M.	64		

1890. D. Ephrem Guy — — — — — g. 66-48-40

—‹3›—

		M.	A.	R.	P.
1665.	D. BEDE WITHAM	G.		17	
1669.	D. ADRIAN BARNARD	A.D.		10	
1745.	D. RICHARD ISHERWOOD	A.D.		61	

—‹4›—

		M.	A.	R.	P.
1735.	D. VINCENT PALIN	L.		19	
1767.	D. BERNARD PRICE	L.		31	
1768.	D. AUGUSTINE SULYARD	L.		61	
1842.	D. RALPH RADCLIFFE	G.	70	46	40

—‹5›—

		M.	A.	R.	P.
1661.	LAY S. ANNE TAVERN	B.V.M.	58	21	
1684.	D. THOMAS STOURTON	G.		40	
1778.	D. GREGORY MACKAY	G.		55	
1811.	D. ADRIAN GURNAL	A.D.	69	49	44

—‹6›—

		M.	A.	R.	P.
1654.	D. JOHN OWEN	Sp.			
1699.	D. AMBROSE LINDLEY	A.D.		30	
1726.	D. SCHOLASTICA HOUGHTON	B.V.M.	70	52	
1730.	D. BENEDICT COMBERLEDGE	A.D.		28	
1787.	D. DUNSTAN KNIGHT	A.D.	73	56	

January.

—‹ 7 ›—

M. A. R. P.

		M.	A.	R.	P.
1851.	D. CLARE CRILLY	B.V.M.	79	52	
1883.	D. BENEDICT LYNASS	L.	60	40	33

1896. D. Placid Sinnott

—‹ 8 ›—

1626.	BR. JOHN TOUDELLE	L.	2		
1636.	D. ANSELM WILLIAMS	L.	15		
1636.	BR. LEANDER NEVILLE	L.	9		
1655.	D GEO. DE S. ILDEPHONSO	G.	34		
1738.	D. JOSEPH KENNEDY	E.	77	47	44
1759.	D. MAURUS RIGMAIDEN	L.	87	67	
1815.	D. AUGUSTINE CALDWELL	G.	79	59	
1859.	D. GREGORY HOLDEN	G.	68	51	43

1906 – D. Benedict Mackey — G. 60. 41. 34

—‹ 9 ›—

| 1794. | D. BENEDICT CAWSER | E. | 31 | | |

—‹ 10 ›—

| 1694. | D. JOSEPH FRERE | G. | 96 | 75 | |
| 1800. | D. JOSEPH CROOK | A.D. | 46 | 30 | |

1906. D. Augustine Bury — G. 77. 61. 54

—‹ 11 ›—

1701.	D. BRUNO JENNINGS	G.	33		
1740.	D. WILLIAM CHAMPNEY	L.	30		
1805.	D. BONIFACE TAYLOR	A.D.	30	14	

1896. Rt. Benedict White Laghlike — G. 78. 57
1895. D. Maurus Wilson — G. 52. 32. 25

—‹ 12 ›—

1651.	D. ANTHONY BATT	L.	37	47	
1674.	D. MELLITUS HESKETH	L.	30	11	
1814.	D. DUNSTAN GARSTANG	E.	78	62	

1913 – 8th Jan. Dom Jarom Pearson (L) 69 – 50 –

January.

—< 13 >—

M. A. R. P.

1640.	D. HENRY STILES	Cass.
1774.	D. AUGUSTINE SOUTHCOT	G. 67
1794.	D. AUGUSTINE WALKER, Pres. Gen.	E. 74 52
1876.	D. ATHANASIUS ALLANSON, Prov. of York.	L. 71 56 48

1907 D. aloysius Wilkinson — *& - 7 0 - 50 - 43*

—< 14 >—

1633.	BR. CELESTINE DE LANDRES	L. 4
1731.	D. FELIX TASBURG	E. 50
1794.	D. ANSELMA ANN	B.V.M. 79

—< 15 >—

1692.	D. WILLIBRORD WILSON	A.D. 9
1824.	D. EDWARD FISHER	L. 76 59 52
1837.	D. BEDE RIGBY	A.D. 63 40
1870.	D. ALBAN CALDWELL	L. 66 45 40

1884. D. Cuthbert Smith — *G. 6 9 - 44 - 40*

—< 16 >—

1660.	D. BONIFACE CHANDLER	L. 46
1712.	D. JAMES FERREYRA	L. 37
1720.	S. PLACIDA PULLEYNE	B.V.M. 67 43
1724.	D. JAMES MATHER	L. 57
1795.	D. PLACID NAYLOR	L. 53
1851.	M. JULIANA HORSMAN	B.V.M. 82 51

—< 17 >—

| 1665. | D. ROBERT SHERWOOD | G. 77 53 |
| 1746. | D. PAULA GASCOIGNE | B.V.M. 56 32 |

1905. D. Benedict Snow — *& - 66 - 49 - 40*

January.

—‹ 18 ›—

		M.	A.	R.	P.
1665.	D. ROBERT CORHAM	G.	23		
1714.	LAY BR. FRANCIS WEST	L.	51		
1715.	D. ALBAN BERRIMAN	E.	55		
1735.	D. BARTHOLOMEW HAVERS	G.	7		
1780.	D. BENEDICT STEARE	G.	61		
1869.	D. CUTHBERT SPAIN	G.	72	56	50

—‹ 19 ›—

1681.	D. FAUSTUS SADLER	L.	77	60	
1707.	D. JAMES NELSON	E.	69	48	
1775.	D. TERESA WILKS	B.V.M.	29	12	

—‹ 20 ›—

1605.	D. AUSTIN DE S. FACUNDO	Sp.			
1680.	D. WINEFRID CONSTABLE	B.V.M.			
1799.	D. ANSELM BRADSHAW	A.D.	57	40	

—‹ 21 ›—

1633.	D. MAURUS SMITH	G.	9		
1665.	D. WILLIAM WALGRAVE	G.	77	16	
1755.	LAY S. ANNE MOODY	B.V.M.			
1794.	D. TERESA WALMESLEY	B.V.M.	55		

1905. D fregory Brown — *L. 52 33 25*

—‹ 22 ›—

1675.	D. PETER SALVIN	G.	70	44	
1689.	LAY S. TERESA GURNEY	B.V.M.	63	37	
1723.	BR. JOHN OSLAND	A.D.	22		

—‹ 23 ›—

| 1865. | D. TERESA FRANS. SAYLES | B.V.M. | 69 | 47 | |

January.

—‹24›—

		M.	A.	R.	P.
1629.	D. BEDE HELME	Sp			
1648.	D. FRANCIS GICOW	B.	63	32	

—‹25›—

		M.	A.	R.	P.
1641.	D. FRANCES LUCY	B.V.M.	20	1	
1676.	D. BENEDICT BRYCHAN	G.	68	52	
1695.	D. GREGORY HESKETH	L.		43	
1774.	M. JOSEPHA GASCOIGNE	B.V.M.	75	57	
1872.	BR. MAURUS McKENNA	G.	38	17	

—‹26›—

		M.	A.	R.	P.
1675.	D. GERTRUDE WRISDEN	B.V.M.	66	40	
1676.	D. MECHTILDIS FRERE	B.V.M.	64	48	
1724.	D. PLACID NELSON	L.		46	
1684.	D. BARBARA CONSTABLE	B.V.M.	57	44	
1725.	D. ANTHONY ORD	G.		41	
	Pr. of St. Greg.				

—‹27›—

		M.	A.	R.	P.
1653.	D. THOMAS WOODHOPE	G.		32	
1711.	D. BERNARD GREGSON	L.	60	44	
	Prov. of Cant.				
1747.	D. WILLIAM HEWLETT	E.		49	
1793.	D. JOHN FISHER	L.	83	68	
1829.	BR. ALBAN BANKS	G.	52	14	

—‹28›—

		M.	A.	R.	P.
1615.	D. ROBERT EDMUNDS	Miss.			
1760.	D. CONSTANCE LANGDALE	B.V.M.	83	65	

January.

—< 29 >—

		M.	A.	R.	P.
1668.	D. MICHAEL CAPE Pr. of St. Ed.	L.	58	41	35
1694.	M. MARINA APPLETON Abbess.	B.V.M.	70	48	
1702.	D. CHARLES SUMPNER	G.	57	31	
1733.	LAY BR. PETER DEVAL	G.			
1753.	S. MARGARET LEE	B.V.M.			
1796.	D. BENEDICT GARNER	A.D.	60	39	
1812.	LAY S. FRANCES HELME	B.V.M.		5	
1814.	D. MAURUS SHAW	E.		58	
1845.	D. OSWALD ORRELL	L.	46	27	22
1874.	D. BEDE SMITH	L.	73	56	49

—< 30 >—

1668.	D. FRANCIS CAPE	G.	66	49	
1670.	D. MATTHEW CHERITON	L.		15	
1773.	D. BENEDICT BOLAS	A.D.		30	
1877.	D. WILFRID COOPER	L.	58	42	33
1885.	*D. Laurence Shepherd*	*L.*	*59.*	*41.*	*35*

—< 31 >—

1642.	D. ALBAN ROE	L.	60	31	
1749.	LAY S. MAG. TOLDERWINE	B.V.M.	74	48	
1807.	LAY S. ANN LE FEURE	B.V.M.	72	50	

February.

‹1›—

		M.	A.	R.	P.
1692.	D. ANNE GILL	B.V.M.	52	24	
1701.	LAY S. ANN BATEMANSON	B.V.M.	53	21	
1761.	D. ALEXIUS LATHAM	A.D.		19	

—‹2›—

		M.	A.	R.	P.
1638.	D. CUTHBERT FURSDEN	G.		19	
1662.	D. MAURUS ROBINSON	L.		10	
1665.	LAY S. FLAVIA BROWN	B.V.M.	61	39	
1755.	D. AMBROSE BROWN	G.	56	49	
1776.	D. AMBROSE WAREING	L.		16	
1786.	D. CUTHBERT GRIME	G.	42	23	2
1832.	D. ANSELM LORYMER	G.	81	65	

—‹3›—

		M.	A.	R.	P.
1723.	D. MICHAEL PULLEIN	G.		52	

—‹4›—

		M.	A.	R.	P.
1688.	D. EDMUND HAWET	E.		6	
1789.	D. BEDE SCOTT	A.D.	46	27	
1764.	D. BENEDICTA MEYNELL	B.V.M.	87	69	38
1868.	D. CLEMENT CROFT	L.	63	46	
1876.	LAY BR. FRANCIS REA	G.	71	46	

1899 . D. Aloysius Leavy (b) - 80 __ A 55 _ R 50 P - -

1901 _ Nᵢ Anselm Karnewall (g) - 80 _ . 56 __ _ _ . _

February.

—‹5›—

		M.	A.	R.	P.
1631.	D. John Norton	G.		8	
1728.	Lay Br. Jerome Six	L.		44	
1738.	D. Augustine Brigham	G.		8	
1814.	D. Ralph Ainsworth, Prov. of Cant.	E.	50	31	26
1869.	D. Augustine Lowe	L.	63	39	34
1870.	D. Bernard Paillet	G.	60	37	31
1877.	D. Benedict Murphy	L.	43	23	15

—‹6›—

		M.	A.	R.	P.
1668.	D. Thomas Tanke	G.	70	46	
1670.	Lay S. Hilda Percy	B.V.M.	74	39	
16—.	S. Josepha Soutnez	B.V.M.			
1720.	D. Maura Harrington	B.V.M.	36	19	
1727.	D. Joseph Wyche	A.D.	55	37	
1759.	D. Gregory Selby	A.D.		34	
1794.	Lay S. Ann Pennington	B.V.M.	60		

—‹7›—

		M.	A.	R.	P.
1669.	D. David Guilliam	L.		18	
1709.	D. George Whall	L.		44	
1737.	Lay B. Gabl. de Bocquet	G.		34	
1740.	D Joseph D'Ognate	E.		41	

—‹8›—

		M.	A.	R.	P.
1650.	D. Robert Haddock	Sp.			
1717.	Lay Br. Austin Rumley	L.		46	

February.

		M.	A.	R.	P.
1738.	D. Thomas Nelson	G.		36	31
1807.	D. Michael Lacon	G.	63	47	
1852.	D. Edmund Marsh	E.	50	29	26

◄ 9 ►

		M.	A.	R.	P.
1711.	D. Jerome Farnworth	E.		16	

◄ 10 ►

		M.	A.	R.	P.
1650.	D. Dunstan Everard	B.		35	
1707.	Lay S. Benedicta Taylor	B.V.M.	43	14	
1718.	D. James Poyntz	E.		31	
1726.	D. Anthony Turberville	E.		58	
1739.	D. Placid Robinson	A.D.		39	

◄ 11 ►

		M.	A.	R.	P.
1737.	D. Bede Halsall	G.		51	

◄ 12 ►

		M.	A.	R.	P.
1631.	Lay Br. Anselm Hamoy	B.		12	
1655.	D. Gregory Moore	G.		34	
1688.	D. Hugh Starkey	A.D.	70	40	
1703.	D. Joseph Hesketh	G.		23	
1735.	D. Bernard Bartlett	G.		44	
1738.	D. Odo Duddell	A.D.	68	50	
1772.	Lay S. Josepha Tookey	B.V.M.			
1818.	M. Augustina Shepherd, Abbess.	B.V.M.	54		
1865.	D. Benedict Blount	G.	44	25	16
1878.	D. Laurence Wright	L.	29	11	3

D. Basil Hurworth (2) ---- 71 - 51 -- 43

D. Basil Hurworth (2) ---- 71 - 51 -- 43

february.

— 13 —

		M.	A.	R.	P.
1610.	D. Nicholas Sadler				
1610.	D. Nicholas Hutton				
1728.	D. Maurus Barber	G.		46	
1798.	D. Robert Goolde	E.	63	63	
1830.	Lay S. Scholastica Caton	B.V.M.	81		

— 14 —

| 1689. | D. Euphrasia Tempest | B.V.M. | 67 | 49 | |
| 1706. | D. Anselm Brown | B. | | 19 | |

— 15 —

1743.	D. Benedict Knight	A.D	27	11	
1743.	D. Bernard Wythie	G.	36	27	
1854.	D. George Turner	G.	84	65	54

— 16 —

1677.	D. Ildeph. Willoughby	G.		10	
1798.	D. Jerome Marsh	L.	55	38	
1870.	D. Bede Day	L.	79	64	

— 17 —

| 1653. | D. Placid Carey | E. | | 13 | |
| 1733. | D. Alban Dawney | A.D. | | 51 | |

— 18 —

1656.	D. Viviana Yaxley	B.V.M.	53	36	
1657.	D. Wilfrid Selby	G.		38	
1727.	Lay S. Mary Gaudelier	B.V.M.	56	34	
1787.	D. Laurence Hardisty	A.D.	73	56	49

February.

		M.	A.	R.	P.
1733.	D. Agnes Widdrington	B.V.M.	67	46	
1847.	D. Ambrose Feraud	G.	61	46	37
1872.	D. Placid Morris, Bp. of Troy.	G.	78	62	54

—‹ 19 ›—

| 1837. | D. Alexius Pope | L. | 82 | 62 | |

—‹ 20 ›—

1626.	D. Placid Hilton	L.		17	17
1657.	D. Hilarion Wake	G.		19	
1748.	D. Paul Gilmore	A.D.		64	
1769.	D. Laurence Turck	A.D.		19	
1776.	Lay B. Andrew Barquet	G.	73	38	
1872.	D. Anselm Cockshoot	L.	67	50	42

—‹ 21 ›—

| 1676. | D. Augustine Kinder | G. | 80 | 56 | |
| 1733. | D. Isabella Kennet | B.V.M. | 79 | 50 | |

—‹ 22 ›—

1610.	D. Sigebert Buckley	Westm.	93		
1641.	D. John Lone	G.		22	
1691.	D. Alban Fuller	L.		18	
1736.	D. Joseph Riddell	A.D.		18	
1881.	D. Bernard Jackson	L.	66	46	42

—‹ 23 ›—

| 1843. | D. Richard Marsh | L. | 81 | 61 | 57 |
| 1857. | Lay S. Aloysia Bridge | B.V.M. | 74 | 41 | |

D. Edmund Moore --- § - 74 - 55 - 45
D. Alphonsus Morall -- § - 85 - 66 - 57

February.

‹ 24 ›—

		M.	A.	R.	P.
1635.	S. Barbara Smith	B.V.M.	18	1	

—‹ 25 ›—

1656.	Lay Br. John Gratian	L.		26	
1786.	D. Edward Hussey	G.		56	
1832.	D. Alexius Chew	L.	61	41	37

—‹ 26 ›—

| 1789. | D. Bernard Davis | A.D. | 75 | 55 | 51 |

—‹ 27 ›—

| 1601. | D. Mark Barkworth | | | | |
| 1777. | D. Bede Newton | A.D. | 63 | 46 | 40 |

—‹ 28 ›—

| 1710. | D. John Dakins | E. | 42 | 23 | 15 |
| 1745. | Lay B. Lau. Delattre | E. | | 47 | |

—‹ 29 ›—

| 1626. | D. Richard Hodgson | G. | | 13 | |

March.

‹1›

		M.	A.	R.	P.
1730.	D. Gregory Riddell	A.D.		43	
1789.	M. Agnes Ingleby, Abbess.	B.V.M.	81	62	
1795.	D. Placid Bennet	L.	54	39	
1798.	Lay Br. Joseph Valentine	E.	75	49	

‹2›

| 1614. | D. Bede Merriman | L. | | 5 | |
| 1813. | D. Josepha Knight | B.V.M. | 70 | 48 | |

‹3›

| 1640. | D. Vincent Latham | G. | | 19 | |

‹4›

1626.	D. Augustine Richardson	G.		9	
1655.	D. Agnes More	B.V.M.	60	31	
1667.	Lay S. Mary Hoskins	B.V.M.	64	44	
1746.	D. Anselm Carthorne	A.D.		44	
1865.	D. Benedict Hoole	E.	66	42	40

‹5›

1690.	Lay B. Benedict Hankinson	E.		43	
1798.	D. Thomas Barker	G.	30	9	
1814.	D. Adrian Towers	A.D.	62	43	39

897 - D. Edmund Caldwell (E) - - 79 - 60 - 50
908 - D. Josephus Fitzgerald (J) - - 44 . 24 . 16

- Lay Bro. Benedict (No Votes) (J) - - 81 - . 54

97 - D. Ceolfrid Treharne (e) - - 35 - 15 - . 8

888 - D. Anselm Gillett (S) - - - - 64 . 43 . . 38
898 - D. Benedict Rowley (e) - - - - 64 - 44 - 35

1909. D. Placid Wray (S) — — — — 44 — 25 — 18 —

885. D. Placid Newhall (L) — — — — 75, 52 — 49

888. D. Anselm Gillett (S) — — — — 64 — 43 — 38

1900. D. Maurus Anderson (S) — — — — 72 — 52 — 46 —

1896. D. Gregory Smith (S) — — — 50 — 38 — 32

March.

—< 6 >—

		M.	A.	R.	P.
1648.	S. Benedicta Roper	B.V.M.	17	1	
1650.	D. Francis Blakestone	G.	25		
1846.	D. Augustine Harrison	G.	76	55	46

—< 7 >—

| 1720. | D. John Rous | L. | 10 | | |
| 1723. | D. Maurus Wilson | A.D. | 36 | | |

—< 8 >—

1722.	D. Augustine Townson	A.D.	35		
17—.	D. Etheldreda Delattre	B.V.M.			
1807.	Br. Augustine Atkinson	G.	22	6	

—< 9 >—

| 1658. | D. Bernard Salkeld | G. | 9 | | |
| 1744. | Lay Br. Adrian Muller | A.D. | 30 | | |

—< 10 >—

1635.	D. Maurus Atkins	G.	22		
1689.	Br. Maurus Fermor	L.	4		
1733.	Lay Br. Joseph Bateson	L.	44		
1737.	D. Edmund Batchelor	E.	28	12	
1739.	D. Teresa Chilton	B.V.M.	67	43	

—< 11 >—

1707.	D. Patrick Curwen	L.	40		
1776.	D. Peter Wilcock	L.	40		
1869.	D. Joseph Hewitt	G.	57	29	23

March.

‹ 12 ›

		M.	A.	R.	P.
1646.	D. Boniface Wilford	G.	90	38	
1690.	Lay S. Bridget Lusher	B.V.M.	57	39	
1701.	D. Eugenia Houghton	B.V.M.	80	60	
1762.	D. Robert Robinson	A.D.		41	
1790.	D. Peter Walmesley	G.	73	55	
1812.	D. Cyril Mather	A.D	43	23	
1837.	D. Basil Bretherton	L.		18	13

‹ 13 ›

1651.	D. Cecily Hall	B.V.M.	24	3	
1741.	D. Francis Moore	E.		44	
1745.	D. Edward Sherburne	E.		47	
1810.	D. Bernard Slater	L.	66	50	
1871.	Br. Hilary Taylor	L.	24	3	

‹ 14 ›

1658.	D. Mark Crowther	G.		50	
1729.	Br. Thomas Short	E.	59	41	
1753.	D. Maurus Coupe	E.		23	
1754.	D. Joseph Starkey	G.		52	
1865.	D. Francis Kershaw	A.D.	54	32	29

‹ 15 ›

1630.	D. Maurus Hanson	Sp.			
1689	D. Francis Porter	A.D.		32	
1754.	D. Benedicta Warwick	B.V.M.	76	43	

D. Kennard (χι (2) _ _ _ 70 _ _ 50 _ _ 43

D. Kennard (χι (2) _ _ _ 70 _ _ 50 _ _ 43

1895 – Dom. Dunstan Chambers (S) –   a_ _ _.R_ P
                                             – _50 _SL_25 _

889. Dom. Bernard Ullathorne (Y) –   –   83 — 65 _ 43 –
1910 – Dom Leo Sense. (F. a)   –   _ _ _   61 _. 42 ../
       1st Abbot of Fort Augustus

March.

—< 16 >—

		M.	A.	R.	P.
1745.	D. Edward Bulmer	A.D.		61	
1751.	D. Dunstan Pigott	G.		25	
1875.	M. Scholastica Gregson	B.V.M.	69	49	
1877.	D. Bede Polding, Archbp. of Sydney.	G.	83	67	

—< 17 >—

1651.	D. Clement Reyner, Abb. of Lambspring.	L.	62	43	
1690.	D. Maura Hall	B.V.M.	56	39	
1834.	Br. Maurus Grafton	E.	21	4	

—< 18 >—

1712.	D. Ildephonsus Aprice, Prov. of Cant.	L.		45	
1770.	D. Dunstan Worswick	L.		12	
1827.	Lay Br. Joseph Loughry	G.			

—< 19 >—

1745.	D. Edmund Cox	E.	83	48	
1750.	D. Francis Rookwood	G.		71	
1780.	D. Charles Smith	G.	53	35	

—< 20 >—

| 1705. | D. Elphege Skelton | A.D. | | 18 | |

—< 21 >—

| 1669. | D. Peter Hunt | L. | | 55 | |

—< 22 >—

| 1634. | D. Boniface Blandy | Sp. | | | |

March.

—< 23 >—

		M.	A.	R.	P.
1671.	D. Teresa Timperley	B.V.M.	65	41	
1795.	D. Anselm Geary	A.D.	81	64	57
1878.	D. Wilfrid Price	A.D.	59	43	29

—< 24 >—

1673.	D. Basil Roan	G.		20	
1792.	D. Edmund Duckett	E.		33	
1807.	D. Edmund Hadley	G.	63	47	
1878.	D. Vincent Spears	E.	54	35	28

—< 25 >—

1662.	Lay Br. Anthony Lovel	L.		43	
1669.	Br. Benedict Sparrey	L.		2	
1755.	Lay Br. Bede Houghton	L.		27	
1807.	D. Placid Harsnip	A.D.	54	38	
1875.	Br. Francis McElroy	L.	21	2	

—< 26 >—

1814.	D. Peter Kendal, Pr. of S. Greg.	G.	56	36	32
1876.	D. Augustine Atkinson	L.	61	39	34

—< 27 >—

1637.	D. Dunstan Grove	E.		4	

—< 28 >—

1878.	M. Magdalen Le Clerc	B.V.M.		62	

—< 29 >—

1673.	D. Gregory Grainge	G.		50	
1853.	Lay S. Felicitas Daniel	B.V.M.	35	11	

March.

—<30>—

—<31>—

		M.	A.	R.	P.
1635.	D. Gabriel Latham	E.		14	8
1640.	D. Augustine Lee	G.		17	
1777.	D. Anselm Lynch	G.	84	64	
1859.	D. Ignatius Callaghan	L.	29	11	5

April.

—‹ 1 ›—

		M.	A.	R.	P.
1631.	Lay S. Martha Martin	B.V.M.	43	7	
1636.	D. Bernard Edmunds	L.		27	
1660.	D. Gertrude Swinburne	B.V.M.			
1808.	D. James Sharrock, Pr. of S. Greg.	G.	58	41	

—‹ 2 ›—

| 1634. | D. Felix Thompson | B. | | 21 | |
| 1863. | D. Basil Duck | G. | 50 | 33 | 24 |

—‹ 3 ›—

1640.	D. Thomas Preston	Cass.		51	
1794.	D. Margaret Burgess	B.V.M.	73		
1824.	Lay Br. Francis Tegetmeyer	A.D.		46	
1855.	D. Maurus Philips	G.	61	44	36
1858.	D. Francis Cook	E.	43	19	13

—‹ 4 ›—

1663.	D. George Bacon	G.	66		
1718.	D. Placid Anderton	E.		23	
1744.	D. Scholastica Addison	B.V.M.			
1880.	D. Charles Fairclough	L.	92	63	60

D. Konrad Fay Norby (8) - - 65 - - 42 - 32
D. Oswald Kunchall (8) - - 68 - - 43 - 36

Mr. Joseph. Cornwell (0) Leighton -- -- - 56

April.

‹5›

		M.	A.	R.	P.
1692.	D. Placid Scroggs	G.	59		
1740.	D. Francis Rich	G.	49	42	
1747.	D. Augustina Jenison	B.V.M.	44	24	
1773.	D. Edward Tempest	A.D.	55		
1822.	D. John Atkinson	E.	62	42	37

‹6›

		M.	A.	R.	P.
1641.	D. Gervase Gray	Cass.			
1823.	D. Augustine Hatton	A.D.	85	66	
1869.	D. Augustine Kitchen	E.	45	19	10

‹7›

		M.	A.	R.	P.
1825.	D. Jerome Digby	G.	81	65	

‹8›

		M.	A.	R.	P.
1664.	D. Laurence Reyner	L.	82	56	
1720.	Lay Br. Anthony Doutch	A.D.	6		
1748.	D. Alban Ashton	E.	68	50	
1797.	D. Joachim Swinburne	A.D.	43	22	
1802.	Lay B. Sylvester Quince	G.	24		

‹9›

		M.	A.	R.	P.
1667.	D. Bernard Millington	L.	40	17	
1697.	D. Joseph Sherburne, Pres. Gen.	E.	69	46	
1699.	D. Dominic Green	E.	34	12	
1705.	D. Basil Smeaton	A.D.	42		
1721.	M. Cecily Hussey	B.V.M.	69	49	

April.

		M.	A.	R.	P.
1816.	D. Stephen Hodgson	L.	53	33	26
1821.	D. James Calderbank	L.	51	30	28

—< 10 >—

1629.	D. Gabriel Giffard, Archbp. of Rheims.	L.	75	21	
1694.	D. Bede Foster	B.		61	
1733.	D. Gertrude Chilton	B.V.M	62	39	

—< 11 >—

1608.	D. George Gervase	Miss.	37	2	5
1683.	Lay S. Jane Cellar	B.V.M.	80	53	
1770.	S. Catherine Palliser	B.V.M.			
1865.	D. Bernard O'Sullivan	G.	42	25	15

—< 12 >—

1682.	D. Bede Taylard	L.	89	61	52
1712.	D. Paul Chandler	G.		8	2
1770.	D. Basil Bradshaw	A.D.		9	
1820.	Lay Br. Francis Holderness	G.		44	
1847.	D. Wilfrid Fisher	A.D.	80	61	57
1880.	D. Joseph Brown, Bp. of Newport.	G.	84	67	57

—< 13 >—

1679.	D. Anselm Collingwood	A.D.		17	
1718.	D. Cuthbert Tatham	G.		41	
1760.	Br. Anselm Macdonald	G.		22	4

D. Cuthbert Murphy (8) - - 65 - - 44 - - 36

1890 - D. Maurus Shepherd (2) - - - , 72 . 52 . 43
18-3 - D. Stanislaus Holzhaur (?) - - - - ., 53 . 44

April.

—‹ 14 ›—

		M.	A.	R.	P.
1609.	D. ANDREW SHIRLEY	Sp.			
1736.	D. WILLIAM PESTEL	G.		55	
1830.	M. CHRISTINA CHARE	B.V.M.	52	29	

—‹ 15 ›—

1645.	D. ANSELM TURBERVILLE	Sp.			
1787.	LAY BR. DUNSTAN OSBALDESTONE	G.		50	
1822.	LAY BR. AMBROSE PAPE	A.D.	66	50	

—‹ 16 ›—

1685.	D. EDWARD SHELDEN	G.		42	
1883.	D. NORBERT SWEENEY, Prov. of Cant.	G.	62	45	35

—‹ 17 ›—

1749.	D. JAMES BUCKLEY	E.		42	
1777.	LAY BR. CHRISTOPHER OSBALDESTONE	L.			

—‹ 18 ›—

1619.	D. GREGORY GRAINGE	Sp.			
1640.	D. BENEDICTA MORGAN	B.V.M.	36	17	
1650.	D. CATHERINE SHELDON	B.V.M.	34	9	
1663.	D. MILDRED LATCHMORE	B.V.M.	67	36	
1668.	D. AUGUSTINE STOKER	G.	70	48	
1713.	D. WOLSTAN CROSBY	G.		54	
1822.	D. BEDE BREWER, Pres. Gen.	L.	80	65	

—‹ 19 ›—

1667.	D. FRANCIS CRATHORNE	G.	69	47	

April.

—◄ 20 ►—

		M.	A.	R.	P.
1713.	D. Anna Ayvay	B.V.M.	59	41	
1740.	Lay Br. Henry Lawson	G.	80	55	
17—	D. Margaret Swinburne	B.V.M.			
1770.	D. Laurence York, Bp. of Niba.	G.	83	65	59

—◄ 21 ►—

| 1732. | D. Laurence Champney | L. | 65 | 49 | |
| 1847. | D. Oswald Talbot | L. | 79 | 59 | 55 |

—◄ 22 ►—

1657.	D. Maurus Hames	B.		28	
1763.	D. Benedicta Reeves	B.V.M.			
1808.	D. Maurus Chaplin	A.D.	63	46	

—◄ 23 ►—

1635.	D. Justus Edner	Sp.			
1735.	D. Bede Moore	E.		54	
1758.	D. Josepha Bate	B.V.M.			
1830.	D. Augustine Lawson	G.	72	52	47

—◄ 24 ►—

1736.	D. Benedict Winter	G.		45	29
1752.	D. Gregory Metcalfe	A.D.	28	13	
1758.	D. Bridget Coffin	B.V.M.	80	54	

—◄ 25 ►—

| 1657. | D. James Sherburne | G. | | 44 | |
| 1860. | D. Augustine Shann | L. | 59 | 42 | 36 |

April.

‹ 26 ›

		M.	A.	R.	P.
1671.	D. Clementina Cary	B.V.M.	56	30	
1761.	D. Placid Ashton	E.	54	37	

‹ 27 ›

		M.	A.	R.	P.
1807.	D. Bernard Warmoll	G.	89	71	
1812.	D. Boniface Taylor	A.D.	60	41	
1875.	D. Aelred Kearns	G.	33	12	4

‹ 28 ›

		M.	A.	R.	P.
1708.	D. Maurus Knightley, Abbot of Lambspring	A.D.		32	
1768.	D. Bernarda Plompton	B.V.M.	68	51	
1792.	D. Jerome Heatly	A.D.	35	16	

‹ 29 ›

		M.	A.	R.	P.
1732.	D. Basil Warwick, Pr. of St. Greg.	G.		35	
1747.	D. Thomas Eaves	L.	88	64	
1760.	S. Olivia Darell	B.V.M.			
1785.	D. Basil Eyston	G.		53	

‹ 30 ›

		M.	A.	R.	P.
1672.	D. John Martin	G.		12	
1906.	D. Richard O'Hare	S.	62	47	36

May.

—❧1❧—

		M.	A.	R.	P.
1721.	D. Celestine Shaftoe	A.D.		50	
1733.	D. Augustine Delattre	E.		28	
1767.	Lay Br. Benedict Monpas	G.		12	
1882.	Br. Celestine Froes	L.		22	4
1883.	D. Ambrose Cotham	E.	73	54	49

—❧2❧—

		M.	A.	R.	P.
1723.	D. Anselm Blakey	A.D.		42	
1801.	D. Benedict Simpson	L.		49	
1837.	D. Gregory Robinson, Prov. of York	L.	58	34	30
1864.	D. Benedict Bonney	A.D.	50	30	25

—❧3❧—

		M.	A.	R.	P.
1690.	D. Maurus Nelson	E.		10	-

—❧4❧—

		M.	A.	R.	P.
1618.	D. Augustine Bradshaw	Sp.	42	24	18

—❧5❧—

		M.	A.	R.	P.
1644.	D. Matthew Sandford	B.		32	
1666.	D. Anselm Crowther, Prov. of Cant.	G.	78	56	

15 — D. Clement Worsley — L -- 73 .. 54 -- 48
40 — D. Aloysius Bayer — — — L -- 48 -. 29 -- 21
5 D. Wilfred Brown — L -- 73 - 54 - 4,

08 . D. Bernard Caldwell C __ 82 .. 64 - 5

D. Bernard Morris (C) — __ — — .. 40 -- 20 -- 13

1908 Dom. Benedict Scarisbrick.__6 Jan—64—58—

1898 - D. Bernard Saunders (l) _ _ _ _56_ _39_ _29

May.

		M.	A.	R.	P.
1666.	D. JOHN MEUTISSE	G.		61	
1688.	D. HELEN BRENT	B.V.M.	77	53	
1700.	D. CATHERINE KENNET	B.V.M.	49	17	

—< 6 >—

| 1702. | D. CUTHBERT HUTTON | G. | | 18 | |
| 1816. | D. AUGUSTINE MITCHELL | L. | 49 | 29 | 25 |

—< 7 >—

1640.	M. FRANCES GAWEN	B.V.M.	64	40	
1684.	LAY S. ELIZABETH LUSHER	B.V.M.	55	33	
1763.	LAY S. AGNES BATCHELL	B.V.M.			
1831.	D. DUNSTAN SHARROCK	L.	77	57	

—< 8 >—

1732.	D. PLACID FRERE	G.		9	1
1848.	D. DUNSTAN WEBB	A.D.	84	65	59
1848.	S. BENEDICTA CHAPMAN	B.V.M.	28	3	

—< 9 >—

1658.	LAY BR. ANTHONY TENANT				
1679.	LAY BR. THOMAS PICKERING	G.	58	15	
1805.	D. LEWIS HEATLEY	A.D.	53	30	
1858.	D. FRANCIS COOPER	L.	79	59	55

—< 10 >—

| 1688. | D. NICHOLAS HESKETH | L. | | 21 | |

—< 11 >—

| 1636. | D. BENEDICT D'ORGAINE | L. | | 25 | |
| 1662. | D. BASIL CHERITON | E. | | 12 | |

May.

		M.	A.	R.	P.
1669.	D. Edward Wolseley	G.		38	
1690.	D. Scholastica Hodson	B.V.M.	69	48	
1782.	Lay Br. John Jansen	A.D.		39	

—‹ 12 ›—

| 1735. | D. Anselm Walmesley | L. | | 26 | |

—‹ 13 ›—

| 16— | Lay Br. John Barbierre | B. | | | |
| 1774. | D. Anselm Eastham | E. | | 44 | |

—‹ 14 ›—

1645.	Lay S. Margaret Kenyon	B.V.M.		23	
1834.	D. Benedict Glover	L.	47	31	23
1855.	D. Romuald Demonchy	E.	45	10	6

—‹ 15 ›—

1658.	Lay Br. William Tahon				
1762.	D. Nicholas Richardson	L.		26	
1867.	Br. Wulstan Barton	L.	23	6	

—‹ 16 ›—

1652.	D. Nicholas Fitzjames	G.	92	45	51
1726.	D. William Banester	G.		39	
1755.	D. Hugh Frankland	G.		56	50

—‹ 17 ›—

1677.	D. Wolstan Shuttleworth	E.		38	
1690.	D. Justina Gascoigne	B.V.M.	67	51	
1712.	Lay Br. Peter Gregson	L.		12	

-- D. Ignatius Dewhurst (1.D) -- ⌐ °--. 5°--- '43

o - D. Francis Davis (ly) - - - - 84 -- 66 -- 58

1887 – D. Kedoswale ... – – – 79 – – 60 – – 75 –

1901 – D. Norbert Ward (6) 57 – – 38 – 00

May.

		M.	A.	R.	P.
1755.	D. PLACID HUTTON	A.D.		42	35
1854.	D. CHARLES DAVIS, Bp. of Maitland	G.	39	23	14

—< 18 >—

17—.	D. GERTRUDE MANSFIELD	B.V.M.			
1875.	D. EPHREM PRATT	G.	73	56	48

—< 19 >—

1664.	D. GEORGE BERINGTON	Sp.	88		
1829.	D. CUTHBERT WILKS	E.	86	66	57

—< 20 >—

1658.	LAY BR. JOHN BRADSTOCK				
1723.	D. BERNARD BARR	G.	84	66	
1837.	S. AUGUSTINA SINNOT	B.V.M.		1	

—< 21 >—

1676.	M. CATHERINE GASCOIGNE	B.V.M.	73	53	
1851.	D. AUGUSTINE WILKINSON	E.	40	24	14

—< 22 >—

1646.	D. JOHN MOUNDEFORD	G.		33	
—	D. TERESA MANSFIELD	B.V.M.			
1827.	D. JEROME COUPE	L.	73	53	

—< 23 >—

1648.	D. BENEDICT COX	L.		37	

—< 24 >—

1714.	LAY BR. BERNARD HUNTLEY	L.		42	
1730.	D. AUGUSTINE SOUTHCOT	E.		42	
1762.	D. TERESA SWINBURNE	B.V.M.	74	55	

May.

—‹ 25 ›—

		M.	A.	R.	P.
1631.	D. Joseph Prater	Sp.			

—‹ 26 ›—

1747.	D. Francis Bruning	A.D.	72	49	
1840.	D. Ignatius Greenough	E.		14	11
1847.	D. Francis Appleton	E.	43	21	17

—‹ 27 ›—

| 1633. | Lay Br. Edmund Arrowsmith | G. | | 20 | |
| 1746. | D. Dunstan Rogers | E. | | 33 | |

—‹ 28 ›—

| 1654. | D. Francis Constable | L. | | 40 | |

—‹ 29 ›—

| 1654. | D. Mellitus Bapthorpe | L. | | 46 | |
| 1756. | D. Bede Hutton | A.D. | | 44 | 38 |

—‹ 30 ›—

1612.	D. Maurus Scott	Sp.			
1655.	D. Placid Hartburn	G.		39	46
1805.	D. Laurence Hadley	G.	66	49	

—‹ 31 ›—

1655.	D. William Palmer	Cass.	80		
1803.	D. Laurence Barnes	G.	53	36	
1832.	D. Maurus Robinson	A.D.	54	41	
1847.	D. Augustine Gilbert	E.	27	8	2
1872.	D. Alban Dunn	L.	75	28	25

02 _ D. Francis Brown (C) _ _ _ _ _ _ 61 _ 29 _ 32

D Romuald Turner _ (8) _ _ _ _ 72 _ 50 _ 43

_ D. Benedict Talbot (2) _ _ _ _ 57 _ 28 _ 21

June.

—‹1›—

		M.	A.	R.	P.
1699.	D. Columban Phillips	E.	87	68	60
1711.	Lay Br. Andrew Townson	G.	17		
1794.	D. Edmund Pennington	L.	37	17	
1817.	D. Jerome Alcock	A.D.	42	26	
1842.	D. Anselm Appleton	E.	77	55	53

—‹2›—

		M.	A.	R.	P.
1724.	D. Clement Paston	E.	42		

—‹3›—

		M.	A.	R.	P.
1828.	D. Martin Levaux	G.	82	31	
1876.	D. Laurence Vrignon	G.	54	33	19

—‹4›—

		M.	A.	R.	P.
1631.	D. Francis Foster	Miss.			33
1662.	S. Agnes Errington	B.V.M.	20	1	
1687.	D. Augustine Mather	L.	22		
1746.	D. Laurence Fenwick	G.	62		
1787.	D. Thomas Patten	G.	60	42	

—‹5›—

		M.	A.	R.	P.
1669.	D. Bernard Sanderson	A.D.		7	
1702.	D. Benedict Hemsworth	G.	46		
1715.	Lay Br. Robert Richardson	L.	55		

Iune.

—‹6›—

		M.	A.	R.	P.
1629.	D. Bede Banester	G.		10	
1811.	D. Louisa Hagan	B.V.M.	71	49	
1874.	D. Winefrid Morrall	B.V.M.	65	40	

—‹7›—

1810.	D. John Dawber	L.	41	23	
1869.	D. Paulinus Heptonstall	G.	71	54	42

—‹8›—

1653.	D. Amandus Southcot	G.		30	
1809.	D. Augustine Kellet	E.	77	59	

—‹9›—

1663.	D. Maurus Davis	E.		22	
1810.	D. Richard Harris	E.		56	
1866.	D. Oswald Tindall	L.	32	12	4

—‹10›—

1626.	D. Francis Atrobas	Sp.			
1660.	D. Mary Watson	B.V.M.	52	37	

—‹11›—

1646.	D. Joseph Latham	G.		30	
1697.	D. Laurence Wolfe	E.	65	42	
1830.	D. Agnes Robinson	B.V.M.	69		

—‹12›—

1642.	D. Thomas Monington	G.		33	
1809.	D. Teresa Shepherd	BVM.	47		
1816.	D. Dunstan Tarllton	E.	45	23	

P. 1. D. Oswald O'Neill — 6 _ 66 _ _ 48 _ 41

1. Wilfrid Raynal - - { - - - 74th - - - 56th - 47th
2. Wulstan Perkins - 6 - - '67 - - 40 - - 34

3. D. Anselm Glassbrook - - 6 - - - 78 - - 62 - - 54

1891 _ D. Edmund Roche (?) _ _ _ _ _ 65 _ _ 38 _ _ _ 30

1902 . D. Kede Bigly . (?) _ _ _ _ 58 _ _ 42 _ 31 _

June.

—< 13 >—

		M.	A.	R.	P.
1640.	D. Scholastica Timperley	B.V.M. 35	16		

—< 14 >—

1618.	D. Anthony Winchcomb	G.	5

—< 15 >—

1720.	D. William Philipson	E.	37	
1775.	D. Augustine Moore, Pr. of S. Greg.	G. 51	36	

—< 16 >—

1664.	D. Bernard Ribertierre	B.	44	
1773.	D. Ambrose Elliot	G	55	
1792.	D. Gregory Watkinson	G. 65	47	

—< 17 >—

1669.	Lay Br. Francis Chamberlain	B.			
1799.	D. Jane Alexander	B.V.M. 84			
1802.	Lay S. Magdalen Kimberley	B.V.M. 57	33		
1877.	D. Augustine Dowding	G. 71	53	46	

—< 18 >—

—< 19 >—

1653.	Lay Br. Claude Moliner	L	34	
1799.	D. Gregory Cowley, Pres. Gen.	L. 67	51	

—< 20 >—

1635.	D. Maurus Curre	G.	22

June.

—‹ 21 ›—

		M.	A.	R.	P.
1621.	D. ROBERT SADLER, Prov. of Cant.	West.		15	
1706.	BR. RICHARD LANNING	G		9	
1743.	D. BEDE POTTS	A.D.	69	53	

—‹ 22 ›—

		M.	A.	R.	P.
1691.	D. MARY LEGGE	B.V.M.	48	22	
1726.	BR. MAURUS DALE	E.		48	

—‹ 23 ›—

		M.	A.	R.	P.
1667.	D. THOMAS SWINBURNE	G.	60	43	
1720.	D. BERNARD LOWICK	E.	18	2	

—‹ 24 ›—

		M.	A.	R.	P.
1624.	D. JOSEPH HAWORTH	L.		16	
1731.	D. CHARLES DELATTRE	A.D.		21	16

—‹ 25 ›—

		M.	A.	R.	P.
1782.	D. DUNSTAN HOLDERNESS	L.		42	

—‹ 26 ›—

		M.	A.	R.	P.
1690.	D. JOSEPH SHERWOOD, Abb. of Lambs.	A.D.		38	
1847.	D. VINCENT DALE	E.	47	17	14

—‹ 27 ›—

		M.	A.	R.	P.
1632.	D. GREGORY HAYWARD	G.	30	12	4
1866.	D. WILFRID BURCHALL	E.	48	28	23

—‹ 28 ›—

97 - D. Paul Penton (L) - - - 27 --- 8 --- 1

D. Maurus Margison (L) - - - 77 --- 5g -- 54
D. Audan Howlett (g) -   -   53 -- 33 - :6

1894 -- D. Stanislaus Giles (6) --- 81 -- 61

June.

—‹ 29 ›—

		M.	A.	R.	P.
1689.	S. Alexia Fenwick	B.V.M.			
1747.	D. Francis Walmesley	L.	30	13	

—‹ 30 ›—

1635.	D. John Allen	G.		12	
1646.	D. Philip Powel	G.	53	27	
1777.	D. Ambrose Kaye	L.		43	
1832.	S. Augustina Spencer	B.V.M.	19	2	

1890 D. Placid Hall   a. D 71.56-46

July.

—<1>—

		M.	A.	R.	P.
1651.	D. Jocelin Elmer, Pr. of St. Bened.	L.	42		
1653.	Br. John Barter	G.	1		
1737.	D. Benedict Lawson	A.D.	53		
1871.	D. Benedict Wassell	G.	80	64	55

—<2>—

		M.	A.	R.	P.
1664.	D. Richard King	E.	26	25	
1689.	D. Mellitus Walmesley, Pr. of St. Lau.	L.	11		
1760.	D. Cuthbert Hutchinson	G.	38		
1774.	D. Benedict Shuttleworth	A.D.	52		
1788.	D. Cyprian Barnewall	A.D.	27	6	
1825.	D. Bernard Butler	G.	77	50	

—<3>—

		M.	A.	R.	P.
1682.	Lay S. Catherine Trevelyan	B.V.M.	59	26	
1725.	D. Benedicta Englefied	B.V.M.	49	30	
1841.	D. Alexius Pope	G.	46	28	21

—<4>—

		M.	A.	R.	P.
1636.	Br. Boniface Martin	L.	13		
1697.	D. Teresa Meynell	B.V.M.	25	8	

.. Don Lawrence Burges (2) - -- 81 -- 60 -- 56

.. Don Lawrence Burges (2) - -- 81 -- 60 -- 56

1901 – D. Francis Penton (d) – – – – 33 – 15 – 7.
'909 – D. Bernard Davey (d) – – – – 81 – 46 40

1893. D. Anselm Walker (d) – – – – 72 – 56 – 48

July.

		M.	A.	R.	P.
1718.	D. John Townson	A.D.		45	
1725.	D. Ambrose Eastgate	L.		11	
1726.	D. Augustine Fenwick	G.		34	32
1828.	Lay Br. Joseph Sharrock	G.	72	51	

—❮5❯—

		M.	A.	R.	P.
1764.	D. Thomas Simpson	L.		28	
1766.	D. Placid Howard, Pres. Gen.	G.	67	48	
1779.	D. Bede Anderton	G.	39	23	
1780.	D. Placid de la Fontaine	G.		50	

—❮6❯—

		M.	A.	R.	P.
1632.	D. Placid Muttleberry	L.		23	31
1776.	D. Anne Rigby	B.V.M.	56	31	
1786.	D. Placida Pullen	B.V.M.			
1843.	D. Augustine Baines, Bishop of Siga.	L.	57	40	
1871.	D. Cyprian Tyrer	L.	72	50	43

—❮7❯—

		M.	A.	R.	P.
1740.	D. Thomas Riddell	A.D.	42	26	

—❮8❯—

		M.	A.	R.	P.
1725.	D. Benedict Wilson	G.		48	
1817.	D. Henry Parker, Pr. of St. Ed.	E.		65	45

—❮9❯—

		M.	A.	R.	P.
1652.	D. Cuthbert Risden	E.		13	
1772.	D. Maurus Scroggs	G.	55	39	

July.

		M.	A.	R.	P.
1714.	D. Edmund Taylor	G.	35		
1723.	D. Joseph Johnson	E.	49		
1864.	D. Athanasius Clarkson	E.	48	28	24

—< 10 >—

1705.	Lay Br. Thomas Brabant	G.	41		
1774.	D. Maurus Westbrooke	A.D.	49		
1775.	D. Benedict Daniel	L.	43		
1801.	D. Vincent Wearden	A.D.	32	15	

—< 11 >—

1653.	D Christopher Anderton	G.	46	30	

—< 12 >—

1617.	D. Thomas Minshall	Miss.			9

—< 13 >—

1766.	D. Ambrose Boucher	A.D.	49	23	
1844.	D. John Turner	E.	80	59	54

—< 14 >—

1718.	D. Edward Chorley	G.		21	14
1782.	Lay Br. Andrew Burn	L.			
1808.	D. Frances Sheldon	B.V.M.	88	68	

—< 15 >—

1718.	Br. Bede Knight	G.	5		
1752.	D. James Hawkins	A.D.	48		
1796.	Lay S. Josepha Miller	B.V.M.	30	1	
1832.	D. Bede Slater, Bishop of Ruspa	L.	58	39	34

1884 -- D. Jerome Watmough (2) -- .47-- 28

July.

—< 16 >—

		M.	A.	R.	P.
1704.	Lay Br. Anthony Dandy	G.	· 5		
1815.	D. Alban Clarkson	A.D.	49	29	

—< 17 >—

1738.	D. William Metcalfe	G.		49	40
1741.	D. Denis Bulmer	A.D.		10	5
1779.	D. Augustine Gregson	L.		55	
1882.	D. Evangelista Weetman	B.V.M.	76	42	

—< 18 >—

1743.	D. Laurence Kirby	L.		34	

—< 19 >—

1669.	Lay Br. Paul Waty	L.		31	
1877.	D. Gregory Gregory	A.D.	64	44	40
1878.	D. Edmund Poole	E.	59	41	33

—< 20 >—

1641.	D. Laurence Mabbs	G.		22	
1697.	D. Placid Skinner	G.		36	
1780.	Lay Br. Anthony Parkinson	G.	81	45	

—< 21 >—

1637.	D. Benedict Smith	E.		21	
1829.	D. Henry Lawson	G.	65	45	41
1879.	D. Vincent Dinmore	L.	74	56	49

—< 22 >—

1656.	D. Emilian Throckmorton	E.		34	29
1749.	S. Amanda Barrister	B.V.M.			
1799.	D. Adrian Horsman	A.D.	34	13	

July.

—< 23 >—

		M.	A.	R.	P.
1811.	D. Gregory Ballyman	A.D.	77	58	

—< 24 >—

1681.	D. Placid Gascoigne, Abbot of Lambs.	L.	82	66	58
1828.	D. Richard Pope	L.	68	48	
1878.	D. Jerome Jenkins	G.	82	66	58
1881.	Lay Br. Joseph Lawson	L.	65	41	

—< 25 >—

1624.	Br. Epiphanius Stapylton	G.		5	
1699.	Br. Augustine Lumley	E.		2	
1703.	D. Joseph Aprice	L.	53	38	

—< 26 >—

1644.	D. Boniface Kemp	Sp.			
1644.	D. Alphonsus Hesketh	G.		32	
1644.	D. William Middleton	Miss.			

—< 27 >—

1709.	Br. Joseph Roskow	G.		2	
1715.	D. Placid Francis	A.D.		46	
1769.	Lay Br. Jerome Clarkson	A.D.		22	
1876.	M. Josepha Spencer	B.V.M.	75	58	

—< 28 >—

1687.	Lay S. Frances Lusher	B.V.M.	63	43	
1732.	D. Mary Eves	B.V.M.			
1850.	D. Anselm Kenyon	A.D.	79	64	56
1871.	D. Teresa Sumner	B.V.M.	62	41	

Laurence Farrant (S) _ _ _ 53 _ _ 34 _ _ 27

Laurence Farrant (S) _ _ _ 53 _ _ 34 _ _ 27

July.

—<29>—

| | | M. | A. | R. | P. |

1814.   D. Benedict Macdonald   G. 75 57

—<30>—

1710.   D. Robert Killingbeck   A.D.   58

1757.   D. Augustine Turner   A.D. 37 18

—<31>—

1657.   D. Maurus Pritchard   G.   38

1791.   D. Benedict Catteral   E. 67 49

August.

—‹1›—

		M.	A.	R.	P.
1710.	D. Gregory Dalyson	A.D.		41	
1754.	D. Ambrose Davis	E.		67	57
1762.	D. John Aspenwall	E.		49	
1802.	D. Thomas Turner	L.	59	42	

—‹2›—

		M.	A.	R.	P.
1792.	D. Catherine Throckmorton	B.V.M.	97		
1837.	D. Augustine Birdsall, Pres. Gen.	A.D.	62	42	36

—‹3›—

		M.	A.	R.	P.
1636.	D. Alexius Bennet	L.		22	
1744.	D. Gregory Greenwood	G.		57	
1755.	D. Alexius Shepherd, Pr. of S. Greg.	G.		35	
1792.	M. Christina Hooke	B.V.M.	77	58	

—‹4›—

		M.	A.	R.	P.
1680.	D. Benedict Stapylton Pres. Gen.	G.	57	38	33
1741.	D. Benedicta Fairclough	B.V.M.			
1770.	D. James Crook	E.		32	

August.

—‹5›—

			M.	A.	R.	P.
1649.	D. Nicholas Curre	L.	40			
1688.	D. Benedicta Middleton	B.V.M.	57	38		

—‹6›—

1667.	D. Paul Robinson	L.	66	43		
1668.	S. Etheldreda Stapleton	R.V.M.	43	18		
1670.	D. Denis Sanderson	A.D.	7			
1698.	Lay Br. Gregory Wilkinson	E.	49			
1719.	D. Thomas Bruning	E.	24			
1795.	D. Thomas Ballyman	A.D.	58	40		
1840.	D. Joseph Glover	E.	49	34	26	

—‹7›—

1636.	D. Joseph Foster	L.	7			
1644.	D. Thomas Hill	G.	84	32	53	
1720.	D. Josepha O'More	B.V.M.	46	12		

—‹8›—

1623.	D. Augustine Owen	G.	8			
1624.	D. Thomas Green	Sp.				
1654.	S. Gertrude Shaftoe	B.V.M.	22	1		
1836.	D. Gregory Flinn	L.	13	6		

—‹9›—

| 1641. | D. Augustine Baker | West. | 66 | 36 | | |

—‹10›—

1674.	D. Serenus Cressy	G.	69	26	24	
1711.	D. William Hitchcock	G.	94	62		
1655.	D. Alexius Jones	G.	74	57	50	

August.

—< 11 >—

| M. | A. | R. | P. |

1667.	D. John Barter	G.	68	15	
1681.	D. Bridget Radcliffe	B.V.M.			
1696.	D. Gregory Helme	L.	11		

—< 12 >—

1665.	D. Gabriel Brett	B.	66	51	38
1816.	M. Lucy Blyde	B.V.M.	87		
1877.	D. Edith Palmer	B.V.M.	51	13	

—< 13 >—

1664.	Lay Br. Peter Huitson	G.	55		
1829.	Br. Raymund Eldridge	G.	38		
1862.	D. Maurus Francomme	E.	39	9	5
1865.	Br. Cyprian Hubbersty	L.	22		

—< 14 >—

| 1680. | D. Margaret Smith | B.V.M. | 44 | | |
| 1824. | Lay Br. James Minns | E. | 52 | | |

—< 15 >—

1634.	D. Romuald Danvers	G.	15	15	
1636.	D. Aldhelm Phillips	L.	17		
1665.	D. Dunstan Pettinger	L.	79	51	
1684.	Lay Br. Peter Street	A.D.	29		
1725.	D. George Fitzwilliams	G.	31		
1729.	D. John Girlington	E.	77		
1733.	D. Francis Watmough, Pr. S. Lau.	L.	68	50	

- D. Cuthbert Proctor (2) - - 63 - - 39 - - 34

- D. Cuthbert Proctor (2) - - 63 - - 39 - - 34

1883 — D. Bede Vaughan .. &c. — — — — . 50 — — 30 — — 10 6
     Archbishop of Sydney
1895 — D. Hildebrand Hoadley — &c. — — — 37 — — 18 — 11

August.

		M.	A.	R.	P.
1760.	D. Maurus Langdale	G.	26	10	
1802.	D. Maurus Heatley	A.D.	80	63	56

—< 16 >—

		M.	A.	R.	P.
1637.	D. Margaret Gascoigne	B.V.M.	29	8	
1705.	D. Bede Addy	A.D.		41	

—< 17 >—

		M.	A.	R.	P.
1633.	D. Gertrude More	B.V.M.	28	10	
1718.	D. Laurence Swale	A.D.		49	
1726.	D. Dorothy More	B.V.M.			
1816.	Br. Basil Knapp	G.	20	3	

—< 18 >—

		M.	A.	R.	P.
1676.	D. Catherine Vavasour	B.V.M.	66	48	

—< 19 >—

		M.	A.	R.	P.
1633.	D. Sigebert Bagshaw, Pres. Gen.	West.		37	
1638.	D. Wolstan Ingham	E.		9	4
1643.	D. John Hutton	Sp.			
1774.	D. Bernard Bradshaw, Prof. Cant.	A.D.		52	

—< 20 >—

		M.	A.	R.	P.
1657.	D. Maurus Roe	L.		32	
1675.	D. Rowland Dunn	Miss.			
1709.	B. Bernard Bradley	L.		3	
1749.	D. Gregory Pigott	G.		39	
1778.	D. Mary Mooney	B.V.M.			

August.

		M.	A.	R.	P.
1790.	D. Thomas Welsh	E.	47		
1856.	D. Anselm Bradley	E.	37	17	10

—‹ 21 ›—

1657.	D. Peter Warnford	Miss.	38		

—‹ 22 ›—

1694.	Br. Bernard Hornyold	E.	26	7	
1707.	D. Philip Blakey	A.D.	18		
1837.	D. Bede Burgess	L.	69	49	45
1879.	D. Gregory Kendal	G.	31	13	6

—‹ 23 ›—

1876.	D. Bede Cummins	L.	29	11	3

—‹ 24 ›—

1717.	D. Wilfrid Hutchinson	A.D.	39		
1775.	D. Augustina Widdrington	B.V.M.	70	49	

—‹ 25 ›—

1679.	D. Ambrose Booth	L.	7		
1685.	D. Lucy Vavasour	B.V.M.	73	56	
1807.	D. Paul Grimbaldestone	A.D.	52	32	
1848.	D. Euphrasia Weetman	B.V.M.	42	13	

—‹ 26 ›—

1718.	D Augustine Howard	G.	74	57	50
1751.	D. Edward Houghton	L.	42	31	
1829.	D. Denis Allerton	A.D.	75	29	

B. Ambrose Brindle (S) — — 73 — — 52 — — 47

1886 _ D. Ignatius Sutton (J) _ _ _ _ _ _ 74 _ 53 _ _ 49

1895 _ Dom. Stanislaus Nugent (J) _ 28 _ 10 _ 2

August.

—‹ 27 ›—

		M.	A.	R.	P.
1646.	D. JAMES ANDERTON	G.	24		

—‹ 28 ›—

| 1700. | D. JOSEPH ASHTON | G. | 13 | | |
| 1823. | D. CYPRIAN KEARTON | A.D. | 45 | 28 | |

—‹ 29 ›—

| 1701. | D. JOHN BYFLEET | G. | 78 | | |
| 1867.· | D. JEROME HAMPSON   - | L. | 65 | 49 | 41 |

—‹ 30 ›—

| 1722. | S. SCHOLASTICA RYDER | B.V.M. | 53 | 22 | |
| 1769. | D. HENRY WYBURNE, Prov. of Cant. | E | 47 | | |

—‹ 31 ›—

1636.	BR. BENEDICT JERNINGHAM	L	12		
1739.	LAY BR. JAMES DRAPER	L.	21		
1801.	D. THOMAS SLATER	E.	45	25	
1882.	D. MAURUS POTTER	L.	34	15	8

September.

—‹1›—

		M.	A.	R.	P.
1731.	D. BERNARD QUYNEO	L.	39		
1734.	D. LEANDER DAVIES	A.D.	64	46	

—‹2›—

1647.	LAY BR. DOMINIC TAYLOR	B.	33	—	
1691.	LAY BR. JOSEPH BLAKEY	A.D.	26		
1847.	D. STEPHEN BARBER	G.	63	46	38
1869.	D. PAULINUS KIRTLAN	E.	29	9	3

—‹3›—

1699.	D. BENEDICT NELSON	E.	81	60	
1737.	D. AMBROSE GAWEN	A.D.	48		
1750.	D. ELPHEGE DOBSON	A.D.	42		
1783.	D. JOSEPH CARTERET	G.	61		

—‹4›—

| 1776. | S. PLACIDA WILSON | B.V.M. | | | |
| 1820. | D. TERESA PARTINGTON | B.V.M. | 75 | | |

—‹5›—

1706.	LAY BR. THOMAS TUCKER	A.D.	44		
1732.	D. LAURENCE CASSE	E.	44		
1760.	BR. BENEDICT HARSNIP	E.	23	8	
1812.	D. AMBROSE ALLAM	G.	45		

R.P.

10 _ Dom Conrad Banekaert (J) - 67 _ _ 31 _ _ _ 24

_ Dom Wilfrid Sumner. O.S.B (L)   _ 68 46 40.

September.

—‹6›—

		M.	A.	R.	P.
1636.	D. Robert Ingleby	L.		11	
1681.	D. Gregory Mallet, Prov. of Cant.	L.	77	57	54
1716.	D. George Brent	A.D.		21	
1775.	D. John Barnes	E.	45	30	
1801.	D. Bernard Young	A.D.	60	42	
1879.	D. Gerard Tiernan	E.	25	8	1

—‹7›—

1737.	S. Martha Smith	B.V.M.			
1853.	D. Basil Thomas	L.	39	18	15

—‹8›—

1665.	D. Leander Normington	G.		17	
1669.	D. Francis Morgan	L.	69	47	
1702.	Lay Br. Joseph Mosse	E.	77	46	
1719.	D. Jerome Wilson	G.	67	52	42
1734.	D. Gilbert Knowles	G.	67	43	34
1872.	D. Placid Corlett	L.	65	47	28

—‹9›—

1715.	D. Sylvester Metham, Pr. of St. Greg.	G.	33		
1764.	D. Wilfrid Witham	A.D.		50	
1780.	D. Placid Metcalfe	A.D.	57	41	
1781.	D. Bernard Catteral	L.		57	

September.

—< 10 >—

		M.	A.	R.	P.
1788.	D. Maurus Bulmer	L.	74	56	
1800.	D. Vincent Gregson	E.	79	60	

—< 11 >—

| 1730. | D. Alexius Wall | A.D. | | 16 | |

—< 12 >—

1667.	D. Goderic Blount, Pr. of St. Greg.	G.	50	10	
1781.	D. Robert Daniel	L.		47	
1854.	Br. Dunstan Arkwright	L.	24	2	

—< 13 >—

| 1623. | D. Columban Malone, Pr. of St. Lau. | G. | | 15 | |

—< 14 >—

1625.	D. Edward Mayhew	West.	55	10	
1638.	D. William Gordon	Miss.			
1689.	Br. Jerome Bruning	E.		2	
1700.	D. Christina Brent	B.V.M.	99	70	
1758.	D. Teresa Young	B.V.M.			
1761.	D. Adrian Hardisty	A.D.	75	59	

—< 15 >—

| 1678. | D. Cuthbert Middleton | G. | | 36 | |

—< 16 >—

| 1733. | D. Joseph Howard | G. | | 22 | |
| 1770. | D. Scholastica Burgess | B.V.M. | | | |

1895 . D. Aloysius Ridgeway (E) — 81 - 61 - 57 -

1897 - D. Egbert Turner (E) - - - 45 - 25 - 18 -

September.

—< 17 >—

		M.	A.	R.	P.

—< 18 >—

1739.	D. John Philipson	G.	64		
1844.	D. Bernard Gore	E.	27	8	2.
1848.	D. Ambrose Duck	G.	51	33	24

—< 19 >—

1656.	D. Rudesind Barlow	Sp.	72	51	48
1786.	Lay Br. Joseph Johnson	L.			
1870.	Br. Cuthbert Collins	E.	29	3	

—< 20 >—

1641.	D. Ambrose Barlow	G.	55	27	25
1726.	D. Agatha Fazakerley	B.V.M.	68	43	
1880.	D. Placid McAuliffe	L.	31	15	7

—< 21 >

1685.	D. Clare Cook	B.V.M.	74	58	
1689.	Lay Br. John Lockers	L.	27		
1708.	D. Frances Gascoigne	B.V.M.	71	53	
1726.	D. John Baptist Savory	G.	30		
1870.	D. Adrian Hankinson, Bishop of Port Louis.	A.D.	53	35	29

—< 22 >—

1631.	D. Ebba Brown	B.V.M.	22	2	
1693.	D. Mary Cary	B.V.M.	72	53	
1698.	D. John Huddlestone	Miss.	90		

—< 23 >—

| 1732. | D. Augustine Hudson | L. | 47 | | |

September.

—‹24›—

		M.	A.	R.	P.
1764.	D. Placid Rigby	E.	40		

—‹25›—

| 1855. | Lay S. Catherine Crookall | B.V.M. | 74 | 40 | |
| 1880. | D. Oswald Davis | G. | 61 | 42 | 32 |

—‹26›—

1676.	Br. Cuthbert Brent	L.	3		
1699.	Br. John Green	L.	7		
1841.	D. Bernard Ryding	L.	88	72	65
1848.	D. Maura Rayment	B.V.M.	44	13	

—‹27›—

| 1839. | Lay S. Benedicta Foley | B.V.M. | 36 | 14 | |
| 1873. | D. Bede Almond | L. | 52 | 36 | 28 |

—‹28›—

| 1689. | D. Barbara Breton | B.V.M. | 53 | | |
| 1864. | D. Augustine Rolling | G. | 75 | 57 | 49 |

—‹29›—

| 1770. | D. Mary Coffin | B.V.M. | | | |

—‹30›—

1669.	D. Leander Thompson	G.	35		
1694.	D. Martin Stone	E.	38	10	
1797.	D. Anselm Bolas	A.D.	65	47	
1912	D. Placid Corlett	L	58.	39.	31

1.

1888. D. Peter Wilson (g) — — — — — — —go—— 69—61 —.

October.

—‹1›—

		M.	A.	R.	P.
1807.	D. Joseph Burden	G.	30	11	6
1858.	Br. Wolstan Rowley	L.	22	3	

—‹2›—

| 1669. | D. Maurus Flutot | L. | 59 | 40 | |
| 1706. | Br. Dunstan Porter | G. | | 31 | |

—‹3›—

1748.	D. John Stourton	G.		56	49
1772.	D. James Le Grand	A.D.	61	36	38
1819.	Lay Br. Paul Wilson	G.		39	

—‹4›—

| 1704. | D. Cuthbert Wall | A.D. | | 37 | |
| 1786. | D. Joseph Whittel | E. | 79 | 61 | |

—‹5›—

| 1874. | D. Ambrose Gillett | E. | 54 | 35 | 29 |

—‹6›—

—‹7›—

| 1652. | Lay S. Gertrude Hodson | B.V.M. | 26 | 3 | |
| 1708. | D. Placid Bagnal | L. | | 16 | |

October.

—‹ 8 ›—

		M.	A.	R.	P.
1688.	D. Andrew Whitfield	G.	51		
1797.	Br. Maurus Eastham	E.	23	4	
1860.	D. Joseph Sheridan	L.	59	25	22

—‹ 9 ›—

1671.	D. Thomas Anderton	E.	60	42	35
1777.	D. Alexius Pope	L.	29		
1851.	D. Bernard Robinson	L.	85	66	61

—‹ 10 ›—

1634.	D. Thomas Emerson	Sp.			
1659.	Lay S. Benedicta Boult	B.V.M.	53	26	
1725.	D. Edward Salisbury	A.D.	40	23	
1873.	D. Alphonsus Fleming	E.	45	24	17

—‹ 11 ›—

1692.	D. Bridget More	B.V.M.	83	62	
1750.	S. Gertrude Belerby	B.V.M.			
1753.	D. Ildephonsus Byerley	G.	46	42	
1872.	D. Dunstan Scott *12 Oct.*	G.	81	57	48

—‹ 12 ›—

1872 D Dunstan Scott   81-57-48

—‹ 13 ›—

1633.	D. Laurence Lowick	L.	14		
1678.	D. Lionel Sheldon	G.	45	26	21
1692.	Br. William Sheldon	G.	3		
1860.	D. Alban Molyneux	L.	78	58	54

1899 - Mr. Robert Adams (St Michaeli) - 84 - -34. Lay Br

1911. D. Gregory Rathe (?) __54 __35 __28   —.

1901 – D. Anselm O'Forman b. 69 __52 _42 __ __ __

October.

—‹ 14 ›—

		M.	A.	R.	P.
1655.	D. Claude White, Pres. Gen.	L.	72	50	50
1711.	D. Augustine Llewellyn	E.	54		
1800.	D. Bede Bennet	G.	77	60	
1826.	D. Dunstan Scott	A.D.	86	67	
1826.	Br. Gregory Philipson	G.	18	2	
1835.	D. Francis Fairclough	L.		18	13
1878.	Lay S. Martha Chew	B.V.M.	68	45	

—‹ 15 ›—

1793.	D. Oswald Eaves	L.	54	39	
1856.	Br. Placid Styles	L.	23	2	
1881.	D. John Carroll	E.	53	30	22

—‹ 16 ›—

1725.	D. Denis Bishop	A.D.		44	
1803.	D. Boniface Hall	A.D.	66	48	

—‹ 17 ›—

1657.	D. Michael Gascoigne	G.		36	
1809.	D. Gregory Sharrock Bp. of Telmessus.	G.	67	52	43
1824.	D. Clement Grimbaldestone	A.D.	72	51	
1871.	D. Bede Sumner	G.	68	39	35

—‹ 18 ›—

1800.	D. Gregory Gregson	L.	72	59	

October.

‒‹ 19 ›‒

		M.	A.	R.	P.
1639.	D. Benedict Jones	Sp.			
1790.	D. Bede Barton	E.	52	34	
1793.	D. Frances Beswick	E.	28	8	

‒‹ 20 ›‒

		M.	A.	R.	P.
1699.	Lay Br. John Green	G.		15	
1702·	D. Nicholas Colston	A.D.		30	
1773.	S. Bathildis Du Perry	B.V.M.		48	

‒‹ 21 ›‒

		M.	A.	R.	P.
1618.	D. George Brown	Sp.			
1650.	D. Bernard Warren	E.		3	1

‒‹ 22 ›‒

		M.	A.	R.	P.
1663.	Br. Bede Sherburne	E.		4	
1694.	D. Thomas Hesketh	E.	40	23	
1721.	D. Gregory Skelton, Prov. of York	G.		41	25
1843.	D. Augustine Clifford	D.	40	21	16
1854.	D. Placida Le Cleve	B.V.M.	42	23	
1875.	D. Bernard Williams	A.D.	76	39	33

‒‹ 23 ›‒

		M.	A.	R.	P.
1633.	D. William Kemble	G.		14	
1723.	D. Agnes Kennet	B.V.M.	38	21	
1794.	D. Daniel Spencer	E.	28	7	
1846.	Br. Clement Gibson	L.	23	3	

1898 _ D. Placid O'Brien (S) 7

October.

—‹ 24 ›—

		M.	A.	R.	P.
1631.	D. Augustine Heath	L.	20		
1640.	D. Lucy Cape	B.V.M.			
1748.	D. Thomas Southcot	G.	78	61	
1877.	D. Vincent Dowding	G.	68	48	41

—‹ 25 ›—

1629.	D. Celestine Trembie	B.	38	16	
1703.	D. John Lumley	L.	48		
1746.	Br. Maurus Blount	G.	19	1	
1749.	D. Gregory Robinson	L.	39	20	

—‹ 26 ›—

1674.	Lay Br. Peter Holmes	G.			
1726.	Lay S. Josepha Dwerihouse	B.V.M.	25	6	
1855.	D. Edith Saul	B.V.M.	41	15	
1870.	D. Ignatius Greenough	L.	69	52	45
1877.	D. Wilfrid Ryan	L.	75	55	51

—‹ 27 ›—

| 1774. | S. Winefrid Ball | B.V.M. | | | |
| 1795. | Br. Benedict Marsh | L. | 24 | 3 | |

—‹ 28 ›—

1629.	D. Rupert Guillet	B.	34	13	
1663.	D. William Johnson	Sp.	80		
1671.	D. Anselm Cassey	G.	61	46	

—‹ 29 ›—

| 1776. | D. Philip Jefferson | E. | 44 | 27 | |

October.

—‹ 30 ›—

		M.	A.	R.	P.
1602.	D. Gregory Sayr	Cass.		14	
1618.	D. Nicholas Becket	Sp.			
1689.	D. Ursula Radcliffe	B.V.M.	56	34	
1694.	D. Francis Fenwick	E.	49	31	
1697.	D. Benedict Sies	A.D.		9	
1705.	D. Cuthbert Parker	E.		33	
1792.	M. Clare Knight, Abbess.	B.V.M.		52	

—‹ 31 ›—

		G.	A.	R.	P.
1693,	Br. Wilfrid Reeve	G.	51	18	
1867.	Lay Br. Cuthbert Heptonstall	E.	63	37	
1900	D. Joseph Davis	G.	73	55	46

Right Rev. Peter Augustine O'Neill (b) 69 [a] - 49 [b] - 43 [p] - 15 [c]

November.

—❤1❤—

		M.	A.	R.	P.
1650.	D. Magdalen Cary	B.V.M.	31	10	
1785.	D. Cuthbert Simpson	E	61	40	
1861.	D. Anselm Collyer	G.	69	46	40

—❤2❤—

| 1639. | D. Bernard Berington | Sp. | | | |
| 1669. | Lay Br. John Sherwood | A.D. | | 14 | |

—❤3❤—

1668.	D. Placid Johnson	D.		17	
1671.	D. Gregory Scroggs	G.	56	38	
1788.	D. Josepha Carrington	B.V.M.			

—❤4❤—

| 1726. | Lay Br. Robert Rowston | L. | | 8 | |
| 1786. | D. James Berry | E. | 28 | 8 | |

—❤5❤—

| 1662. | D. Winefrid Colton | B.V.M. | 55 | 34 | |

—❤6❤—

1616.	Br. Joseph Brooks	L.		2	
1668.	D. Francis Walgrave	L.		61	
1761.	D. Joseph Rokeby, Abbot of Lambs.	A.D.	74	59	

November.

—‹7›—

		M.	A.	B.	P.
1845.	D. Benedict Deday	G.	74	52	45

—‹8›—

| 1704. | D. Leander Green | A.D. | | 45 |
| 1772. | D. Placid Naylor, Pres. Gen. | L. | | 62 |

—‹9›—

1632.	D. Michael Blakestone	G.		8
1662.	D. Magdalen Enve	B.V.M.	52	35
1662.	D. Anne More	B.V.M.	62	37
1818.	D. Oswald Johnson	A.D.	68	47

—‹10›—

1657.	Lay S. Helen Kenyon	B.V.M.	53	25
1663.	D. Elphege Sherwood	L.		38
1734.	Lay S. Anne Aston	B.V.M.	46	18
———	D. Teresa Conquest	B.V.M.		
1821.	D. Ambrose Naylor	G.	83	65

—‹11›—

| 1705. | Lay S. Elizabeth Complin | B.V.M. | | 27 |
| 1880. | S. Anastasia Richardson | B.V.M. | 59 | 6 |

—‹12›—

1712.	D. Augustine Constable	G		64
1833.	Lay S. Monica Crookall	B.V.M.	56	34
1863.	D. Benedict Dullard	A.D.	68	32	40

18896 - Don Francis Barz - (E) _ _ 61-.39

4 D. Romuald Magan (L) - 61- 40

1901_D. Normand Kulbeck. 2_76_51_.42

1901_D. Normand Kulbeck. 2_76_51_.42

November.

—< 13 >—

		M.	A.	R.	P.
1640.	Br. Benedict Preston	G.		2	
1652.	D. Andrew Simpson	E·		12	
1677.	D. Augustine Latham, Pr. of St. Ed.	E.	58	38	35
1695.	D. George Beare	G.		26	
1794.	Lay Br. Joseph Sharrock	G.		57	

—< 14 >—

—< 15 >—

		M.	A.	R.	P.
1712.	D. Francis Lawson	G.		63	
1792.	D. Jerome Berry	L.	78	62	

—< 16 >—

		M.	A.	R.	P.
1726.	D. Michael Ellis, Bishop of Aureopolis.	G.	73	57	

—< 17 >—

		M.	A.	R.	P.
1632.	D. Jerome Porter	G.		11	
1682.	D. Augustina Cary	B.V.M.	65	42	
1729.	D. Augustine Tempest, Abb. of Lambs.	A.D.		65	
1797.	Lay Br. James Johnson	L.	83	38	
1846.	M. Gertrude Westhead	B.V.M.	65	40	
1875.	D. Bernard Short	G.	74	56	48

—< 18 >—

		M.	A.	R.	P.
1662.	Br. Dunstan Duck	L.		8	
1749.	D. Benedict Rigmaiden	L.		43	
1871.	D. Gregory Lane	G.	53	32	26

November.

—‹ 19 ›—

		M.	A.	R.	P.
1683.	D. Edward Johnson	L.	21		
1686.	D. Benedicta Conquest	B.V.M.	27	9	
1716.	D. Placid Haggerstone	G.		16	8
1742.	D. Benedict Shaftoe	E.	28		

—‹ 20 ›—

1628.	D. Amandus Verner	L.	15	19	
168—	Br. Augustine Cornwallis	E.			
1806.	D. Benedict Pembridge	G.	81	66	

—‹ 21 ›—

1634.	D. George Gaire	G.	24		
1682.	Lay Br. Laurence Brocast	L.	43		
1695.	Lay Br. Bede Barnes	A.D.	31		
1783.	S. Benedicta Walker	B.V.M.			

—‹ 22 ›—

1650.	D. John Garter	E.	12	7	
1763.	D. Denis Wareham	A.D.	31		
1850.	D. Leo Spain	G.	60	44	

—‹ 23 ›—

| 1713. | Br. Benedict Welden | E. | 39 | 22 | |
| 1729. | D. Thomas Witham | G. | 45 | | |

—‹ 24 ›—

| 1681. | D. Placid Shaftoe | A.D. | 47 | 27 | 22 |

R. P.   35. D. Ignatius Stuart (b) —   80 — 62 ... 56

21

9

16

28

15 16

66
                                                    â   a   p

     85. D. Aidan Hiddy (d) — — — — 60 ... 40 — 33
4   90. D. Bernard Collier (b) — —   89 — 67 — — — 51
3

1903 - Dom. Benedict Paxton (E) 68 - 44

1902 - D. Dunstan Ross (E) 65 - 46 - 39
1903 - D. Bede Preet (E) - 72 - 54 - 48

November.

—‹25›—

		M.	A.	R.	P.
1666.	D. Placida Yaxley	B.V.M.			
1727.	D. Placid Acton	G.		43	
1797.	D. Charles Walmesley Bp. of Rama.	E.	74	59	

—‹26›—

| 1655. | D. Richard Huddlestone | Cass. | 72 | | 48 |

—‹27›—

1644.	Br. William Sheldon	E.		5	
1645.	D. Paulinus Greenwood Prov. of Cant.	G.		34	
1753.	D. Alathea Clifton	B.V.M.			
1779.	D. Anselm Bromley	L.		14	

—‹28›—

| 1639. | D. John Harper | Sp. | | | |

—‹29›—

| 1694. | Br. John Smith | E. | 62 | 18 | |
| 1694. | Br. Richard Yoward | E. | 49 | 32 | |

—‹30›—

1672.	D. Benedict Winchcomb	L.	29	13	
1764.	D. Anselm Mannock	G.	83	65	
1768.	D. Paul Allanson	A.D.		56	

December.

—‹1›—

M. A. R.

—‹2›—

1730. D. Dunstan Hutchinson   A.D.   46

—‹3›—

1794. D. Maurus Barret   L. 59 42

—‹4›—

1703. D. Charles Barker   L.   16
1705. D. Susanna Philips   B.V.M. 57 32
1734. D. Winefrid Howet   B.V.M. 49 32

—‹5›—

16—   Lay Br. Benedict Galli
1782. D. Wilfrid Strutt   A.D. 72 40
1815. D. Laurence Forshaw   A.D. 47 28
1860. D. Ambrose Prest   L. 60 42
1862. D. Maurus Hodgson   G. 47 29

—‹6›—

1641. Lay S. Angela Mullins   B.V.M. 25 2
1720. D. Francis Mildmay   A.D.   47
1736. D. Augustine Dunscombe   A.D. 34 15
1792. D. Bernard Nechills   E. 81 64
1878. D. Monica Mordle   B.V.M. 65 44

R. P.

805 - D. Ambrose Turner (L) -   51 __ 32 __ 25 -
16   911 - D. Dunstan Green (f) - --- 70 - 51 __ 42

12
      883 - D. Nicholas Kendal (g) - - - 78 -- 58 -- 53

16
32
32

40
28
42
29 22

2
47
15
64
11

Vincent Murphy (C) — — 43 — 16 —. 13

Dom Vincent Murphy

December.

—< 7 >—

		M.	A.	R.	P.
1699.	D. Maurus Poss	G.		50	
1712.	D. James Winton	A.D.	40	23	
1786.	D. John Charlton	G.	76	51	
1808.	D. Placid Waters	G.	68	52	

—< 8 >—

| 1711. | D. John Tempest | A.D. | | 51 | |
| 1715. | Lay S. Josepha Dodd | B.V.M. | 63 | | |

—< 9 >—

1640.	Br. Jerome Hesketh	G.		2	
1704.	D. Vincent Craven	L.		19	
1744.	Lay S. Elizabeth Fairclough	B.V.M.	46	24	
1836.	D. Clement Rishton	L.		34	31

—< 10 >—

1610.	D. John Roberts	Sp.		16	9
16—	D. Teresa Conquest	B.V.M.			
1829.	D. Bernard Clarkson	L.		13	6

—< 11 >—

| 1664. | D. Benedict Meryng | A.D. | 66 | 7 | |
| 1683. | D. Benedict Constable | A.D. | | 15 | |

—< 12 >—

1657.	D. Michael Witham	G.		22	
1709.	D. Gregory Timperley	E.	78	33	
1719.	D. Magdalen Moore	B.V.M.	61	44	
1755.	D. Francis Howard	L.		48	

December.

		M.	A.	R.	P.
1774.	Lay S. Alexia Elerby	B.V.M.			
1802.	D. Basil Brindle	L.	56	38	
1873.	D. Placid de Paiva	G.	37	18	9

—< 13 >—

1646.	D. Placid Loader	G.		27	22
1835.	D. James Higginson	G.	71	51	

—< 14 >—

1866.	D. Bede Jolley	E.	42	22	13

—< 15 >—

1640.	D. Swithbert Latham	L.		27	
1803.	D. Joseph Collins	A.D.	45	21	
1856.	D. Augustine Marsh	E.	62	33	30
1864.	D. Hilary Dowding	L.		32	30

—< 16 >—

1720.	D. Bernard Greaves, Prov. of York	G.		45	

—< 17 >—

1685.	Br. Adrian Kirke	A.D.		33	
1867.	D. Ignatius Abram	G.	71	54	47

—< 18 >—

1717.	D. Richard Holmes	G.		42	
1792.	Lay Br. Bernard Beckman	A.D.		58	
1803.	D. George Johnson	G.	55	36	

—< 19 >—

1624.	D. Torquatus Latham	Sp.			
1799.	D. Joseph Storey	A.D.		49	

4. D. Paulonus Thomas (b) - - 36_ 15 _ _ _ 8

2. D. Wilfrid Drongool (P) _ _ 81 _ _ 50 — 41

305-
Dom Willibrord Van Volckxsom (g) 61--31-24 :-

December.

—‹ 20 ›—

		M.	A.	R.	P.
1715.	Lay Br. John Armston	G.		11	
1738.	Lay Br. Maurus Graincourt	G.		12	
1779.	D. Angela Plompton	B.V.M.	83	66	
1878.	Lay S. Agnes Lacy	B.V.M.	72	52	

—‹ 21 ›—

1645.	D. Pudentiana Deacons	B.V.M.	64	37	
1677.	D. Cuthbert Horsley	L.	80	52	
1738.	Br. Mark Le Doux	G.			
1831.	S. Edith Breen	B.V.M.		1	

—‹ 22 ›—

1715.	D. Maurus Corker	A.D.	79	60	
1805.	D. Anselm Bolton	L.	70	53	

—‹ 23 ›—

1677.	D. Thomas Fursden	L.	92	58	

—‹ 24 ›—

1639.	D. Stanislaus Tanke	G.		15	

—‹ 25 ›—

1663.	D. Bernard Palmes	G.		21	
1880.	D. Jerome Lynch	L.	31	13	6

—‹ 26 ›—

1725.	D. Oswald Smithers	A.D.		32	
1824.	Lay Br. John Knacksterdt	A.D.		29	

December.

—‹27›—

		M.	A.	R.	P.
1635.	D. Leander Jones, Pres. Gen.	Sp.	60	35	
1700.	D. Placida Sheldon	B.V.M.			
1741.	D. Robert Hardcastle	L.		52	
1764.	D. Wilfrid Constable	E.	58	49	

—‹28›—

1635.	D. Anselm Beech	Cass.		45	
1790.	Br. Robert Copsey	A.D.	73	58	
1826.	D. Benedicta Partington	B.V.M.	75		

—‹29›—

1709.	D. Joseph Kennet	L.		26	
1758.	D. Leander Raffa	G.		26	
1850.	D. Bernard Barber, Pres. Gen.	G.	61	44	36

—‹30›—

| 1784. | D. Anselm Chaplin | A.D. | 30 | 14 | |

—‹31›—

| 1645. | D. Francis Hull | L. | | 31 | |
| 1723. | Lay Br. Peter Moncy | | | | |

07 - Dom Romuald Woods (S) - 75 - 57

91 - Dom Clifton (S) - - 73 - 50

ALPHABETICAL LIST

OF THE

DECEASED MEMBERS

OF THE

ENGLISH CONGREGATION

OF THE

Order of Saint Benedict.

b. signifies lay-brother.   *c.*, circiter, about.

ABRAM, Ignatius.   1867.   Dec. 17th.

Acton, Augustine.   1695.

Acton, Placid.   1727.   Nov. 25th.

Addison, Scholastica.   1744.   April 4th.

Addy, Bede.   1705.   Aug. 16th.

Adelham, Placid.   1681-5.

Ainsworth, Ralph.   1814.   Feb. 5th.

Alcock, Jerome.   1817.   June 1st.

Alexander, Jane.   1799.   June 17th.

Allam, Ambrose.   1812.   Sep. 5th.

Allanson, Athanasius. 1876. Jan. 13th.

Allanson, Paul. 1768. Nov. 30th.

Allen, John. 1635. June 30th.

Allerton, Denis. 1829. Aug. 26th.

Almond, Bede. 1873. Sep. 27th.

Anderton, Bede. 1779. July 5th.

Anderton, Celestine. 1697.

Anderton, Christopher. 1653. July 11th.

Anderton, James. 1646. Aug. 27th.

Anderton, Placid. 1718. April 4th.

Anderton, Robert. 1677-81.

Anderton, Thomas. 1671. Oct. 6th.

Ann, Anselma. 1794. Jan. 14th.

Appleby, Paulinus. 1645.

Appleton, Anselm. 1842. June 1st.

Appleton, Francis. 1847. May 26th.

Appleton, Laurence. 1664.

Appleton, Marina. 1694. Jan. 29th.

Aprice, Ildephonsus. 1712. Mar. 18th.

Aprice, Joseph. 1703. July 25th.

Arkwright, Dunstan. 1854. Sep. 12th.

Armston, John. l. 1715. Dec. 20th.

Arrowsmith, Edmund. l. 1633. May 27th.

Ashe, Edward. 1629. c.

Ashton, Alban. 1748. April 8th.

Ashton, Joseph. 1700. Aug. 28th.

Ashton, Placid. 1761. April 26th.

Ashton, Robert.   1677-81.

Aspenwall, John.   1762.   Aug. 1st.

Aston, Ann.   1734.   Nov. 10th.

Atkins, Maurus.   1635.   Mar. 10th.

Atkinson, Augustine.   1807.   Mar. 8th

Atkinson, Augustine.   1876.   Mar 26th.

Atkinson, John.   1822.   April 5th.

Atrobas, Francis.   1626.   June 10th.

Augustine de S. Facundo.   1605.   Jan. 20th.

Ayvay, Anna.   1713.   April 20th.

ACON, George.   1663.   April 4th.

Bagnall, Placid.   1708.   Oct. 7th.

Bagshaw, Sigebert.   1633.   Aug. 19th.

Baines, Augustine.   1843.   July 6th.

Baker, Augustine.   1641.   Aug. 9th.

Ball, Winefrid.   1774.   Oct. 27th.

Ballyman, Gregory.   1811.   July 23rd.

Ballyman, Thomas.   1795.   Aug. 6th.

Banester, Bede.   1629.   June 6th.

Banester, William.   1726.   May 16th.

Banks, Alban.   1829.   Jan. 27th.

Bapthorpe, Mellitus.   1654.   May 29th.

Barber, Bernard.   1850.   Dec. 29th.

Barber, Maurus.   1728.   Feb. 13th.

Barber, Stephen.   1847.   Sep. 2nd.

Barbierre, John.   1.   166--.   May 13th.

Barguet, Andrew. 1. 1776. Feb. 20th.

Barker, Charles. 1703. Dec. 4th.

Barker, Joseph. 1. 1782.

Barker, Thomas. 1798. March 5th.

Barkworth, Mark. 1601. Feb. 27th.

Barlow, Ambrose. 1641. Sep. 20th.

Barlow, Theodore. 1633.

Barlow, Rudesind. 1656. Sep. 19th.

Barnard, Adrian. 1699. Jan. 3rd.

Barnes, Bede. 1. 1695. Nov. 21st.

Barnes, John. 1775. Sep. 6th.

Barnes, Laurence. 1803. May 31st.

Barnewall, Bernarda. 18—.

Barnewall, Cyprian. 1788. July 2nd.

Barr, Bernard. 1823. May 20th.

Barret, Maurus. 1794. Dec. 3rd.

Barrister, Amanda. 1749. July 22nd.

Barter, John. 1653. July 1st.

Barter, John. 1667. Aug. 11th.

Bartholomew, Dom. 1616. c.

Bartlet, Bernard. 1735. Feb. 12th.

Barton, Bede. 1790. Oct. 19th.

Barton, Wolstan. 1867. May 15th.

Batchell, Agnes. 1763. May 7th.

Batchelor, Edmund. 1737. March 10th.

Bate, Josepha. 1758. April 23rd.

Batemanson, Anne. 1701. Sep. 14th.

Bateson, Joseph. I. 1733. March 10th.

Batt, Anthony. 1751. Jan. 12th.

Beare, George. 1695. Nov. 13th.

Becket, Nicholas. 1618. Oct. 30th.

Beckman, Bernard. I. 1792. Dec. 18th.

Beech, Anselm. 1635. Dec. 28th.

Belerby, Gertrude. 1750. Oct. 12th.

Bell, Bernard. 1879. Oct. 6th.

Bennet, Alexius. 1636. Aug. 3rd.

Bennet, Bede. 1800. Oct. 14th.

Bennet, Claude. 1655. Oct. 14th.

Bennet, Maurus. 1663. June 9th.

Bennet, Placid. 1795. March 1st.

Benson, Robert. 1650. Feb. 8th.

Berington, Bernard. 1659. Nov. 2nd.

Berington, George. 1664. May 19th.

Berriman, Alban. 1715. Jan. 18th.

Berriman, Joseph. 1715.

Berry, James. 1786. Nov. 4th.

Berry, Jerome. 1792. Nov. 15th.

Beswick, Francis. 1793. Oct. 19th.

Betenson, Placid. 1689.

Birdsall, Augustine. 1837. Aug. 2nd.

Bishop, Denis. 1725. Oct. 16th.

Blakestone, Francis. 1650. March 6th.

Blakestone, Michael. 1632. Nov. 9th.

Blakey, Anselm. 1723. May 2nd.

Blakey, Joseph. 1. 1691. Sep. 2nd.

Blakey, Philip. 1707. Aug. 22nd.

Blundy, Boniface. 1634. March 22nd.

Blount, Benedict. 1865. Feb. 12th.

Blount, Godric. 1667. Sep. 12th.

Blount, Maurus. 1746. Oct. 25th.

Blyde, Lucy. 1816. Aug. 12th.

Bocquet, Gabriel. 1. 1737. Feb. 7th.

Bolas, Anselm. 1797. Sep. 30th.

Bolas, Benedict. 1773. Jan. 30th.

Bolton, Anselm. 1805. Dec. 22nd.

Bonney, Benedict. 1864. May 2nd.

Booth, Ambrose. 1679. Aug. 25th.

Boucher, Ambrose. 1766. July 13th.

Brabant, Thomas. 1. 1705. July 10th.

Boult, Benedicta. 1659. Oct. 13th.

Bradley, Anselm. 1856. Aug. 20th.

Bradley, Bernard. 1709. Aug. 20th.

Bradshaw, Anselm. 1799. Jan. 20th.

Bradshaw, Augustine. 1618. May 4th.

Bradshaw, Basil. 1770. April 12th.

Bradshaw, Bernard. 1774. Aug. 19th.

Bradstock, John. 1. 1658. May 20th.

Breen, Edith. 1831. Dec. 21st.

Brent, Christina. 1700. Sep. 14th.

Brent, Cuthbert. 1676. Sep, 26th.

Brent, Elizabeth. 1660. Jan. 1st.

Brent, George.   1716.   Sep. 6th.

Brent, Helen.   1688.   May 5th.

Bretherton, Basil.   1837.   Mar. 12th.

Breton, Barbara.   1689.   Sep. 28th.

Brett, Gabriel.   1665.   Aug. 12th.

Brewer, Bede.   1822.   April 18th.

Bride, Ambrose.   1669.   c.

Bridge, Aloysia.   1857.   Feb. 23rd.

Bridgeman, Wilfrid.   1782.   Dec. 5th.

Brigham, Augustine.   1738.   Feb. 5th.

Brindle, Basil.   1802.   Dec. 12th.

Brocast, Laurence.   l.   1682.   Nov. 21st.

Bromley, Anselm.   1779.   Nov. 27th.

Brooks, Joseph.   1616.   Nov. 6th.

Broughton, Anselm.   1666.   May 5th.

Broughton, Mark.   1658.   Mar. 14th.

Brown, Ambrose.   1755.   Feb 2nd.

Brown, Anselm.   1706.   Feb. 14th.

Brown, Ebba.   1631.   Sep. 22nd.

Brown, Flavia.   1665.   Feb. 2nd.

Brown, George.   1618.   Oct. 21st.

Brown, Joseph.   1880.   April 12th.

Brown, Macarius.   1699.

Bruning, Francis.   1747.   May 26th.

Bruning, Jerome.   1689.   Sep. 14th.

Bruning, Placid.   1720.

Bruning, Thomas.   1719.   Aug 6th.

Brychan, Benedict. 1676. Jan. 25th.

Buckley, James. 1749. April 17th.

Buckley, Maurus. 1729.

Buckley, Sigebert. 1610. Feb. 22nd.

Budd, Placid. 1649. c.

Bulmer, Denis. 1741. July 17th.

Bulmer, Edward. 1745. Mar 16th.

Bulmer, Maurus. 1788. 'Sep. 10th.

Burchall, Wilfrid. 1866. June 27th.

Burden, Joseph. 1807. Oct. 1st.

Burgess, Bede. 1837. Aug. 22nd.

Burgess, Margaret. 1794. April 3rd.

Burgess, Scholastica. 1770. Sept. 16th.

Burn, Andrew. 1. 1782. July 14th.

Butler, Bernard. 1825. July 2nd.

Butler, Jerome. 1792. Nov. 15th.

Byerley, Ildephonsus. 1753. Oct. 12th.

Byfleet, John. 1701. Aug. 29th.

CALDERBANK, James. 1821. April 9th.

Caldwell, Alban. 1870. Jan. 15th.

Caldwell, Augustine. 1815. Jan. 8th.

Callaghan, Ignatius. 1859. Mar. 31st.

Canning, George. 1695.

Cape, Benedict. 1619. c.

Cape, Francis. 1668. Jan. 30th.

Cape, Lucy. 1643. Oct. 24th.

Cape, Michael. 1668. Jan. 29th.

Carnaby, Gregory. 1673. Mar. 29th.

Carrington, Josepha. 1788. Nov. 3rd.

Carroll, John. 1881. Oct. 15th.

Carter, Anselm. 1727.

Carteret, Joseph. 1783. Sep. 3rd.

Cary, Augustina. 1682. Nov. 17th.

Cary, Clementina. 1671. April 26th.

Cary, Magdalen. 1650. Nov. 1st.

Cary, Mary. 1693. Sep. 22nd.

Cary, Placid. 1653. Feb. 17th.

Caryl, Alexius. 1677. c.

Casse, Laurence. 1732. Sep 5th.

Cassey, Anselm. 1671. Oct. 28th.

Caton, Scholastica. 1830. Feb. 13th.

Catteral, Benedict. 1791. July 31st.

Catteral, Bernard. 1781. Sep. 9th.

Cawser, Benedict. 1794. Jan. 9th.

Celler, Jane. 1683. April 11th.

Chamberlain, Francis. 1. 1669. June 17th.

Chambers, William. 1663. Oct. 28th.

Champney, Laurence. 1732. April 21st.

Champney, William. 1740. Jan. 11th.

Chandler, Boniface. 1660. Jan. 16th.

Chandler, Paul. 1712. April 12th.

Chaplin, Anselm. 1784. Dec. 30th.

Chaplin, Maurus. 1808. April 22nd.

Chapman, Benedicta.   1848.   May 8th.

Chare, Christina.   1830.   April 14th.

Charlton, John.   1786.   Dec. 7th.

Cheriton, Basil.   1662.   May 11th.

Cheriton, Matthew.   1670.   Jan. 30th.

Chew, Alexius.   1832.   Feb. 25th.

Chew, Martha.   1878.   Oct. 14th.

Chilton, Gertrude.   1733.   April 10th.

Chilton, Teresa.   1739.   Mar. 10th.

Chorley, Edward.   1718.   July 14th.

Clarkson, Alban.   1815.   July 16th.

Clarkson, Athanasius.   1864.   July 9th.

Clarkson, Bernard.   1829.   Dec. 10th.

Clarkson, Jerome.   1.   1769.   July 27th.

Clerc Le, Magdalen.   1878.   Mar. 28th.

Clerc Le, Placida.   1843.   Oct. 22nd.

Cliffe, Ildephonsus.   1657.

Clifford, Augustine.   1843.   Oct. 22nd.

Clifton, Alathea.   1753.   Nov. 27th.

Clifton, Lambert.   1621.   c.

Cockshoot, Anselm.   1872.   Feb. 20th.

Codner, David.   1631.   c.

Coffin, Bridget.   1758.   April 24th.

Coffin, Mary.   1770.   Sep. 29th.

Collingwood, Anselm.   1679.   April 13th.

Collins, Cuthbert.   1870.   Sep. 19th.

Collins, Joseph.   1803.   Dec. 15th.

Collyer, Anselm.   1861.   Nov. 1st.

Colston, Nicholas.   1702.   Oct. 20th.

Colton, Winefrid.   1662.   Nov. 5th.

Commings, Placid.   1655.   May 30th.

Complin, Elizabeth.   1705.   Nov. 11th.

Conquest, Benedicta.   1686.   Nov. 19th.

Conquest, Teresa.   ———   Dec. 10th.

Constable, Augustine.   1712.   Nov. 12th.

Constable, Barbara.   1684.   Jan. 26th.

Constable, Benedict.   1683.   Dec. 11th.

Constable, Francis.   1654.   May 28th.

Constable, Philip,   1681.   c.

Constable, Wilfrid.   1764.   Dec. 27th.

Constable, Winefrid.   1680.   Jan. 20th.

Conyers, Augustine.   1681.   c.

Cook, Clare.   1685.   Sep. 21st.

Cook, Francis.   1858.   April 3rd.

Cooper, Francis.   1850.   May 9th.

Cooper, Maurus.   1869.   Jan. 1st.

Cooper, Wilfrid.   1877.   Jan. 30th.

Copsey, Robert.   1790.   Dec. 28th.

Cordonnier, Paul.   l.   1876.   Nov. 13th.

Corham, Robert.   1665.   Jan. 18th.

Corker, Maurus.   1715.   Dec. 22nd.

Corlett, Placid.   1872.   Sep. 8th.

Cornwallis, Augustine.   1684.   c.

Cotham, Ambrose   1883.   May 1st.

Coupe, Jerome. 1827. May 22nd.

Coupe, Maurus. 1753. Mar. 14th.

Cowley, Gregory. 1799. June 19th.

Cowper, Ildephonsus. 1657.

Cox, Benedict. 1648. Mar. 23rd.

Cox, Edmund. 1745. Mar. 19th.

Craffe, Dunstan. 1637. Mar. 27th.

Crathorne, Anselm. 1746. Mar. 4th.

Crathorne, Francis. 1667. April 19th.

Craven, Vincent. 1704. Dec. 9th.

Cressy, Serenus. 1674. Aug. 10th.

Crilly, Clare. 1851. Jan. 7th.

Croft, Clement. 1868. Feb. 4th.

Crook, James. 1770. Aug. 4th.

Crook, Joseph. 1800. Jan. 10th.

Crookall, Catherine. 1855. Sep. 25th.

Crookall, Monica. 1833. Nov. 12th.

Crosby, Wolstan. 1713. April 18th.

Crowther, Anselm. 1666. May 5th.

Crowther, Mark. 1658. Mar. 14th.

Cumberlege, Benedict. 1730. Jan. 6th.

Cummins, Bede. 1876. Aug. 23rd.

Curre, Maurus. 1635. June 20th.

Curre, Nicholas. 1649. Aug. 5th.

Curwen, Patrick. 1707. Mar. 11th.

AKINS, John.   1710.   Feb. 28th.

Dale, Maurus.   1726.   June 22nd.

Dale, Vincent.   1847.   June 26th.

Dalton, Wolstan.   1677.   May 17th.

Dalyson, Gregory.   1710.   Aug. 1st.

Dandy, Anthony.   1.   1704.   July 16th.

Daniel, Benedict.   1775.   July 10th.

Daniel, Felicitas.   1853.   Mar. 29th.

Daniel, Robert.   1781.   Sep. 12th.

Danvers, Romuald.   1634.   Aug. 15th.

Darell, Maurus.   1774.   July 10th.

Darell, Olivia.   1760.   April 29th.

Davis, Ambrose.   1754.   Aug. 1st.

Davis, Bernard.   1789.   Feb. 26th.

Davis, Henry.   1854.   May 17th.

Davis, Leander.   1734.   Sep. 1st.

Davis, Maurus.   1663.   June 9th.

Davis, Oswald.   1880.   Sep. 25th.

Dawber, John.   1810.   June 7th.

Dawney, Alban.   1733.   Feb. 17th.

Day, Bede.   1870.   Feb. 16th.

Deacons, Pudentiana.   1645.   Dec. 21st.

Deday, Benedict.   1845.   Nov. 7th.

Delattre, Augustine.   1733.   May 1st.

Delattre, Charles.   1731.   June 24th.

Delattre, Etheldreda.   17—   Mar. 8th.

Delattre, Laurence. 1. 1745. Feb. 28th.

Demonchy, Romuald. 1855. May 14th.

Deval, Peter. 1. 1733. Jan. 29th.

Digby, Jerome. 1825. April 7th.

Dinmore, Vincent. 1879. July 21st.

Dobson, Elphege. 1750. Sep. 3rd.

Dodd, Josepha. 1715. Dec. 8th.

D'Ognate, Joseph. 1740. Feb. 7th.

D'Orgaine, Benedict. 1636. May 11th.

Doutch, Anthony. 1. 1720. April 8th.

Dowding, Augustine. 1877. June 17th.

Dowding, Hilary. 1864. Dec. 15th.

Dowding, Vincent. 1877. Oct. 24th.

Draper, James. 1. 1739. Aug. 31st.

Duck, Ambrose. 1848. Sep. 18th.

Duck, Basil. 1863. April 2nd.

Duck, Dunstan. 1662. Nov. 18th.

Duckett, Edmund. 1792. Mar. 24th.

Duddell, Odo. 1738. Feb. 12th.

Dullard, Benedict. 1863. Nov. 12th.

Dunn, Alban. 1872. May 31st.

Dunn, Rowland. 1675. Aug. 20th.

Dunscombe, Augustine. 1736. Dec. 6th

Du Pery, Bathildis. 1773. Oct. 20th.

Duviviers, Placid. 1808. Dec. 7th.

Dwerihouse, Josepha. 1726. Oct. 26th

Dyer, Thomas. 1615.

ASTGATE, Ambrose.   1725.   July 4th.

Eastham, Anselm.   1774.   May 13th.

Eastham, Maurus.   1797.   Oct. 8th.

Eaves, Oswald.   1793.   Oct. 15th.

Eaves, Thomas.   1747.   April 29th.

Edmunds, Bernard.   1636.   April 1st.

Edmunds, Robert.   1615.   Jan. 28th.

Edner, Justus.   1635.   April 23rd.

Eldridge, Raymund.   1829.   Aug. 13th.

Elerby, Alexia.   1774.   Dec. 12th.

Elliott, Ambrose.   1773.   June 16th.

Ellis, Philip.   1726.   Nov. 16th.

Elmer, Jocelin.   1651.   July 1st.

Emerson, Thomas.   1630.   Oct. 10th.

Englefield, Benedicta.   1725.   July 3rd.

Enve, Magdalen.   1662.   Nov. 9th.

Errington, Agnes.   1662.   June 4th.

Errington, Laurence.   1654.   c.

Everard, Dunstan.   1650.   Feb. 10th.

Eves, Mary.   1732.   July 28th.

Eyston, Basil.   1785.   April 29th.

ACUNDO, Augustine de S.   1605.   Jan. 20th.

Fairclough, Benedicta.   1741.   Aug. 4th.

Fairclough, Charles.   1880.   April 4th.

Fairclough, Elizabeth.   1744.   Dec. 9th.

Fairclough, Francis.   1835.   Oct. 14th.

Fairfax, Placid.   1739.   Feb. 10th.

Farnaby, Bede.   1687.

Farnworth, Cuthbert.   1754.   Jan. 1st.

Farnworth, Jerome.   1711.   Feb. 9th.

Fazakerley, Agatha.   1726.   Sep. 20th.

Fenwick, Alexia.   1689.   June 29th.

Fenwick, Augustine.   1726.   July 4th.

Fenwick, Francis.   1694.   Oct. 30th.

Fenwick, Laurence.   1746.   June 4th.

Feraud, Ambrose.   1847.   Feb. 18th.

Fermor, Amandus.   1628.   Nov. 20th.

Fermor, Maurus.   1689.   Mar. 10th.

Ferreyra, James.   1712.   Jan. 16th.

Fesand, Edward.   1630.   c.

Fisher, Alexius.   1777.   Oct. 9th.

Fisher, Edward.   1824.   Jan. 15th.

Fisher, John.   1793.   Jan. 27th.

Fisher, Wilfrid.   1847.   April 12th.

Fitzjames, Nicholas.   1652.   May 16th.

Fitzwilliams, George.   1725.   Aug. 15th.

Fleming, Alphonsus.   1873.   Oct. 10th.

Flinn, Gregory.   1836.   Aug. 8th.

Flutot, Maurus.   1669.   Oct. 2nd.

Foley, Benedicta.   1839.   Sep. 27th.

Fontaine, Placid de la.   1780.   July 5th.

Foorde, Placid.   1655.   May 30th.

Forshaw, Laurence.   1815.   Dec. 5th.

Foster, Bede.   1694.   April 10th.

Foster, Francis.   1631.   June 4th.

Foster, Joseph.   1636.   Aug. 7th.

Francis, Placid.   1715.   July 27th.

Francomme, Maurus.   1862.   Aug. 13th.

Frankland, Hugh.   1755.   May 16th.

Frere, Joseph.   1794.   Jan. 10th.

Frere, Mechtildis.   1676.   Jan. 26th.

Frere, Placid.   1632.   May 8th.

Froes, Celestine.   1881.   May 1st.

Fryar, Martha.   1825.   Jan. 2nd.

Fuller, Alban.   1691.   Feb. 22nd.

Fursden, Cuthbert.   1633.   Feb. 2nd.

Fursden, Thomas.   1677.   Dec. 23rd.

AILE, Bede.   1629.   June 6th.

Gaire, George.   1634.   Nov. 21st.

Galli, Benedict.   1.   1649.   c.   Dec. 5th.

Garner, Benedict.   1796.   Jan. 29th.

Garstang, Dunstan.   1814.   Jan. 12th.

Garter, John.   1650.   Nov. 22nd.

Gascoigne, Catherine.   1676.   May 21st.

Gascoigne, Frances.   1708.   Sep. 21st.

Gascoigne, Josepha.   1774.   Jan. 25th.

Gascoigne, Justina.   1690.   May 17th.

Gascoigne, Margaret.   1637.   Aug. 16th.

Gascoigne, Michael.   1657.   Oct. 17th.

Gascoigne, Paula.   1746.   Jan. 17th.

Gascoigne, Placid.   1681.   July 24th.

Gaudelier, Mary.   1727.   Feb. 18th.

Gawen, Ambrose.   1737.   Sep. 3rd.

Gawen, Frances.   1640.   May 17th.

Geary, Anselm,   1795.   Mar. 23rd.

George, de S. Ildephonso.   1655.   Jan. 8th.

Gervase, George.   1608.   April 11th.

Gibbon, Benedict.   1723.   Jan. 1st.

Gibson, Clement.   1846.   Oct. 23rd.

Gibson, Dunstan.   1636.   c.

Gicou, Francis.   1648.   Jan. 24th.

Gifford, Gabriel.   1629.   April 10th.

Gifford, Peter.   1649.   c.

Gilbert, Augustine.   1847.   May 31st.

Gill, Anne.   1692.   Feb. 1st.

Gillett, Ambrose.   1874.   Oct. 5th.

Gilmore, Paul.   1748.   Feb. 20th.

Girlington, John.   1729.   Aug. 15th.

Glasscock or Gloster, Edward.   1652.

Glover, Benedict.   1834.   May 14th.

Glover, Vincent.   1840.   Aug. 6th.

Goaverdt, Christian.   1643.   c.

Godfrey, Michael.   1626.   c.

Goolde, Robert.   1798.   Feb. 13th.

Gordon, William.   1638.   Sep. 14th.

Gore, Bernard.   1844.   Sep. 18th.

Grafton, Maurus. 1834. Mar. 17th.

Graincourt, Maurus. l. 1738. Dec. 20th.

Grand, James le. 1772. Oct. 3rd.

Grange, Gregory. 1619. April 18th.

Grange, Gregory. 1673. Mar. 29th.

Gratian, John. l. 1656. Feb. 25th.

Gray, Gervase. 1641. April 6th.

Greaves, Bernard. 1720. Dec. 16th.

Green, Dominic. 1699. April 9th.

Green, John. 1699. Sep. 26th.

Green, John. l. 1699. Oct. 20th.

Green, Leander. 1704. Nov. 8th.

Green, Thomas. 1624. Aug. 8th.

Greenough, Ignatius. 1840. May 26th.

Greenough, Ignatius. 1870. Oct. 26th.

Greenwood, Gregory. 1744. Aug. 3rd.

Greenwood, Paulinus. 1645. Nov. 27th.

Gregory, Gregory. 1877. July 19th.

Gregson, Augustine. 1779. July 17th.

Gregson, Bernard. 1711. Jan. 27th.

Gregson, Gregory. 1800. Oct. 18th.

Gregson, Peter. l. 1712. May 17th.

Gregson, Scholastica. 1875. Mar. 16th.

Gregson, Vincent. 1800. Sep. 10th.

Grimbaldeston, Clement. 1824. Oct. 17th.

Grimbaldeston, Paul. 1807. Aug. 25th.

Grime, Cuthbert. 1786. Feb. 2nd.

Grossier, Romanus.   1649. c.

Grove, Dunstan.   1637.   Mar. 27th.

Guillet, Rupert.   1629. Oct. 28th.

Guilliam, David.   1669.   Feb. 7th.

Gurnall, Adrian.   1811.   Jan. 5th.

Gurney, Teresa.   1678.   Jan. 22nd.

HADDOCK, Robert.   1650.   Feb. 8th.

Hadley, Edmund.   1807.   Mar. 24th.

Hadley, Laurence.   1805.   May 30th.

Hagan, Louisa.   1811.   June 6th.

Haggerston, Elizabeth.   1795-1807.

Haggerston, Placid.   1716.   Nov. 19th.

Hall, Boniface.   1803.   Oct. 16th.

Hall, Cecily.   1651.   Mar. 13th.

Hall, Maura.   1690.   Mar. 17th.

Halsall, Bede.   1737.   Feb. 11th.

Hames, Maurus.   1657.   April 22nd.

Hamoy, Anselm.   1.   1621.   Feb. 12th.

Hampson, Jerome.   1867.   Aug. 29th.

Hankinson, Adrian.   1870.   Sep. 21st.

Hankinson, Benedict.   1.   1690.   Mar. 5th.

Hanmer, Joseph.   1754.   Mar. 14th.

Hanson, Alphonsus.   1644.   July 26th.

Hanson, Maurus.   1630.   Mar. 15th.

Hardcastle, Robert.   1741.   Dec. 27th.

Hardisty, Adrian.   1761.   Sep. 14th.

Hardisty, Laurence.   1787.   Feb. 18th.

Harper, John,   1639.   Nov. 28th.

Harrington, Maura.   1720.   Feb. 6th.

Harris, Richard.   1810.   June 9th.

Harrison, Augustine.   1846.   Mar. 6th.

Harrison, Maurus.   1717.

Harsnip, Benedict.   1760.   Sep. 5th.

Harsnip, Placid.   1807.   Mar. 25th.

Hartburne, Cuthbert.   1646.

Hartburne, Placid.   1655.   May 30th.

Hathersall, George.   1633.   c.

Hatton, Augustine.   1823.   April 6th.

Havers, Bartholomew.   1735.   Jan. 18th.

Hawet, Edmund.   1688.   Feb. 4th.

Hawkins, James.   1752.   July 15th.

Haworth, Joseph.   1624.   June 24th.

Hayward, Gregory.   1632.   June 27th.

Heath, Augustine.   1631.   Oct. 24th.

Heatley, Jerome.   1792.   April 28th.

Heatley, Lewis.   1805.   May 9th.

Heatley, Maurus.   1802.   Aug. 15th.

Helme, Bede.   1629.   Jan. 24th.

Helme, Frances.   1812.   Jan. 29th.

Helme, Gregory.   1696.   Aug. 11th.

Helme, Wilfrid.   1742.   Jan. 2nd.

Hemsworth, Benedict.   1702.   June 5th.

Heptonstall, Cuthbert.   1.   1867.   Oct. 31st.

Heptonstall, Paulinus. 1869. June 7th.

Hesketh, Alphonsus. 1644. July 26th.

Hesketh, Gregory. 1695. Jan. 25th.

Hesketh, Jerome. 1640. Dec. 9th.

Hesketh, Jerome. 1693.

Hesketh, Joseph. 1703.

Hesketh, Mellitus. 1674. Jan. 12th.

Hesketh, Nicholas. 1688. May 10th.

Hesketh, Thomas. 1694. Oct. 22nd.

Hethcote, William. 1644. July 26th.

Hewitt, Joseph. 1869. Mar. 11th.

Hewlett, William. 1747. Jan. 27th.

Higginson, James. 1835. Dec. 13th.

Higgs, Alexius. l. 1700. c.

Hill, Thomas. 1644. Aug. 7th.

Hilton, Placid. 1626. Feb. 20th.

Hird, Paulinus. 1645.

Hitchcock, William. 1711. Aug. 10th.

Hodgson, Maurus. 1862. Dec. 5th.

Hodgson, Richard. 1626. Feb. 29th.

Hodgson, Stephen. 1816. April 9th.

Hodson, Gertrude. 1652. Oct. 7th.

Hodson, Scholastica. 1690. May 11th.

Holden, Gregory. 1859. Jan. 8th.

Holderness, Dunstan. 1782.

Holderness, Francis. l. 1820. April 12th.

Holme, Richard. 1717. Dec. 18th.

Holmes, Peter. l. 1674. Oct. 26th.

Hooke, Christina. 1792. Aug. 3rd.

Hoole, Benedict. 1865. Mar. 4th.

Hornyold, Bernard. 1694. Aug. 22nd.

Horsley, Cuthbert. 1677. Dec. 21st.

Horsman, Adrian. 1799. July 22nd.

Horsman, Juliana. 1851. Jan. 16th.

Hoskins, Mary. 1667. Mar. 4th.

Houghton, Bede. 1687.

Houghton, Bede. l. 1755. Mar. 25th.

Houghton, Edward. 1751. Aug. 26th.

Houghton, Eugenia. 1701. Mar. 12th.

Houghton, Scholastica. 1726. Jan. 6th.

Houghton, Thomas. 1624. Aug. 8th.

Howard, Augustine. 1718. Aug. 26th.

Howard, Francis. 1755. Dec. 12th.

Howard, Joseph. 1733. Sep. 16th.

Howard, Placid. 1766. July 5th.

Howet, Winefrid. 1734. Dec. 4th.

Hubberstey, Cuthbert. 1865. Aug. 13th.

Huddlestone, John. 1698. Sep. 22nd.

Huddlestone, Richard. 1655. Nov. 26th.

Hudson, Augustine. 1732. Sep. 23rd.

Huitson, Peter. l. 1664. Aug. 13th.

Hull, Francis. 1645. Dec. 31st.

Hungate, Augustine. 1672. Jan. 2nd.

Hungate, Gregory. 1657, c.

Hungate, Thomas. 1657. c.

Hunt, Peter. 1669. Mar. 21st.

Huntley, Bernard. l. 1714. May 24th.

Hussey, Cecily. 1721. April 9th.

Hussey, Edward. 1786. Feb. 25th.

Hutchinson, Cuthbert. 1760. July 2nd.

Hutchinson, Dunstan. 1730. Dec. 2nd.

Hutchinson, Wilfrid. 1717. Aug. 24th.

Hutton, Bede. 1756. May 29th.

Hutton, Cuthbert. 1702. May 6th.

Hutton, John. 1643. Aug. 19th.

Hutton, Nicholas. 1610. Feb. 13th.

Hutton, Placid. 1755. May 17th.

ILDEPHONSO, George de S. 1655. Jan. 8th.

Ingham, Wolstan. 1638. Aug. 19th.

Ingleby, Robert. 1636. Sept. 6th.

Ireland, Placid. 1646. Dec. 13th.

Isherwood, Richard. 1745. Jan. 3rd.

JACKSON, Bernard. 1881. Feb. 22nd.

Jackson, Gregory. 1681. Sep. 6th.

Jackson, Leander. 1669. Sep. 30th.

Jansen, John. l. 1782. May 11th.

Jefferson, Philip. 1776. Oct. 29th.

Jenison, Augustine. 1747. April 5th.

Jenkins, Jerome. 1878. July 24th.

Jennings, Bruno.   1701.   Jan. 11th.

Jerningham, Benedict.   1636.   Aug. 31st

Johnson, Augustine.   1640.   Mar. 31st.

Johnson, Edward.   1683.   Nov. 19th.

Johnson, George.   1803.   Dec. 18th.

Johnson, James.   1.   1797.   Nov. 17th.

Johnson, Joseph.   1.   1786.   Sep. 19th.

Johnson, Oswald.   1818.   Nov. 9th.

Johnson, Placid.   1668.   Nov. 3rd.

Johnson, William.   1663.   Oct. 28th.

Johnstone, Joseph.   1723.   July 9th.

Jolley, Bede.   1868.   Dec. 14th.

Jones, Alexius.   1755.   Aug. 10th.

Jones, Benedict.   1639.   Oct. 19th.

Jones, Leander.   1635.   Dec. 27th.

AYE, Ambrose.   1777.   June 30th.

Kearns, Aelred.   1875.   April 27th.

Kearton, Cyprian.   1823.   Aug. 28th.

Kellet, Augustine.   1809.   June 8th.

Kemble, William.   1633.   Oct. 23rd.

Kemp, Boniface.   1644.   July 26th.

Kendal, Gregory.   1879.   Aug. 22nd

Kendal, Peter.   1814.   March 26th.

Kennedy, Joseph. 1738.   Jan. 8th.

Kennet, Agnes.   1723.   October 23rd.

Kennet, Catherine.   1700.   May 5th.

Kennet, Isabella.   1733.   Feb. 21st.

Kennet, Joseph.   1709.   Dec. 29th.

Kennet, Samuel.   1612. c.

Kenyon, Anselm.   1850.   July 28th.

Kenyon, Helen.   1657.   Nov. 10th.

Kenyon, Margaret.   1645.   May 14th.

Kershaw, Francis.   1865.   March 14th.

Killingbeck, Robert.   1710.   July 30th.

Kimberley, Magdalen.   1802.   June 17th.

Kinder, Augustine.   1676.   Feb. 21st.

King, Richard.   1664.   July 2nd.

Kipton, Boniface.   1644.   July 26th.

Kirby, Laurence.   1743.   July 18th.

Kirke, Adrian.   1685.   Dec. 17th.

Kirke, Bernard.   1789.   Feb. 26th.

Kirtlan, Paulinus.   1869.   Sept. 2nd.

Kitchen, Augustine.   1869.   April 6th.

Knacksterdt, John. 1.   1824.   Dec. 26th.

Knapp, Basil.   1816.   Aug. 17th.

Knight, Bede.   1718.   July 15th.

Knight, Benedict.   1743.   Feb. 15th.

Knight, Clare.   1792.   Oct. 30th.

Knight, Dunstan.   1787.   Jan. 6th.

Knight, Josepha.   1813.   March 2nd.

Knightly, Maurus.   1708.   April 28th.

Knowles, Gilbert.   1734.   Sept. 8th.

 ACON, Michael. 1807. Feb. 8th.

Lacy, Agnes. 1878. Dec. 20th.

Landres, Celestine de. 1633. Jan. 14th.

Lane, Gregory. 1871. Nov. 18th.

Langdale, Constance. 1760. Jan. 28th.

Langdale, Maurus. 1760. Aug. 15th.

Langevin, Deodatus. 1645. c.

Langton, Ambrose. 1619. c.

Lanning, Richard. 1706. June 21st.

Latchmore, Mildred. 1663. April 18th.

Latham, Alexius. 1761. Feb. 1st.

Latham, Augustine. 1677. Nov. 13th.

Latham, Gabriel. 1635. Mar. 31st.

Latham, Joseph. 1646. June 11th.

Latham, Swithbert. 1640. Dec. 15th.

Latham, Torquatus. 1624. Dec. 19th.

Latham, Vincent. 1640. Mar. 3rd.

Laton, Paulinus. 1645.

Lawson, Augustine. 1830. April 23rd.

Lawson, Benedict. 1737. July 1st.

Lawson, Francis. 1712. Nov. 15th.

Lawson, Henry. 1829. July 21st.

Lawson, Henry. 1. 1740. April 20th.

Lawson, Joseph. 1. 1881. July 24th.

Le Clerc, Magdalen. 1878. Mar. 28th.

Le Clerc, Placida. 1843. Oct. 22nd.

Le Doux, Mark. 1. 1738. Dec. 21st.

Lee, Augustine. 1640. Mar. 31st.

Lee, Margaret. 1753. Jan. 29th.

Le Feure, Mary Ann. 1807. Jan. 31st.

Legatt, Amatus. 1633. c.

Legge, Mary. 1691. June 22nd.

Legrand, James. 1772. Oct. 3rd.

L'Estrange, Teresa. 16—.

Levaux, Martin. 1828. June 3rd.

Lindley, Ambrose. 1699. Jan. 6th.

Llewellyn, Augustine. 1711. Oct. 14th.

Loader, Placid. 1646. Dec. 13th.

Lockers, John. 1. 1689. Sept. 21st.

Lone, John. 1641. Feb. 22nd.

Lorymer, Anselm. 1832. Feb. 2nd.

Loughry, Joseph. 1. 1827. March 18th.

Lovel, Anthony. 1. 1662. March 25th.

Lowe, Augustine. 1869. Feb. 5th.

Lowick, Bernard. 1720. June 23rd.

Lowick, Laurence. 1633. Oct. 13th.

Lucy, Frances. 1641. Jan. 25th.

Lumley, Augustine. 1699. July 25th.

Lumley, John. 1703. Oct. 25th.

Lusher, Bridget. 1690. March 12th.

Lusher, Elizabeth. 1684. May 7th.

Lusher, Frances. 1687. July 28th.

Lynass, Benedict. 1883. Jan. 7th.

Lynch, Anselm. 1777. March 31st.

Lynch, Jerome.   1880.   Dec. 25th.

ABBS, Laurence.   1641.   July 20th.

Macdonald, Anselm.   1760.   April 13th.

Macdonald, Benedict.   1814.   July 29th.

Mackay, Gregory.   1778.   Jan. 5th.

Maihew, Edward.   1625.   Sept. 14th.

Mallet, Gregory.   1681.   Sept. 6th. .

Malone, Columban.   1623.   Sept. 13th.

Mannock, Anselm.   1764.   Nov. 30th.

Mansfield, Gertrude.   17—   May 8th.

Mansfield, Teresa.   May 22nd.

Marsh, Augustine.   1856.   Dec. 15th.

Marsh, Benedict.   1795.   Oct. 27th.

Marsh, Cuthbert.   1704.   Oct. 4th.

Marsh, Edmund.   1852.   Feb. 8th.

Marsh, Jerome.   1798.   Feb. 16th.

Marsh, Richard.   1843.   Feb. 23rd.

Martin, Athanasius.   1625. c.

Martin, Boniface.   1636.   July 4th.

Martin, John.   1672.   April 30th.

Martin, Martha.   1631.   April 1st.

Mather, Augustine.   1687.   June 4th.

Mather, Cyril.   1812.   March 12th.

Mather, James.   1724.   Jan. 16th.

Matthews, Constantius.   1649.

McAuliffe, Placid.   1880.   Sept. 20th.

McElroy, Francis. 1875. March 25th.

Merriman, Bede. 1614. March 2nd.

Merriman, Hilarion. 1657. Feb. 20th.

Mervin, John. 1610. Dec. 10th.

Meryng, Benedict. 1664. Dec. 11th.

Metcalfe, Gregory. 1752. April 24th.

Metcalfe, Placid. 1780. Sept. 9th.

Metcalfe, William. 1738. July 17th.

Metham, Sylvester. 1715. Sept. 9th.

Meunier, James. l. 1658. c.

Meutisse, Clement. 1686.

Meutisse, John. 1666. May 5th.

Meynell, Benedicta. 1764. Feb. 4th.

Meynell, Teresa. 1697. July 4th.

Middleton, Benedicta. 1688. Aug. 5th.

Middleton, Cuthbert. 1678. Sept. 15th.

Middleton, Maurus. l. 1724. Feb. —

Middleton, Michael. 1646. c.

Middleton, William. 1644. July 26th.

Mildmay, Francis. 1720. Dec. 6th.

Miller, Joseph. 1796. July 15th.

Millington, Bernard. 1667. April 9th.

Minns, James. l. 1824. Aug. 14th.

Minshall, Thomas. 1617. July 12th.

Mitchell, Augustine. 1816. May 6th.

McKenna, Maurus. 1872. Jan. 25th.

Moliner, Claudius. l. 1653. June 19th.

Molyneux, Alban. 1860. Oct. 13th.

Money, Peter. l. 1723. Dec. 31st.

Monington, Thomas. 1642. June 12th.

Mompas, Benedict. l. 1767. May 1st.

Moody, Anne. 1755. Jan. 21st.

Mooney, Mary. 1778. Aug. 20th.

Moore, Augustine. 1775. June 15th.

Moore, Bede. 1735. April 23rd.

Moore, Francis. 1740. Mar. 13th.

Moore, Gregory. 1655. Feb. 12th.

Moore, Magdalen. 1719. Dec. 12th.

Mordlle, Monica. 1878. Dec. 6th.

More, Agnes. 1655. Mar. 4th.

More, Anne. 1662. Nov. 9th.

More, Bridget. 1692. Oct. 12th.

More, Dorothy. 1726. Aug. 17th.

More, Gertrude. 1633. Aug. 17th.

Morgan, Benedicta. 1640. April 18th.

Morgan, Francis. 1669. Sep. 8th.

Morgan, Philip. 1646. June 30th.

Morrall, Winefrid. 1874. June 6th.

Morris, Placid. 1872. Feb. 18th.

Mosse, Joseph. l. 1702. Sep. 8th.

Moundeford, John. 1646. May 22nd.

Muller, Adrian. l. 1744. Mar. 9th.

Mullins, Angela. 1641. Dec. 6th.

Murphy, Benedict. 1877. Feb. 5th.

Musgrave, Placid.   1626.   Feb. 20th.

Muttleberry, Francis.   1697.

Muttleberry, Placid.   1632.   July 6th.

ATHAL, Constantius.   1649.

Naylor, Ambrose.   1821.   Nov. 10th.

Naylor, Placid.   1772.   Nov. 8th.

Naylor, Placid.   1795.   Jan. 16th.

Naylor, Teresa.   17—.

Nedam, William.   1711.   Aug. 10th.

Nechills, Bernard.   1792.   Dec. 6th.

Nelson, Anselm.   1717.

Nelson, Benedict.   1699.   Sep. 3rd.

Nelson, James.   1707.   Jan. 9th.

Nelson, Jerome.   1632.   Nov. 17th.

Nelson, Maurus.   1690.   May 3rd.

Nelson, Placid.   1724.   Jan. 26th.

Nelson, Thomas.   1738.   Feb. 8th.

Neville, Laurence.   1658.   c.

Neville, Leander.   1636.   Jan. 8th.

Newton, Bede.   1777.   Feb. 27th.

Nicholls, Maurus.   1699.   Dec. 7th.

Normington, Leander.   1665.   Sep. 8th.

Northall, Clement.   1686.

Northall, John.   1666.   May 5th.

Norton, John.   1631.   Feb. 5th.

ONATE, Joseph d'. 1740. Feb. 7th.

Ord, Anthony. 1725. Jan. 26th.

Orgaine, Benedict d'. 1636. May 11th.

O'More, Josepha. 1720. Aug. 7th.

Orrell, Oswald. 1845. Jan. 29th.

Osbaldeston, Christopher. 1. 1777. April 17th.

Osbaldeston, Dunstan. 1. 1787. April 15th.

Osland, John. 1723. Jan. 22nd.

O'Sullivan, Bernard. 1865. April 11th.

Owen, Augustine. 1623. Aug. 8th.

Owen, John. 1654. Jan. 6th.

PAILLET, Bernard. 1870. Feb. 5th.

Paiva, Placid de. 1873. Dec. 12th.

Palin, Vincent. 1735. Jan. 4th.

Palliser, Catherine. 1770. April 11th.

Palmer, Edith. 1877. Aug. 11th.

Palmer, William. 1655. May 31st.

Palmes, Bernard. 1663. Dec. 25th.

Pape, Ambrose. 1. 1822. April 15th.

Parker, Cuthbert. 1705. Oct. 30th.

Parker, Henry. 1816. July 8th.

Parkinson, Anthony. 1. 1780. July 20th.

Partington, Benedicta. 1826. Dec. 28th.

Partington, Teresa. 1820. Sep. 4th.

Paston, Clement. 1724. June 2nd.

Patten, Thomas. 1787. June 4th.

Pembridge, Benedict.   1806.   Nov. 20th.

Pennington, Ann.   1794.   Feb. 6th.

Pennington, Edmund.   1794.   June 1st.

Percy, Hilda.   1670.   Feb. 6th.

Pery, Bathildis du.   1773.   Oct. 20th.

Pestel, William.   1736.   April 14th.

Peto, Placid.   1649.   c.

Pettinger, Dunstan.   1665.   Aug. 15th.

Philip, Charles.   1674.

Philips, Aldhelm.   1636.   Aug. 15th.

Philips, Columban.   1699.   June 1st.

Philips, Maurus.   1853.   April 3rd.

Philips, Susanna.   1705.   Dec. 4th.

Philips, William.   1736.   April 14th.

Philipson, Gregory.   1826.   Oct. 14th.

Philipson, John.   1739.   Sep. 18th.

Philipson, William.   1720.   June 15th.

Pickering, Thomas.   1679.   May. 9th.

Pigott, Dunstan.   1751.   Mar. 16th.

Pigott, Gregory.   1749.   Aug. 20th.

Placid, Dom.   1616.

Pleiall, William.   1665.   Jan. 21st.

Plompton, Angela.   1779.   Dec. 20th.

Plompton, Bernarda.   1768.   April 28th.

Polding, Bede.   1877.   Mar. 16th.

Poole, Edmund.   1878.   July 19th.

Pope, Alexius.   1777.   Oct. 9th.

Pope, Alexius. 1837. Feb. 19th.

Pope, Alexius. 1841. July 3rd.

Pope, Richard. 1828. July 24th.

Porter, Alban. 1693.

Porter, Dunstan. 1706. Oct. 2nd.

Porter, Francis. 1689. Mar. 15th.

Porter, Jerome. 1632. Nov. 17th.

Poss, Maurus. 1699. Dec. 7th.

Potter, Maurus. 1882. Aug. 30th.

Potts, Bede. 1743. June 21st.

Powel, Mansuetus. 1564.

Powel, Philip. 1646. June 30th.

Poyntz, James. 1718. Feb. 10th.

Prater, Joseph. 1631. May 25th.

Pratt, Ephrem. 1875. May 18th.

Pratt, Felix. 1634. April 2nd.

Prest, Ambrose. 1860. Dec. 5th.

Preston, Benedict. 1640. Nov. 13th.

Preston, Thomas. 1640. April 3rd.

Price, Benedict. 1639. Oct. 19th.

Price, Bernard. 1767. Jan. 4th.

Price, Wilfrid. 1878. Mar. 23rd.

Pritchard, Leander. 1685-9.

Pritchard, Maurus. 1657. July 31st.

Prosser, Philip. 1646. June 30th.

Pugh, Charles. 1674.

Pullen, Placida. 1786. July 6th.

Pullein, Michael.   1723.   Feb. 3rd.
Pulleyne, Placida.   1720.   Jan. 16th.

UINCE, Sylvester.   1.   1802.   April 8th.
Quyneo, Bernard.   1731.   Sep. 1st.

ADCLIFFE, Bridget.   1681.   Aug. 11th.
Radcliffe, Ildephonsus.   1689-93.
Radcliffe, Ralph.   1842.   Jan. 4th.
Radcliffe, Ursula.   1689.   Oct. 30th.

Raffa, Leander.   1758.   Dec. 29th.
Raphael, Dom.   1608.
Rayment, Maura.   1848.   Sep. 26th.
Rea, Francis. 1. 1876.   Feb. 4th.
Reade, Wilfrid.   1657.   Feb. 18th.
Reeve, Wilfrid.   1693.   Oct. 31st.
Reeves, Benedicta.   1763.   April 22nd.
Reyner, Clement.   1651.   Mar. 17th.
Reyner, Laurence.   1664.   April 8th.
Ribertierre, Bernard.   1664.   June 16th.
Rich, Francis.   1740.   April 5th.
Richardson, Anastasia.   1880.   Nov. 11th.
Richardson, Augustine.   1626.   Mar. 4th.
Richardson, Nicholas.   1762.   May 15th.
Richardson, Robert. 1. 1715.   June 5th.
Riddell, Gregory.   1730.   Mar. 1st.

Riddell, Joseph.   1736.   Feb. 22nd.
Riddell, Thomas.   1740.   July 7th.
Rider, Ildephonsus.   1677.   Feb. 16th.
Rigby, Anne.   1776.   July 6th.
Rigby, Bede.   1837.   Jan. 15th.
Rigby, Placid.   1764.   Sep. 24th.
Rigge, Justus.   1635.   April 23rd.
Rigmaiden, Benedict.   1749.   Nov. 18th.
Rigmaiden, Maurus.   1759.   Jan. 8th.
Risden, Cuthbert.   1652.   July 9th.
Rishton, Clement.   1836.   Dec. 9th.
Roan, Basil.   1673.   Mar. 24th.
Roberts, John.   1610.   Dec. 10th.
Robinson, Agnes.   1830.   June 11th.
Robinson, Bernard.   1851.   Oct. 9th.
Robinson, Gregory.   1749.   Oct. 25th.
Robinson, Gregory.   1837.   May 2nd.
Robinson, Maurus.   1662.   Feb. 2nd.
Robinson, Maurus.   1832.   May 31st.
Robinson, Paul.   1667.   Aug. 6th.
Robinson, Placid.   1739.   Feb. 10th.
Robinson, Robert.   1762.   Mar. 12th.
Roe, Alban.   1642.   Jan. 31st.
Roe, Maurus.   1657.   Aug. 20th.
Rogers, Dunstan.   1746.   May 27th.
Rokeby, Joseph.   1761.   Nov. 6th.
Rolling, Augustine.   1864.   Sep. 28th.

Rookwood, Francis. 1750. Mar. 19th.

Roper, Benedicta. 1648. Mar. 6th.

Roskow, Joseph. 1709. July 27th.

Rotton, Serenus. 1697.

Rous, John. 1720. Mar. 7th.

Rowley, Wolstan. 1858. Oct. 1st.

Rowston, Robert. l. 1726. Nov. 4th.

Rumley, Augustine. l. 1717. Feb. 8th.

Ryan, Wilfrid. 1877. Oct. 26th.

Rycaut, Andrew. 1675. c.

Ryder, Scholastica. 1722. Aug. 30th.

Ryding, Bernard. 1841. Sep. 26th.

ADLER, Faustus. 1681. Jan. 19th.
Sadler, Nicholas. 1610. Feb. 13th.
Sadler, Vincent. 1621. June 21st.
Salisbury, Edward. 1725. Oct. 10th.

Salkeld, Bernard. 1658. Mar. 9th.

Salvin, Cuthbert. 1702. May 6th.

Salvin, Peter. 1675. Jan. 22nd.

Sandeford, Matthew. 1644. May 5th.

Sanderson, Bernard. 1669. June 5th.

Sanderson, Denis. 1670. Aug. 6th.

Saul, Edith. 1855. Oct. 26th.

Savory, John Baptist. 1726. Sep. 21st.

Sayles, Frances. 1865. Jan. 23rd.

Sayr, Gregory. 1602. Oct. 30th.

Scott, Bede. 1789. Feb. 4th.
Scott, Dunstan. 1826. Oct. 14th.
Scott, Dunstan. 1872. Oct. 12th.
Scott, Maurus. 1612. May 30th.
Scott, Richard. 1664. July 2nd.
Scroggs, Gregory. 1671. Nov. 3rd.
Scroggs, Maurus. 1672. July 9th.
Scroggs, Placid. 1692. April 5th.
Scudamore, Placid. 1704. Jan. 2nd.
Selby, Gregory. 1759. Feb. 6th.
Selby, Wilfrid. 1657. Feb. 18th.
Shaftoe, Benedict. 1742. Nov. 19th.
Shaftoe, Celestine. 1721.
Shaftoe, Gertrude. 1654. Aug. 8th.
Shaftoe, Placid. 1681. Nov. 24th.
Shann, Augustine. 1860. April 25th.
Sharrock, Dunstan. 1831. May 7th.
Sharrock, Gregory. 1809. Oct. 17th.
Sharrock, Jerome. 1808. April 1st.
Sharrock, Joseph. 1. 1794. Nov. 13th.
Sharrock, William. 1. 1828. July 4th.
Shaw, Maurus. 1814. Jan. 29th.
Sheldon, Catherine. 1650. April 18th.
Sheldon, Edward. 1685. April 16th.
Sheldon, Frances. 1808. July 14th.
Sheldon, Lionel. 1678. Oct. 13th.
Sheldon, Placida. 1700. Dec. 27th.

Sheldon, William.   1644.   Nov. 27th.
Sheldon, William.   1692.   Oct. 13th.
Shepherd, Alexius.   1755.   Aug. 3rd.
Shepherd, Augustina.   1818.   Feb. 12th.
Shepherd, Teresa.   1809.   June 12th.
Sherburne, Bede.   1663.   Oct. 22nd.
Sherburne, Edward.   1745.   Mar. 13th.
Sherburne, James.   1657.   April 25th.
Sherburne, Joseph.   1697.   April 9th.
Sherburne, Richard.   1745.   Jan. 3rd.
Sherburne, Peter.   1790.   Mar. 12th.
Sheridan, Joseph.   1860.   Oct. 8th.
Sherley, Andrew.   1609.   April 14th.
Sherwood, Elphege.   1663.   Nov. 10th.
Sherwood, John.   l.   1669.   Nov. 2nd.
Sherwood, Joseph.   1690.   June 26th.
Sherwood, Robert.   1665.   Jan. 17th.
Short, Bernard.   1875.   Nov. 17th.
Short, Thomas.   1729.   Mar. 14th.
Shuttleworth, Benedict.   1774.   July 2nd.
Shuttleworth, Wolstan.   1677.   May 17th.
Sies, Benedict.   1697.   Oct. 30th.
Simpson, Andrew.   1652.   Nov. 13th.
Simpson, Benedict.   1775.   July 10th.
Simpson, Benedict.   1801.   May 2nd.
Simpson, Cuthbert.   1785.   Nov. 1st.
Simpson, Thomas.   1764.   July 5th.

Sinnot, Augustina.   1837.   May 20th.

Six, Jerome.   1.   1728.   Feb. 5th.

Skelton, Elphege.   1705.   Mar. 20th.

Skelton, Gregory.   1721.   Oct. 22nd.

Skinner, Basil.   1681-5.

Skinner, Placid.   1697.   July 20th.

Slater, Bede.   1832.   July 15th.

Slater, Bernard.   1810.   Mar. 13th.

Slater, Thomas.   1801.   Aug. 31st.

Smeaton, Basil.   1705.   April 9th.

Smith, Augustine.   1631.   c.

Smith, Barbara.   1635.   Feb. 24th.

Smith, Bede.   1874.   Jan. 29th.

Smith, Benedict.   1637.   July 21st.

Smith, Charles.   1780.   Mar. 19th.

Smith, John.   1694.   Nov. 29th.

Smith, Margaret.   1680.   Aug. 14th.

Smith, Martha.   1737.   Sep. 7th.

Smith, Maurus.   1633.   Jan. 21st.

Smith, Maurus.   1759.   Jan. 8th.

Smithers, Oswald.   1725.   Dec. 26th.

Southcot, Amandus.   1653.   June 8th.

Southcot, Augustine.   1730.   May 24th.

Southcot, Augustine.   1774.   Jan. 13th.

Southcot, Thomas.   1748.   Oct. 24th.

Soutnez, Josepha.   ——   Feb. 6th.

Spain, Cuthbert.   1869.   Jan. 18th.

Spain, Leo. 1850. Nov. 22nd.

Sparrey, Benedict. 1669. Mar. 25th.

Spears, Vincent. 1878. Mar. 24th.

Spencer, Augustina. 1832. June 30th.

Spencer, Daniel. 1794. Oct. 23rd.

Spencer, Josepha. 1876. July 27th

Stapleton, Benedict. 1680. Aug. 4th.

Stapleton, Epiphanius. 1624. July 25th.

Stapleton, Etheldreda. 1668. Aug. 6th.

Starkey, Hugh. 1688. Feb. 12th.

Starkey, Joseph. 1754. Mar. 14th.

Steare, Benedict. 1780. Jan. 18th.

Stelling, Augustine. 1729.

Stiles, Henry. 1640. Jan. 13th.

Stoker, Augustine. 1668. April 18th.

Stone, Martin. 1694. Sep. 30th.

Storey, Joseph. 1799. Dec. 19th.

Stourton, John. 1748. Oct. 3rd.

Stourton, Thomas. 1684. Jan. 5th.

Street, Peter. 1. 1684. Aug. 15th.

Strutt, Wilfrid. 1782. Dec. 5th.

Styles, Placid. 1856. Oct. 15th.

Sulyard, Augustine. 1768. Jan. 4th.

Sumner, Bede. 1871. Oct. 17th.

Sumner, Teresa. 1871. July 28th.

Sumpner, Charles. 1702. Jan. 29th.

Swale, Laurence. 1718. Aug. 17th.

Sweeney, Norbert.   1883.   April 16th.

Swinburne, Gertrude.   1660.   April 1st.

Swinburne, Joachim.   1797.   April 8th.

Swinburne, Margaret.   17—.   April 20th.

Swinburne, Teresa.   1762.   May 24th.

Swinburne, Thomas.   1667.   June 23rd.

AHON, William.   1.   1658.   May 15th.

Talbot, Oswald.   1847.   April 21st.

Tanke, Stanislaus.   1639.   Dec. 24th.

Tanke, Thomas.   1668.

Tarleton, Dunstan.   1816.   June 12th.

Tasburg, Felix.   1731.   Jan. 14th.

Tempest, Euphrasia. 1689. Feb. 14th.

Tempest, John. 1711. Dec. 8th.

Tenant, Anthony. l. 1658. May 9th.

Thomas, Basil. 1853. Sep. 7th.

Thomas, Benedict. 1676. Jan. 25th.

Thompson, Felix. 1634. April 2nd.

Thompson, Leander. 1669. Sep. 30th.

Thornton, Bede. 1694. April 10th.

Throckmorton, Œmilian. 1656. July 22nd.

Throckmorton, Catherine. 1792. Aug. 2nd.

Tiernan, Gerard. 1879. Sep. 6th.

Timperley, Gregory. 1709. Dec. 12th.

Timperley, Scholastica. 1640. June 13th.

Timperley, Teresa. 1671. Mar. 23rd.

Tindall, Oswald. 1866. June 9th.

Tolderwine, Magdalen. 1749. Jan. 31st.

Tookey, Josepha. 1772. Feb. 12th.

Touchet, Anselm. 1685-9.

Toudelle, John. 1626. Jan. 8th.

Towers, Adrian. 1844. Mar. 5th.

Townson, Andrew. l. 1711. June 1st.

Townson, Augustine. 1722. Mar. 8th.

Townson, John. 1718. July 4th.

Trembie, Celestine. 1629. Oct. 25th.

Trevelyan, Catherine. 1682. July 3rd.

Tucker, Thomas. l. 1706. Sep. 5th.

Turberville, Anselm. 1645. April 15th.

Turberville, Anthony.   1721.   Feb. 10th.

Turck, Laurence.   1769.   Feb. 20th.

Turner, Augustine.   1757.   July 30th.

Turner, George.   1854.   Feb. 15th.

Turner, John.   1844.   July 13th.

Turner, Thomas.   1802.   Aug. 1st.

Tyrer, Cyprian.   1871.   July 6th.

VAVASOUR, Catherine.   1676.   Aug. 13th.

Vavasour, Lucy.   1685.   Aug. 25th.

Valentine, Joseph.   I.   1798.   Mar. 1st.

Verner, Amandus.   1628.   Nov. 26th.

Vrignon, Laurence.   1876.   June 3rd.

WAKE, Hilarion.   1657.   Feb. 20th.

Walgrave, Francis.   1668.   Nov. 6th.

Walgrave, William.   1665.   Jan. 21st.

Walker, Augustine.   1794.   Jan. 13th.

Walker, Benedicta.   1783.   Nov. 21st.

Wall, Alexius.   1730.   Sep. 11th.

Wall, Cuthbert.   1704.   Oct. 4th.

Walmesley, Anselm.   1735.   May 12th.

Walmesley, Augustine.   1815.   Jan. 8th.

Walmesley, Charles.   1797.   Nov. 25th.

Walmesley, Francis.   1747.   June 29th.

Walmesley, Mellitus.   1689.   July 2nd.

Walmesley, Peter. 1790. Mar. 12th.

Walmesley, Teresa. 1794. Jan. 21st.

Walmesley, Wolstan. 1638. Aug. 19th.

Ward, Edmund. l. 1649.

Wareham, Denis. 1763. Nov. 22nd.

Wareing, Ambrose. 1776. Feb. 2nd.

Warmoll, Bernard. 1807. April 27th.

Warnford, Peter. 1657. Aug. 21st.

Warren, Bernard. 1650. Oct. 21st.

Warwick, Basil. 1732. April 29th.

Warwick, Benedicta. 1754. Mar. 15th.

Wassell, Benedict. 1871. July 1st.

Waters, Placid. 1808. Dec. 7th.

Watkinson, Gregory. 1792. June 16th.

Watmough, Francis. 1733. Aug. 15th.

Watson, Mary. 1660. June 10th.

Waty, Paul. l. 1669. July 19th.

Wearden, Vincent. 1801. July 10th.

Webb, Dunstan. 1848. May 8th.

Weetman, Euphrasia. 1848. Aug. 25th.

Weetman, Evangelista. 1882. July 17th.

Welch, Thomas. 1790. Aug. 20th.

Welden, Benedict. 1713. Nov. 23rd.

Wenham, Denis. 1763. Nov. 22nd.

West, Peter. 1657. Aug. 21st.

West, Francis. l. 1714. Jan. 18th.

Westbrooke, Maurus. 1774. July 10th.

Westhead, Gertrude. 1846. Nov. 17th.

Whall, George. 1709. Feb. 7th.

White, Augustine. 1618. May 4th.

White, Claudius. 1655. Oct. 14th.

White, Thomas. 1653. Jan. 27th.

Whitenhall, Francis. 1632. c.

Whitfield, Andrew. 1688. Oct. 8th.

Whittel, Joseph. 1786. Oct. 4th.

Widdrington, Agnes. 1733. Feb. 18th.

Widdrington, Augustina. 1775. Aug. 24th.

Wilcock, Peter. 1776. Mar. 11th.

Wilcox, Peter. 1619. c.

Wilford, Boniface. 1646. Mar. 12th.

Wilkinson, Augustine. 1851. May 21st.

Wilkinson, Gregory. 1. 1698. Aug. 6th.

Wilks, Cuthbert. 1829. May 19th.

Wilks, Teresa. 1775. Jan. 19th.

Williams, Anselm. 1636. Jan. 8th.

Williams, Anselm. 1693.

Williams, Bernard. 1875. Oct. 22nd.

Willoughby, Ildephonsus. 1677. Feb. 16th.

Wilson, Benedict. 1725. July 8th.

Wilson, Jerome. 1700.

Wilson, Jerome. 1719. Sept. 8th.

Wilson, Maurus. 1723. Mar. 7th.

Wilson, Paul. 1. 1819. Oct. 3rd.

Wilson, Placida. 1776. Sep. 4th.

Wilson, Thomas.   1712-13.

Wilson, Willibrord.   1692. Jan. 15th.

Winchcombe, Anthony.   1618.   June 14th.

Winchcombe, Benedict.   1672.   Nov. 30th.

Windsor, Placid.   1692.   April 5th.

Winter, Benedict.   1736.   April 24th.

Winton, James.   1712.   Dec. 7th.

Witham, Bede.   1665.   Jan. 3rd.

Witham, Michael.   1657.   Dec. 12th.

Witham, Thomas.   1729.   Nov. 23rd.

Witham, Wilfrid.   1764.   Sep. 9th.

Wolseley, Edward.   1669.   May 11th.

Woodhope, Thomas.   1653.   Jan. 27th.

Woolfe, Laurence.   1697.   June 11th.

Worsley, John.   1701.   Aug. 29th.

Worswick, Dunstan.   1770.   Mar. 18th.

Wright, Laurence.   1878.   Feb. 12th.

Wrisden, Gertrude.   1675.   Jan. 26th.

Wyburne, Henry.   1769.   Aug. 30th.

Wyche, Joseph.   1727.   Feb. 6th.

Wythie, Bernard.   1743.   Feb. 15th.

 YAXLEY, Placida.   1666.   Nov. 25th.
Yaxley, Viviana.   1656.   Feb. 18th.
York, Laurence.   1770.   April 20th.
Young, Bernard.   1801.   Sep. 6th.
Young, Teresa.   1758.   Sep. 14th.
Yoward, Richard.   1.   1694.   Nov. 29th.

Requiescant in Pace.

www.ingramcontent.com/pod-product-compliance
Lightning Source LLC
Chambersburg PA
CBHW021330110726
47900CB00005B/1421